MEGALITHIC
Mysteries

MEGALITHIC
Mysteries

AN ILLUSTRATED GUIDE TO EUROPE'S ANCIENT SITES

MICHAEL BALFOUR

WITH PHOTOGRAPHS BY BERND SIERING

FOREWORD BY JOHN MICHELL

DRAGON'S
WORLD

For Elisabeth and Calandra, companions in the field

ACKNOWLEDGEMENTS

I would like to thank the following very much for their
valuable advice and help during the compilation of this
book: Colin Burgess, Celia Dearing, Tom Deas, Paul
Devereux, Lesley Ferguson (Royal Commission on the
Ancient and Historical Monuments of Scotland), Michael
Gibbons (Office of Public Works, Dublin), Cherry Lavell,
Teresa Marques (Department of Archaeology, Instituto
Patremoneo Cultural, Lisbon), Jenny Mulherin, Susan
Vaughan for the Index, and the Librarian and staff of the
Institute of Archaeology, University College, London.
My special thanks to Aubrey Burl, and Sean O'Nuallain
(Ordnance Survey Office, Dublin).
M.B.

DUST JACKET ILLUSTRATIONS:
Front: The Stones of Stenness, Orkney Islands
Back; top left: West Kennet Long Barrow, Wiltshire
top right: Gavr'inis, Morbihan
below: Castlerigg, Cumbria

Dragon's World Ltd
Limpsfield
Surrey RH8 0DY
Great Britain

First published by Dragon's World 1992

© Dragon's World 1992
© Text Michael Balfour 1992
© Photographs Bernd Siering and copyright holders
listed in the Acknowledgements 1992
© Foreword John Michell 1992

Editorial: Jenny Mulherin
Editorial Director: Pippa Rubinstein
Design: Tom Deas
Art Director: Dave Allen
Picture Editor: Celia Dearing

The catalogue record for this book is available from the British Library

ISBN 1 85028 163 7

Typeset by Bookworm Typesetting, Manchester, England

Printed in Portugal.

Contents

Visbeker braut, the Bride of Visbek, one of a pair of hünengraben in Oldenburg, Germany. The Bridegroom lies just to the south-west.

Havelte west, one of the many hunebedden in the Dutch province of Drenthe. They are all numbered, and this ganggraf is D. 53.

Foreword

BY JOHN MICHELL

When the subject of megalithic monuments crops up, everyone knows about Stonehenge and many people have at least heard of Avebury, Newgrange, Callanish, and one or two other famous sites, mostly in the British Isles. In Brittany, the stone alignments of Carnac have become a major tourist attraction, but the thousands of other wonderful relics of French prehistory are comparatively neglected. Further afield, in eastern Europe, Scandinavia, Portugal and the Mediterranean lands, including North Africa, the very existence of their great megalithic structures is sparsely recognized, even in some cases by the natives. Who, for instance, would first think of Holland as a likely place for megalithic explorations? Yet, as we learn from this book, the 'unique and remarkable' *hunebedden* (Huns' beds) in the north-eastern Dutch province of Drenthe outdo in size and interest many of the better known British monuments. We also learn that in little Denmark the number of listed and protected prehistoric sites, some 24,000, is greater than in any other country, and this number represents only a fraction of the total sum.

There is no one obvious reason why modern visitors are increasingly attracted to ancient sites and sanctuaries. These are often located in remote, desolate regions far from any 'facilities' and, once found, they convey little direct information about the lives and thoughts of their founders. Unlike the great cathedrals and galleries they have no history to teach and offer no explicit images. Their aesthetic is simple and minimalist to a degree. Prehistoric sites are certainly an acquired taste, but those who happen to acquire it, whether as archaeologists, historians, artists, pilgrims or antiquarian ramblers, come to experience more satisfaction among the ruins of ancient stones than at the famous historical showplaces.

Far more than is generally realized, local cultures and countrysides are largely formed on patterns laid down by the megalith builders. The early Christian practice of taking over and reconsecrating the sites of pagan shrines and temples has ensured that virtually every old church stands on a place of long pre-Christian sanctity. The calendar round of festivals and saints' days, which England lost at the Reformation but which continues elsewhere in traditional country districts to mark the stages of the agricultural and social year, derives many of its locations and customs from prehistoric times. Even the familiar shapes of hills, adapted by mounds, cairns and earthworks, bear the marks of ancient workmanship.

The megalith builders were the same people as we are and they are separated from us in time by a mere 3,500–4,000 years, but the beliefs or understandings which inspired them to structure wide landscapes with a vast system of inter-related monuments in earth and stone are still deeply mysterious. The mystery deepens further as one reads through this book. Despite its extensive contents, it scarcely does more than scratch the surface; for every site described or mentioned there are thousands of others, a fair number of them still unknown even to archaeologists. And all these great works, both individually and as a whole, were raised up for an unknown purpose!

In this revelation of the wealth and variety of megalithic sites both within and beyond the British Isles, Michael Balfour is continuing a career which he began as a publisher in 1966. In that period of archaeological fervour, when studies by Hawkins, Thom and others were demonstrating the astronomical and scientific skills of the megalith builders, his Garnstone Press published a series of books on the mysteries and folklore of ancient sites, the alignments which they form across country and their possible connection with astrological powers and the subtle energies of the earth.

This is an informative rather than a speculative book, but like the author's previous *Stonehenge and its Mysteries* it stimulates a host of speculations about the riddle of the megaliths. One would like to be able to follow in Balfour's footsteps to the ancient, sacred and often secret places which he has discovered and brought to view, but his geographical range is too wide to be covered in most people's busy lifetimes. The best possible use of this book is as a practical guide for travellers, but those who cannot make the journeys are compensated as far as is possible by these stirring accounts and images of the spots where all traditional cultures had their mysterious origins.

John Michell

Introduction

Till antiquaries are agreed whether the circles are temples or
tombs or observatories, whether the dolmens are monuments
of the dead or altars for sacrificing living men, and whether the
mounds are tombs or law courts, it seems impossible, without
arguing every point, to write anything that will be
generally accepted.

– from James Fergusson's Preface to his Rude Stone Monuments In All Countries :
Their Age and Uses. 1872

This book is intended to be a general introduction to over 200 archaeological sites in Europe and North Africa, which present clear, exciting evidence of the craft of the megalith builders. Map references and travel instructions are provided, with illustrations and accounts of all these monuments.

Far more megalithic sites exist than could be encompassed by any one volume. Denmark, for example, boasts more than 24,000 listed, protected sites. This selection is necessarily eclectic – but I hope that this adds to its interest. There are even included non-megalithic sites, such as SILBURY HILL, Wiltshire, England, because I cannot believe there is no stone structure within its vast pile, and SIDI SLIMANE, Meknès, Morocco, because it is a contemporary replica in mud of a prehistoric North African mortuary house. (NOTE: The use of SMALL CAPITAL LETTERS indicates that the site has its own account in this book).

It is conceivable that no one researcher has visited every one of these sites; I have not been able to do so. Authors must rely upon existing books and publications, archaeologists' reports, and myriad secondary sources. This is why, whenever possible, I have given the names of excavators; they are the heroes. That said, any errors occurring will, I trust, be mine alone. Most facts can be verified, but legends cannot, except for their age, and they are attached to so many megalithic sites across the world. Some of the legends repeated here are among those that I have taken on a degree of trust; but one entirely bogus one is included, just to see how it makes its way in the world!

The language of the megaliths

It was a Dane, Jacob Worsaae (1821–85), an amateur archaeologist, lawyer and politician, who first reached for labels to describe the stages of toolmaking art which were becoming increasingly recognisable. Worsaae is credited with coining the names of the Three Ages : Stone, Bronze and Iron, to describe a National Museum collection by Christian Jurgensen Thomsen (1788–1865) in 1819. The word 'megalith' was devised by an Oxford don, Algernon Herbert, in 1849, for use in his book *Cyclops Christianus*; he had quite logically Anglicized the two Greek words 'megas' (great) and 'lithos' (stone).

The term 'Prehistoric' first appeared in English in the title and text of *The Archaeology and Prehistoric Annals of Scotland*, by Daniel Wilson (1816–92). This was first published in 1851, and Wilson's new word was a welcome replacement for the clumsy 'antehistoria'. The innovative Danes had already evolved 'forhistorisk' in 1837.

General interest in prehistory was really first sprung by a paper read to The Royal Society in London in 1859 by Joseph Prestwich (1812–1896), a Clapham-born wine merchant who became Oxford Professor of Geology at the age of 62. The subject was flint implements and their relationship with extinct animals. *The Origin of Species by Means of Natural Selection* by Charles Darwin (1809–82) was published in the same year to a wide, though initially sceptical, public. The recognition of Early Man, as he was comfortably known, as a toolmaker was widening, within his overall evolution through various cultures, to ever higher levels of manual, intellectual and social achievements.

A few years later, Sir John Lubbock (1834–1913; later the first Lord Avebury), a banker and politician, invented two more words which remain in the archaeologists' vocabulary. They made their appearance in his book *Prehistoric Times as Illustrated by Ancient Remains and The Manners and Customs of Modern Savages*, published in 1865; these words were Palaeolithic and Neolithic.

This book covers sites in more than 20 countries and the descriptions incorporate their indigenous terms for those structures unique to them. Thus we meet some striking nomenclature within the six groups of countries into which they are divided.

Across these countries some epithets recur in the names of sites: those of Devils, Druids, Fairies, Giants, Knights, Huntsmen, Maidens, Pipers, Priests, Trolls and many others. In this way, folk memories from the ancient past remain embedded in the present language of the megaliths. The monuments bearing them in this book are almost all Neolithic, to use Lord Avebury's word. The term is indicative of a certain cultural stage, not a fixed period of time. Very broadly, it implies food producing as opposed to gathering, and the manufacture, export and use of ground and polished stone implements and weapons.

The latter are among the most common finds during an excavation and have much to tell archaeologists. For example, a certain honey-coloured flint is found all over Europe at tomb sites; 'Le Grand Pressigny' constantly appears in excavation reports and it proclaims its presence in tombs far from its quarry south of Tours in Indre-et-Loire, France, which is over 250 miles (400km) south of the coast of England. Those reports also note pottery finds, and these too have a story to tell.

The broken pottery mystery

From America, the islands of the Pacific and Indonesia, as well as all over Europe, has come evidence that, in Neolithic times, the body of a deceased person appears to have gone through two entirely separate rituals. In the first, it seems that all bodily fluids were drained from the corpse into pottery vessels. The corpse was then allowed to decay through putrefaction to the ultimate state of total discarnation. This stage may have taken place on top of a chamber or passage capstone, which could explain why they are so often made flat on top as well as beneath. This natural process was sometimes hastened by the deliberate removal of flesh: evidence for this has been found, for example, on bones in Michelsberg culture burials at the Belgian sites of Spiennes and Furfooz.

The ritualistic act which came next was one of celebration. The spirit of the dead body had by now departed on the next stage of its journey and the purified bones were finally interred in their sepulchre (most often megalithic in Europe). At the same time the used vessels were smashed into pieces and the sherds were buried either with the skeletal remains (together with other burial goods) or near the entrance of the grave. 'Broken pottery near the entrance' is a frequent refrain in the accounts of sites throughout this work. Complete vessels are found very rarely, indeed almost never. In today's world this funerary procedure is reversed. First comes the funeral service (a kind of celebration in remembrance), followed by cremation or burial, and sometimes both. A separate and later service of thanksgiving may follow in a third stage.

In Neolithic times death was believed to be but one stage of the soul's eternal journey. As accounts in this book show, inhumations in burial chambers frequently took place in succession; the disarticulated bones from earlier rituals were unceremoniously piled up in corners or against walls to make room for the next arrival. Odd facts persist. The last arrival is the one an archaeologist discovers with the keenest interest, but even he cannot prove why one skeleton often lies on its left side, with its head to the west, or why another skeleton is in an extended position or flexed. It does seem that if inhumations occurred in succession, they were very rarely collective, but one by one, as if of the same family, tribe or clan. Thus the origins of different pottery sherds at the same location can be so instructive.

Sites and the public

Professor Stuart Piggott has written: 'Archaeology comprises a constantly elaborating set of techniques for obtaining knowledge of communities by means other than the use of written records.' (Piggott 1982). Ever-improving standards of excavation, as well as dating and photography techniques, contribute to this elaboration; site dates are on the retreat, leading to exciting revisions to earlier assessments of the capabilities of prehistoric man.

Were the leaders of these tribes astronomers, priests, surveyors, blood-thirsty thugs with territorial ambitions or perhaps simply men with natural authority elected by the bodies of their communities? In this so-called New Age, public interest in archaeology is greater than ever before. The works of respected archaeologists such as Aubrey Burl and Colin Renfrew have contributed much to this happy situation. There is inevitably a lunatic fringe, but this is healthy in its way. The founder and Editor of *Antiquity*, O.G.S. Crawford refused to publish a review of *The Old Straight Track* by Alfred

MEDICINE WHEELS AND EARTH MOUNDS IN NORTH AMERICA AND CANADA

In North America the Indians in the first millennium BC were living as hunters and food gatherers, with some plant cultivation. They did not use stone in the making of their ceremonial and burial sites. They used timber to construct mortuary houses which were then buried beneath enormous earth mounds. The earthworks of the Hopewell culture, which started about 300 BC and came to an end about AD 700 in Newark, Ohio, and the Illinois valley are notable. The Serpent Mound, of the Adena culture (about 1000 BC to 300 BC) is near Locust Grove, Ohio. It is 1300ft (396m) long, and up to 3ft (0.9m) high; the uncoiling serpent holds an egg-shaped object in its mouth. Is this a dragon enclosing the sun – the place for ritual acts?

Another Adena mound is in Mason County, Kentucky; it is 120ft (37m) in diameter, 17ft (5m) high, and contained 55 cremations and burials. The remarkable settlement site at Koster, Southern Illinois, was continually in use from the extraordinary date of 8000 BC (Early Archaic period) right up to AD 1200; then the Mississippian people built great ceremonial squares, defensive walls and earthen temple mounds. At one edge lies one of North America's oldest cemeteries (about 6400 BC); in one grave an infant was found to be dusted with red ochre (*see* SKARA BRAE, Orkney Islands). Again, no large stones were used: so, no

megalithic mysteries at Koster.

South of this site, in Missouri, is the Cahokia 'Woodhenge', which has been proved to be a solar observatory of great sophistication. Also in the Cahokia Mounds State Park, is the massive Monks' Mound; it is no less than 1000ft (303m) long, 700ft (213m) wide, and 100ft (30m) high.

Cahokia was undoubtedly a Neolithic-type settlement, but the existence of some 50 medicine wheels on the plains of western America and Canada can only have been created by nomadic hunters; moreover it has been shown that they were in use since about 2500 BC. They are confined generally to Alberta (which has most of them), Saskatchewan, Montana, North Dakota, Idaho, and Wyoming. This last state is home to the Bighorn Medicine Wheel, on Medicine Mountain. It is set 9640ft (2938m) up, and is snowfree for only three months in the year. One of the most recently made wheels, it was in use from about AD 1250 to 1750, as a lunar, solar and stellar obsevatory. It has 28 radiating 'spokes' – the days in a lunar month.

The older and larger Moose Mountain Medicine Wheel, in Saskatchewan, Canada, is similar to Bighorn in that both use stone rubble cairns for co-ordinating points around the wheel 'rims'.

*Some of the 1099 menhirs forming
the MÉNEC alignment in Carnac –
north-west France's 'megalithic
wonderland'.*

Watkins in the late 1920s; that book remains in print to this
day. One champion of Watkins and his ley theories has been
John Michell. His own publications have proved very popular
as well, and he was one of the first writers to bring the surveys
and their accounts by Professor Alexander Thom to the general
reader's attention.

Archaeo-astronomy is a discipline of its own these days. See
the accounts here, in Thom's native Scotland, of THE RING OF
BRODGAR, Orkney Islands, CALLANISH, Western Isles (the
'Stonehenge of the North'), THE HILL O' MANY STANES,
Highland Region, and KINTRAW, Strathclyde. Where there is
an elliptical stone ring there is a megalithic mystery; there is
even one in Morocco (*see* M'ZORA). Interest in archaeo-
astronomy in this century can be traced back to the
publications of Sir Norman Lockyer (1836–1920); Alfred
Watkins read his observations on the apparent alignments
between ancient sites. Indeed it was Colonel Johnston,
Director-General of the Ordnance Survey in the 1890s, who
alerted Lockyer to an alignment upon which STONEHENGE
occurred!

The ever-increasing popularity of archaeological sites does,
of course, create problems. STONEHENGE, Wiltshire, can no
longer be touched. Some monuments near Carnac, Morbihan,
France, are having the past trampled out of them but some are
now being protected by wire-netting. The solution would

appear to be to have a few principal sites in each country,
which, once archaeologists have finished with them, are fitted
out with car parks, toilets, visitor centres, multi-language
guide books and a full range of facilities for a curious public.
This has been done at Lough Gur, Co Limerick, Ireland, not
far from THE GREAT STONE CIRCLE there, and at BARNENEZ,
Finistère, France.

In general people do not regard megalithic monuments as
dead, inanimate things. They may bring to them
preconceptions – indeed misconceptions – but I have found
that people often express a liking or disliking for a monument.
And yet how is it possible to 'like' a chamber tomb in other
than architectural terms? Why is a much-restored site held to
have 'lost something'? How can it be so, assuming that the
restoration was sound? As with many man-made
constructions, the answers are linked to the level of personal
attention brought to a site. Truly to 'see' is to feel and
understand the strength or spirit of the place. Conversely,
some monuments seem to lack presence and atmosphere. Two
of my nominations for this mysterious latter category are
TUMULUS ST MICHEL, Morbihan, France, and ST. LYTHAN'S,
South Glamorgan, Wales.

What is certain is that megalithic monuments *always* evoke
responses *of some kind*; I have heard them whenever I am not
alone at a site, and indeed children join in the opinionating.

DROMBEG, Co Cork, Ireland, evoked very mixed emotions and views when I was last there. Personally, I would give this most interesting assembly of stones only two stars out of five – if this was that kind of guide book!

Christianization of megalithic monuments

Controversy about monuments is nothing new. From the earliest days of the Christian church, its leaders have concerned themselves with the problems of dealing with places of so-called pagan worship. In AD 392, the Roman emperor Theodosius I The Great, a Spaniard, ordered such shrines to be dedicated as Christian churches. In 408, Honorius, his second son, issued an edict forbidding the demolition of 'heathen temples' in areas of high population. In 574, St Martin, the first Archbishop of Braga, asked in a famous sermon : '. . . what is lighting candles at stones . . . but the worship of the Devil?' But old ways continued. An edict issued from the Breton city of Nantes in 655 was firm in its direction that 'bishops and their servants . . . dig up and remove and hide in places where they cannot be found those stones which in remote and woody places are still worshipped and where vows are still made'.

St John's Church at YSBYTY CYNFYN, Dyfed, Wales, is a well-known example of a Christian place of worship which incorporates parts of a stone circle. Another is the recumbent stone circle in the churchyard of MIDMAR KIRK, Grampian, Scotland. The best-known churchyard standing stone in Britain is probably the one at All Saints, RUDSTON, Humberside, England. The stone with ogham notches and a cross at BRIDELL, Dyfed, Wales, in the churchyard of St David's is a wondrous curiosity.

The stone standing at the western end of Le Mans Cathedral, Sarthe, France, has a legend that women wishing to bear children should dip a finger in its deep cup-shaped hollow. Jersey's LA HOUGUE BIE carries a chapel on top (which replaced an earlier medieval one), and so does TUMULUS ST MICHEL, Morbihan, France.

The *département* of Morbihan has very many Christianized megaliths. A strange legacy of those early days of doubt among Christian leaders is in La Chapelle de Les Sept Saints, Le Vieux-Marché, just east of Plouaret, Côtes-d'Armor (known as Côtes-du-Nord until 1991). Its southern transept has as its crypt an *allée-couverte*, and the seven saints are inside it. Even more curious is the fact that they are the object of an annual pilgrimage by Islamo-Christians!

There is a similar arrangement in north-west Spain, 40 miles (64km) east of Oviedo, in the Asturias. Below the church of Santa Cruz de la Victoria at Cangas de Onis is a passage-grave, of which the capstone is the altar. Portugal has the remarkable ANTA DE PAVIA, Mora.

LEFT: *The* GARYNAHINE *stone circle, on the Isle of Lewis, Scotland, is in fact oval-shaped. It is noted for the unusual low rectangular stone in its centre.*
RIGHT: *Three of the four remaining* STONES OF STENNESS *in the Orkney Isles. The stone in the foreground, with its strange, steeply sloping top, is 16½ ft (5m) tall.*
FAR LEFT: STONEHENGE *is one of the most important megalithic monuments in Europe. It was constructed over about 1800 years.*

Areas to visit

In England, the Wessex Group (AVEBURY, STONEHENGE and others) would provide many days of happy exploration. To the north, the beautiful Western Isles in Scotland, which include CALLANISH, would be a perfect week; so would a stay in the Orkney Islands. They contain such fine monuments as MAES HOWE, THE RING OF BRODGAR, SKARA BRAE and THE STONES OF STENNESS, (where my very early childhood was spent).

In south-west England, a week touring Cornwall, with another one on the Scilly Isles, would make a worthwhile package. The Boyne Valley group, in eastern Ireland, which contains 25 of the country's 300 and more passage-tombs, offer study for half a lifetime. A whole life's study is to be found in France's Morbihan (the setting of Carnac). In the north-east of the old East Germany, the island of Rügen is littered with megalithic tombs. For an exotic break, and if North Africa appeals, I suggest the vast cemetery of DJEBEL MAZELA — and the services of a guide!

In the end

This book does not pretend to offer solutions to the mysteries displayed — so few are founded on universally accepted facts. Migrations across continents, leaving dateable structures behind them, have been zealously tracked for a few hundred years. Diffusionist theories come and go. The linkage between archaeology and language has been brilliantly explored by Colin Renfrew (1987), who asks if modern European languages are derived from just one Indo-European tongue.

It is no longer conventional to assume that those food-producing stone users, the people of the Neolithic age, spread from south-east Europe in the sixth millennium BC, west into the Mediterranean countries, perhaps across the coastal Mahgreb to Iberia, and also up the Danube into central Europe, and as far as The Netherlands by the end of the fifth millennium BC. Or that they reached Brittany northwards on land, or by sea to its south-west coast, and then moved on to England and Ireland at the same time. The possibility of simultaneous tomb and temple design and construction all over Europe might yet emerge as a plausible fact.

'Dates and Dating', which follows this Introduction, gives a brief account of radiocarbon dating. By the 1970s, the dates being thrown up served to transform our conceptions of the so-called diffusion of megalithic cultures from the Near East (*tholoi* 'beehive' chambers notwithstanding).

The time had come to put on one side the famous reference by Professor Gordon Childe (1892–1957) to 'the irradiation of European barbarism by Oriental civilization'. We now know there are monuments in Brittany and Portugal, for example, which are vastly older than their supposed models in the Near East. The importance of the carving of a Mycenaean-type dagger, which Professor Richard Atkinson so famously discovered on the inner face of Stone 53 in the Great Trilithon Horseshoe at STONEHENGE during the late afternoon of 10th July 1953, became a victim of the calibration curves. Ancient Britons, whether or not covered in paint, were at work with their stones millennia before the dawn of the Mycenaean glories.

In the end, it is perhaps best to think of megalithic monuments as prehistoric handwriting. They were evidence set up to record, forever as we see, rights to territory. Around 7000 years ago these were assumed by a commonly felt instinct, by whole communities, which then related the area of their claims to their own numbers. Such megalithic markers were, we must never forget, most often places of burial. Thus they were dignified with the aura of life, in which death was almost suddenly acknowledged to be merely a stage, as archaeological finds demonstrate.

If such a cognition of this eternal passage of man's spirit did occur at broadly the same time all over the world, then we have the context for the building of physical structures which represented newly formed social orders. I would call it the Society Age.

Michael Balfour LONDON

Dates and Dating

High up in the White Mountains of California there grows the bristlecone pine (*pinus aristata*), which can live for more than 4000 years. This tree plays a central role in the very important story of how the dating of archaeological sites has, in recent years, been drastically revised.

Carbon, together with hydrogen, is an element found in all organic matter and is fundamental to life. Examples of pure carbon are graphite (the lead in a pencil) and diamonds. The possibility that radiocarbon might be detected in living matter was realised by Willard F. Libby (1908–), a Professor of Chemistry at the University of Chicago, in 1946. For his work he was awarded a Nobel Prize in 1960. Here 'C14' signifies one of the three elemental carbons, with an atomic weight of 14. It is not stable, and therefore very slightly radioactive – which is why it is called radiocarbon.

Everybody knows that a tree adds a ring for each year of its life. Once it is felled it ceases to 'exchange' its carbon, in the form of carbon dioxide, with the biosphere (the animal and vegetable worlds), and consequently will not add further rings. Conversely, human bone continues to exchange with the biosphere for about 30 years; animal bones do so for a shorter time span.

The science of the use of tree rings for the calculation of dates is called dendrochronology. Thomas Jefferson (revered for many reasons, and also as a founding father of American archaeology) long urged the use of this science. Their yielded dates, in the early years of research (notably by another American, the astronomer A.E. Douglass, who was investigating the Pueblo Bonito ruins earlier in this century), were then compared with analyses of radiocarbon dates. Considerable discrepancies constantly appeared in calculations which should have matched up. So-called C-variations were responsible for the differences between C14 dates and known historical or calendar dates (from Egypt's Old Kingdom, for example).

The Californian bristlecone pine was used by Wesley Ferguson and other Americans to establish a dendro-chronological sequence about 8000 years long. This was possible because these pines survive when dead, as it were, because of the very dry environment at their altitude of about 9800ft (3000m) and their high content of resin. Thus both dead and living trees were used – with the living samples being acquired by means of bore holes in their trunks. An important dendrochronological factor is that rings in trees do not exchange C14 among themselves, in the same trunks.

Hans Suess's name is forever associated with the first curve he produced, using the pine rings for true calendar dates, and which gave calibrated sets of dates. His curve showed major variations; at the beginning of the fourth millennium BC the variation was about 900 years. Curves using other organic matter followed by the hundred. But why that variation?

The strength of the earth's magnetic fields fluctuates. This strength (called the geomagnetic moment) has a direct effect upon the production of carbon, because cosmic rays are particles which are charged. Therefore, as they arrive, on their spiral path, they are deflected by the earth's magnetic field. So if the geomagnetic moment (the fluctuations) is low, production of carbon on earth rises. It is a fact that the whole direction of the earth's magnetic field is known once to have been reversed. Long ago there was a Magnetic South, but well before the 8000 year old start to Suess's curve. During that time it has been assumed that the C14 level in all living organisms has been constant.

Short term variations also occur on calibration curves – they are known as Suess wiggles or the de Vries effect (after the Dutchman, H. de Vries). These are the results of sunspot activity, which goes in long cycles of 200 years and short ones of 11 years. Wiggles affecting calibrations show decreases in C14 production during times of high sunspot activity. This is because it enlarges magnetic fields between planets, which in turn increases the deflection of cosmic rays.

During such times short wave radio transmissions and indeed communication on a global scale (through computers) are affected; the aurora borealis (the Northern, flickering showers of light) become visible as far south as the tropics. Violent sunspot activity can also cause the magnetic pole to 'wander' by two or three degrees, naturally disturbing the accuracy of compass readings. It is likely that Neolithic man had a need to know when sunspot activity was likely to occur, bearing in the mysterious presence of quartz stone at so many sites (including many that follow in this book).

Man-made alterations to the atmosphere has meant that no post-1950 organic matter can be used in the calibrations for curves. The neutrons in nuclear bomb tests, for example, briefly and sharply increase production of radiocarbon. Some human and natural agencies therefore require a process called fractionation in the correction of the C14 dates which are so essential to archaeologists. Contamination of the earth's atmosphere *is* serious!

There are two main methods used for the detection of C14 in archaeological finds: conventional radiocarbon dating, and the now less acceptable accelerator mass spectrometry (AMS), which can permit dating back through at least 70,000 years.

It is conventional to follow C14 dates, for the years before the birth of Christ, by the lower case bc and the plus and minus symbol ±. BP or bp is also used for an uncalibrated radiocarbon date (where the year 0 BP is taken as AD 1950, the last acceptable year for test matter). Think of it as standing for Before Present. In these ways, the probable time range within which the organic sample material 'died' is indicated. A calibrated or corrected calendar date (using the bristlecone pine curve tables) is stated using the upper case BC.

Passage-grave G in the primary cairn at BARNENEZ, Finistère, France, can provide an example. Charcoal found in it yielded a C14 date of 3800 ± 150 bc (ie: between 3950 and 3650 bc). The corrected calendar or true historical date was found to be about 4600 BC (one of the earliest in this book).

A very simplified C14 calibration table is as follows:

bc	BC
4500	5350
4000	4845
3500	4375
3000	3785
2500	3245
2000	2520
1500	1835
1000	1250

A useful check on C14 dates can be provided by a thermo-luminescence dating technique, commonly referred to as TL. It involves the use of crystals, and is particularly useful for dating pottery.

The dating of obsidian artefacts, both tools and decorative, is easily established. A date of manufacture can be calculated from a measurement of the thickness of the hydration layer on a thin section of a piece. This is because it absorbs water at a rate which depends on its source and the temperature.

Dates for archaeological 'Ages' tend to move about a little, and particularly in different countries. The following table for the British Isles gives a general indication of their spans:

Age	BC
Early Neolithic	5000–4500
Middle Neolithic	4500–3750
Late Neolithic	3750–3000
Final Neolithic	3000–2150
Copper	2150–1700
Early Bronze	1700–1500
Middle Bronze	1500–1150
Late Bronze	1150–1050
Final Bronze	1050–875
Early Iron	875–400

The Council for British Archaeology, London, publishes *Archaeological Site Index To Radiocarbon Dates For Great Britain and Ireland*, with occasional Supplements.

Recent research at the Belfast Conservation Laboratory is expected to provide final confirmation of a tree-ring chronology for the Irish bog oak, going back to the year 5289 BC; radiocarbon dates for between 800 bc and 400 bc are however now being shown to be unusable.

Measuring the Megaliths

In ancient civilizations parts of the human body were used for short measurements – forearms, palms, fingers, feet, etc. In Greece, four fingers' breadth (*daktyloi*), equalled one palm (*palaste*); three palms (*palastai*) equalled one span between thumb and little finger (*spithame*); four palms equalled one foot; one and a half feet equalled one cubit.

In ancient Rome, the smallest unit of measurement was also the breadth of a finger (*digitus*), and 16 of them equalled a foot. Early Egyptians measured the rise and fall of the River Nile in cubits; they regularly surveyed land areas after floods, and this gave rise to 'geometry', which means 'measuring the earth'.

The Rhind mathematical papyrus (bought in Luxor and now in the British Museum) is dated at 1849–1801 BC. It reveals knowledge of some of the properties of right-angled triangles, which were used in the construction of the pyramids. These were square, and positioned (in practically every case) with each side facing a compass point.

Sumerian writing in about 3000 BC recorded numerals, as did the Babylonians (about 2000 BC onwards). Ptolemy (*c.*90–168 AD) noted that records of eclipses were maintained by them from about 747 BC. More than 200 years late the Babylonians had established the Metonic (19 year) cycle for their astronomical calculations.

It was knowledge of such sophisticated facts that brought the mind of Professor Alexander Thom (1894–1985) to the question of just how Neolithic megalithic builders went about their tasks. Britain has more stone circles than any other country in the world, and when Thom retired as Professor of Engineering Science at Oxford in 1961 he started to survey in the most rigorous fashion several of their number. He established that they had an astronomic function, being set to be aligned on significant risings and settings, of (at different sites) the moon, the sun and first order stars. Some were apparently capable of predicting the occurence of eclipses – plainly terrifying events in the prehistoric world.

Alexander Thom's great bequest is his establishment that one unit of measurement was most commonly used. He called it the megalithic yard, and it equalled 2.72ft (0.829m). No summary here can do justice to the scale and detail of his surveys, and the reader is therefore directed to his publications which are listed in 'Further Reading' at the end of this book. Some of his findings and conclusions have been questioned, but he opened out a subject to the general public as well as to the academic archaeological world, and for this he will be remembered for a long time to come. To discover that stone circles are in fact enormously subtle ellipses is to realize that Neolithic man was himself a remarkable instrument. The circles at AVEBURY in Wiltshire are set to an accuracy approaching 1 in 1000.

I

British Isles

Historians through the ages consistently ascribe to the British Isles a possession of 'special' qualities. A map shows them to be tucked away off the massive peninsula of north-west Europe, on the way to nowhere, and with no great natural resources worth the journey to plunder. However, 'this other Eden' (Shakespeare; King Richard II) is home to perhaps the oldest Christian church in the world, at Glastonbury, and its foundation was only the latest (though the most lasting) of a long series of stone constructions across the land which incorporated ancient knowledge. This knowledge is all but lost to us, but enough remains for evidence to be discovered of highly sophisticated engineering. Between four and six thousand years ago more than 1000 stone circles, and countless standing stones and burial chambers were erected with stunning precision in large groups all over the British Isles, from the Shetland Islands in the north to the Isles of Scilly in the south-west of England, and in most parts of Ireland. Britain has a concentration of megalithic remains which is comparable only with Brittany and Denmark.

The legacy of Christianization

For the fact that there still are megalithic mysteries we have partly to be grateful for the Roman attitude to the old places of so-called worship. Until Constantine died in AD 337, the earliest Christian missionaries and their converts destroyed the Britons' existing temples, shrines and idols – and set up their churches elsewhere. But the powers of these sites and the ancient beliefs in them remained considerable, and could be used. So Rome changed its mind, and in AD 601 Pope Gregory gave to Abbot Mellitus a letter to take to Bishop Augustine in England: '. . . I have come to the conclusion that the temples of the idols in England should not on any account be destroyed . . . smash the idols, but the temples themselves should be sprinkled with holy water and altars set up in them'.

That new policy left alone much for us to enjoy and puzzle over today. There are many hundreds of circular, raised churchyards in Britain; it is not difficult to spot unusual, large or alien stones incorporated into their walls or indeed the fabric of churches themselves. Witness the five large stones, one 11ft (3.3m) high, in the churchyard and wall at YSBYTY CYNFYN, Llanbadarn Fawr, Dyfed, in Wales. The huge standing stone in All Saints churchyard in RUDSTON, Humberside, survives to this day, as do the stone circle in MIDMAR churchyard, Aberdeen, and the fine altar table, with strange carvings on the supporting stones, in the churchyard of St Nicholas, Trellech, Gwent. Tremendous sarsen stones

which once topped the elliptical mounded churchyard in Alfriston, East Sussex, are long since broken up and lie ignored beneath a nearby tree – the still visible reason for the very existence of beautiful Alfriston and 'The Cathedral of the South Downs'. Perhaps that Roman policy was responsible for a dramatic fact: there is not a stone circle to be found to the east of a line between Scarborough on the North Yorkshire coast and Southampton on the Hampshire coast.

In the beginning

The story of Britain's prehistory could be said to start with the gradual ending of the Ice Age, about 12,000 years ago. At that time there was no English Channel; remains of mammoth and woolly rhinoceros have been found in the Cheddar Gorge, Somerset; bones of bears, lions and hyenas were discovered in Kent's Cavern, Torquay. Over the next 4,000 years the English Channel, as we know it, slowly came into existence; the Isles of Scilly were one land mass as recently as 2,000 BC, easing the tasks of the megalithic workforce there, in that great concentration of tombs. A distribution map showing the numbers and grouping of burial chambers, circles, standing stones and alignments is more eloquent than words, but it does not betray one remarkable fact; this is that at the time when STONEHENGE I was being made (before the Great Pyramid was even started) it has been estimated that the population of the British Isles may have been no greater than about 20,000. This implies discipline of a very high order, which is why a kind of priesthood must have attained, preserved and passed down the necessary mathematical and astronomical knowledge enshrined in Britain's monuments. It is unsafe to assume that druids had anything to do with them; through the years they have been called up as the true inheritors of the ancient traditions, but they are best left in their sacred groves, where Julius Caesar found and recorded them as such.

Anglesey

Megalith hunters heading for Ireland would do well to leave a day spare for this Welsh island. The carvings in BARCLODIAD-Y-GAWRES are well worth examining, beneath their modern dome overlooking Trecastell Bay. BRYN CELLI DDU, in its restored state, is very instructive, and the blue-green pillar in the chamber (actually a replica) is one of the strangest stones in the British Isles; one puzzle is its height of only 4ft (1.2m). Free-standing pillars are also found in Breton V-shaped passage-graves, such as Ty-ar-Bondiquet, Brennilis, Finistère.

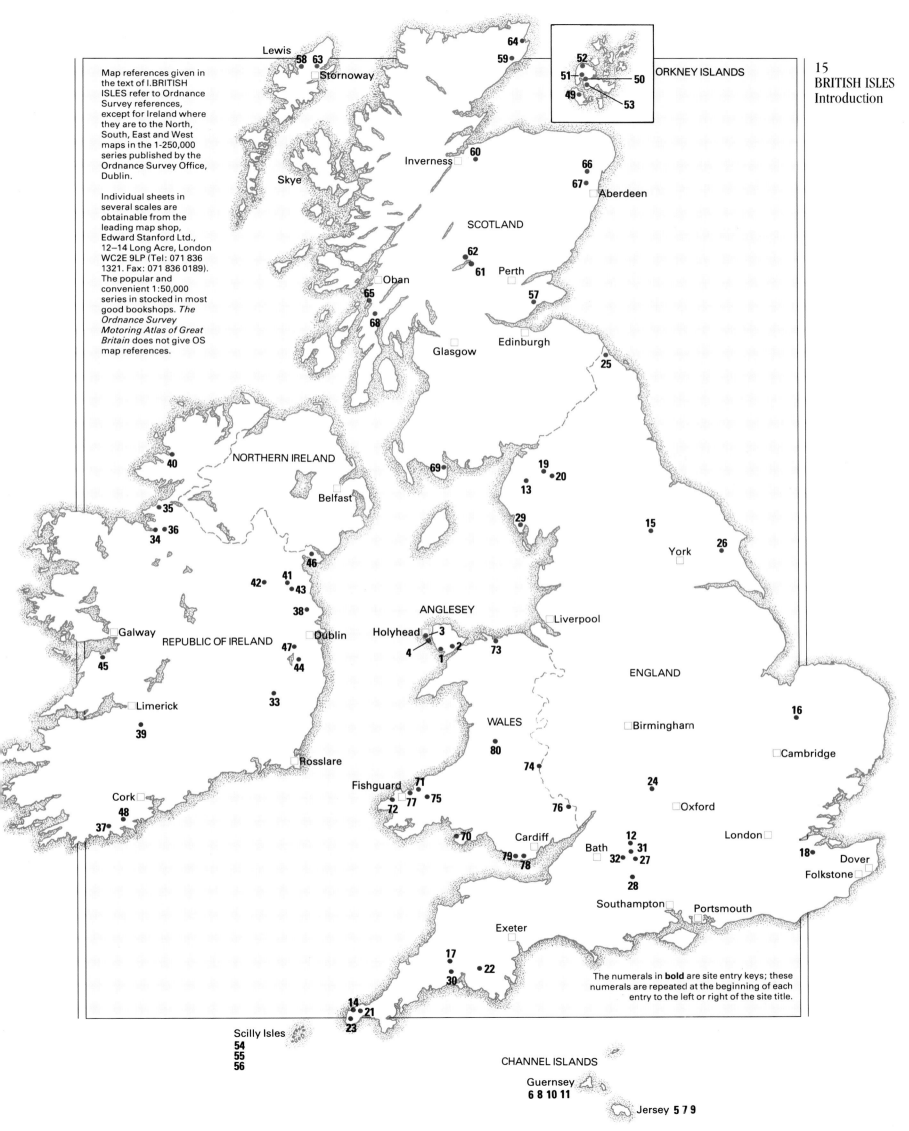

Map references given in the text of I.BRITISH ISLES refer to Ordnance Survey references, except for Ireland where they are to the North, South, East and West maps in the 1-250,000 series published by the Ordnance Survey Office, Dublin.

Individual sheets in several scales are obtainable from the leading map shop, Edward Stanford Ltd., 12–14 Long Acre, London WC2E 9LP (Tel: 071 836 1321. Fax: 071 836 0189). The popular and convenient 1:50,000 series in stocked in most good bookshops. *The Ordnance Survey Motoring Atlas of Great Britain* does not give OS map references.

ORKNEY ISLANDS

Lewis

Stornoway

Skye

Inverness

SCOTLAND

Aberdeen

Perth

Oban

Glasgow

Edinburgh

NORTHERN IRELAND

Belfast

Galway

REPUBLIC OF IRELAND

Dublin

Limerick

Rosslare

Cork

ANGLESEY

Holyhead

Liverpool

ENGLAND

York

Birmingham

Cambridge

WALES

Oxford

London

Fishguard

Cardiff

Bath

Dover

Folkstone

Southampton

Portsmouth

Exeter

The numerals in **bold** are site entry keys; these numerals are repeated at the beginning of each entry to the left or right of the site title.

Scilly Isles
54
55
56

CHANNEL ISLANDS

Guernsey
6 8 10 11

Jersey **5 7 9**

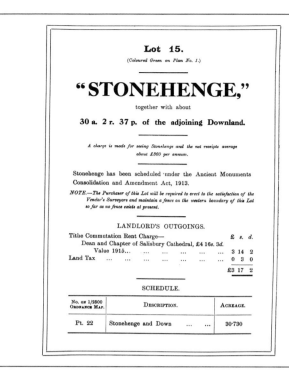

ABOVE LEFT: *A tranquil scene at* AVEBURY, *Wiltshire*.

LEFT: *This natural rock outcrop at* ROUGHTING LINN, *in the far north-east of England, is covered with more than 60 cup-and-ring marks. These mysterious carvings have never been deciphered.*

ABOVE: STONEHENGE *was auctioned by British agents, Knight, Frank & Rutley, on 21 September 1915. This great megalithic site fetched £6600.*

RIGHT: *The Neolithic hut settlement at* SKARA BRAE, *Orkney Islands, revealed after a violent storm in 1850.*

Channel Islands

Jersey and Guernsey were still joined to France in about 7500 BC. Four and a half millennia later the huge passage-grave of LA HOUGUE BIE was going up in Jersey. Much later on it was truly Christianized, with the arrival of a church on top of it (in the manner of TUMULUS ST MICHEL, Morbihan, France. On neighbouring Guernsey, at CÂTEL, stands a 6ft 6in (2m) high statue-menhir, showing a necklace and two breasts. It is about 3000 years old, and its carvings are distinctly similar to others in different parts of France and as far away as Corsica (see FILITOSA). LES FOUAILLAGES is perhaps the oldest of the 60 or so megalithic tombs on Guernsey.

England

England's greatest single glory is of course STONEHENGE, Wiltshire – the most complete megalithic monument of its

kind in the world – and it is a dominating presence among the country's 21 sites described in this first section of the book. Much has been written about this giant calendrical instrument, and it correctly lies towards the centre of any attempt to understand life and times in Neolithic days. As a small, contemporary aside it also lies on a ley (*not* ley line); this is an invisible straight line which connects prehistoric sites; moreover, this fact was first announced in the 1890s by the then Director-General of the Ordnance Survey, Britain's official map-making organization. Parts of the thrilling and important AVEBURY monument complex, also in Wiltshire, also fall on a ley. Single monuments of mysterious purpose are included here: the carved rock face at ROUGHTING LINN, Northumberland, the huge and lonely RUDSTON MONOLITH in Humberside, and the vast yet empty SILBURY HILL, Wiltshire.

Ireland

The Emerald Isle possesses an embarrassment of riches. The capstone on BROWNE'S HILL, Co Carlow, is unforgettable; it is fat and weighs 100 tons! Had more care been taken of it, then CARROWMORE, Co Sligo, might today be rivalling Carnac as a megalithic site; at the last official count it had 42 stone circles, 14 burial chambers, and five cists. There are several indications here which suggest that passage-graves and other tombs in the east and west of Ireland were not the work of migrant north-west European builders, but of local device. The greatest wonder of Ireland is NEWGRANGE, in the Boyne Valley; here there is a description of the unusual stone ring, the massive kerb, the shining quartz roof, and of course the carvings within.

Orkney Islands

In the north of Scotland, among these beautiful islands, lie some of Britain's finest monuments. They include the very rare rock-cut tomb, DWARFIE STANE on Hoy, THE RING OF BRODGAR, Mainland (which Professor Alexander Thom believed to be a prehistoric observatory), the Neolithic settlement of SKARA BRAE, Mainland, and its story of ancient Britons as 'the painted ones', and the romantic 4900 year old STONES OF STENNESS, Mainland.

The stone circle and rows of CALLANISH, in the Western Isles, form a distant yet popular venue for megalith hunters. In its very beautiful setting, there was carefully constructed, so the native Professor Thom argued, a lunar observatory. CLAVA CAIRNS, near the bloody battlefield of Culloden, outside Inverness, provides a set of very unusual features in stone. The recumbent stone circles are unique to Scotland, and one of the most striking of them is probably MIDMAR KIRK, in Grampian. In 1914 a graveyard was established around this ring of stones!

Wales

One of the most moving megalithic landscapes in Britain lies near the foreboding Preseli Mountains (of bluestones fame), in Dyfed. The perfect stone circle and standing stones of GORS FAWR, among the sheep and gorse on the land that has always been common, make a remarkable scene. The village of Trellech, in Gwent, contains HAROLD'S STONES (three of them), a holy well, an earth mound, and a stone table (or pagan altar) in front of a preaching cross in the churchyard. PENTRE IFAN, Dyfed, may be some 5500 years old and has yielded many archaeological secrets; yet one feels there is more to know about this well-excavated megalithic site.

I.1

BARCLODIAD-Y-GAWRES

*Trecastell Bay,
Gwynedd*

CHAMBER TOMB

SH 328708

This site's name 'The Giantess's Apronful' derives from the legend that the stones were scattered here when the strings of a giantess's apron broke; she had been carrying the stones to build a fortification nearby.

There is a car park above this popular beach, on the Bordorgan Estate. The tomb is well signposted, guiding you some 500yds (457m) along a cliff path. Take a torch. This tomb has locked iron gates at its entrance; for a deposit and a small fee the key is obtainable from The Wayside shop up the road in Llanfaelog.

Spirals and circles highlighted in red chalk on the fourth stone to the left inside the chamber.

The name of this fascinating tomb is Welsh for 'The Giantess's Apronful'. After excavation in 1952/53, a concrete dome (now topped with earth and turf) was installed to shelter this apparent jumble of stones, which was clearly so arranged for some purpose.

Just beyond the 23ft (7m) passage, which faces north-north-east and out across a bay, a cruciform chamber contains six or more carved stones (among the 23 and capstone) of great antiquarian interest. They feature chevrons, lozenges, squares, arrows, spirals, grooves, cup marks, a hexagram, and even an ankh-like carving. When last seen by the author in August 1990, these were outlined in red chalk, and they made a dramatic show. Symbolic art such as this connects its creators with the builders of the Irish Boyne Valley cruciform tombs.

In the central hearth of the chamber, the excavators found a most odd collation of burnt remains, including eels, a frog, a hare, a mouse, part of a pig's vertebra, a shrew, a snake, and whiting. A meal for a coven perhaps, but no legends of witches are to be found in these parts.

This is an ideal site at which to study prehistoric carvings — but remember to take a wide-beam torch. With the key you may be left alone in the tomb with the megalithic puzzles.

I.2

BRYN CELLI DDU

*Llanddaniel Fab
Gwynedd*

PASSAGE-GRAVE WITH
CHAMBERED CAIRN

SH 508702

Leave the Menai Bridge on the A5 to Holyhead; then turn left on to the A4080, and right towards Llanddaniel Fab. Park, as directed there, just past the school on the verge. Then walk as signposted, along the broad farm track for about 750yds (686m). Take a torch.

The restored entrance, with kerbstones in the former henge ditch.

Much has been written about this famous megalithic site, which about 4000 years ago was marked with a stone circle, bank and ditch. These were then replaced by a chambered cairn with a 27ft (8.2m) long passage, and the whole was covered by a mound of earth. The present kerb stones stand in the former henge ditch. Beside the unusual pit beyond the chamber lies a carved stone; this is in fact a cast of the original which, together with other finds from the site following the 1928 excavations, is now in the National Museum of Wales in Cardiff. Deliberately smashed white quartz stones were one of the interesting finds here (they also feature in other sites in north Wales). Carvings can also be seen on the inside face of one of the entrance stones.

The chamber itself is about 10ft (3m) wide and 6ft (1.8m) high. Within is discovered a standing stone, one of the most mysterious stones in Britain; it is a 5ft 6in (1.7m) tall column, exceptionally smooth, and of a local blue-green stone.

Fragments of cremated and unburnt human bones were found in the passage and chamber; outside the present mound, post sockets, the skeleton of an ox and a human ear-bone were uncovered. Experts describe this site as a ritual place, and many regard it as a temple rather than a tomb.

PENRHOS FEILW

*Penrhosfeilw,
Trearddur Bay,
Gwynedd*

STANDING STONES

SH 227809

*In Trearddur, turn left off the
B4545; proceed north along
the coast road, and take the
third lane on the right.*

*The two remaining stones (right) of
a possible stone circle, the
colloquial term for a ring.*

This attractive site raises many questions, and answers none. It consists of two Early Bronze Age (2000–1500 BC) standing stones, each 10ft (3m) tall, and placed 11ft (3.3m) apart. Although of the same stone, quarried yards away, they are different in outline yet have the same thickness, and vary only 8ins (20cm) in their base lengths. Weathering could not have produced such a difference. And why are they placed on a north-east-north/south-west-south axis?

Tradition says that these two stones were once part of a circle, a belief which often recurs around the country. Farmers have been known to take down one of a pair of stones, leaving the other as a rubbing post for cattle – but not here. Farmers are also known to erect such a post – but surely not two, so closely together in the same field? Whatever their original purpose, they are an excellent antidote to the horrors of nearby Holyhead, the ferry port.

TREFIGNATH

*Trearddur Bay,
Gwynedd*

BURIAL CHAMBER

SH 258805

Excavations have revealed
both decorated and plain
pottery fragments at this site.

This heavily restored burial chamber is almost literally overshadowed by nearby huge smoking factories and, with excavation, has definitely lost some of its mystery. However, it is an unusual and technically interesting site, and excavation has revealed that there were three constructional phases, each represented by a separate chamber.

The first was at the west end of the present site; its entrance is very short and faces due west, and the chamber was square and simple. Then came the now collapsed rectangular, central chamber; only an entrance stone and the back stone remain standing, but the fallen and broken capstone is there. Its rounded forecourt once had a drystone retaining wall.

The third and final burial chamber is the best preserved. Five uprights support two capstones (with the help of a recently installed plinth); there are two tall and impressive portal-stones (associated with the second building phase) at the south-facing chamber entrance, and these were probably not covered by the original stone mound. They opened on to a horn-shaped, recessed forecourt.

*Travel from Holyhead south-
east along the B4545; turn
left just before the Shell petrol
station, and the site is 1 mile
(1.6km) along the road, past
the houses, on the right, where
it is signposted.*

*There were three different
construction phases at Trefignath.*

—————— **CHANNEL ISLANDS** ——————

LE CÂTEL

I.5

I.5

*Couperon,
Jersey*

EARTHWORK

WV 68915464

*On the north-east of the island
between Pot du Rocher and
Couperon; on the left down a
lane. On private property, so
ask for permission to cross the
farmland.*

This is the finest earthwork in Jersey. Its date is uncertain, but probably late Iron Age. With a height of 19ft 9in (6m), and a width of 32ft 9in (10m), sections of the earthwork survive to a length of 219yds (200m). Like others in the Channel Islands, it was obviously planned to fortify a spit of land jutting out between Bouley Bay to the west, and Rozel Bay. Roman occupation also seems evident since coins from Gaul have been found at this site, which was once known as Caesar's Wall.

Near the north side of the entrance to Ste Marie du Câtel Church, on Guernsey, stands a Neolithic statue-menhir. It is, of course, far older than the church itself, but probably just as old as the churchyard site which may have been used in pagan rituals. The menhir, which is roughly though distinctly human in outline, is about 6ft 6in (2m) high, has no face, but shows a necklace and two breasts.

The best-known statue-menhir on Guernsey is La Gran'-Mère du Chimquière, which has a clear carved face; it stands 5ft 6in (1.7m) high and was remodelled in Roman or medieval times. In France, there is a carved stele of some similarity at the end of the short passage of the *allée-couverte* of CRECH-QUILLÉ at Saint-Quay-Perros, Côtes-d'Armor.

The 3000 year-old statue-menhir in the churchyard of Ste Marie du Câtel.

LES FOUAILLAGES

I.6

I.6

*Chouet,
Guernsey*

PASSAGE-GRAVE WITH
STATUE-MENHIR

WV 33578314

*Take L'Ancresse Road north
from St Michael Du Valle,
and then the second turning on
the left towards Chouet. The
site is on the right.*

*Possibly the earliest passage-grave on
Guernsey, in the first of its four
stages.*

Since excavations in the early 1980s this important site has been thought to pre-date, in its early Neolithic period, all the 70 or so Guernsey tombs. It was found to have been constructed in four stages.

In the first, four structures were built, on a north-east/south-west alignment, and covered by a triangular kerbed earth mound, 65ft 6in (20m) long and 32ft 9in (10m) wide, with a narrow entrance at the east end. There was a small chamber, a rectangular chamber, a cairn over a cist, and, at the east end, a small anthropomorphic statue-menhir. Sherds of

Bandkeramik pottery, giving this first stage its rough date, were found on a circular platform.

Next, the whole interior of the grave was filled in with stones and closed. Then the façade at the eastern end was levelled and an oval shrine erected within concentric kerbstones. Finally, about 2000 BC, use of the shrine is shown by the presence, in pairs of two, of eight superb barbed-and-tanged flint arrowheads. Four of them came from the central French quarry at Le Grand Pressigny, which is 224 miles (360km) away.

LA HOUGUE BIE

*Grouville,
Jersey*

PASSAGE-GRAVE

WV 68205038

*Take the A6 north from St
Helier, and turn right at Five
Oaks on to the B28. The site
is signposted nearly 1 mile
(1.6 km) along on the left.
The Museum of the Société
Jersiaise is on the site.*

*The massive lit interior of this
remarkable passage-grave. Inset:
The second chapel to be built on top
of the enormous mound.*

The features, size and fine condition of this 5000-year-old monument place it among the most exciting in north-west Europe. A medieval chapel was built on top of the tomb, and then another adjoining it: hefty pieces of Christianisation! These were removed during the excavations and restoration in 1924, along with a more recent house built on top of *them*.

The mound is a huge 180ft (54.9m) in diameter, and is 40ft (12.2m) high.

The single cruciform grave within is 70ft (20.4m) long, and lies broadly east to west, towards which end the Great Chamber is set. It is 29ft 6in (9m) long, 9ft 9in (3m) wide, and

6ft 6in (2m) high. There are two small side chambers outside the main one, just to the east on either side of the passage. Roofing is provided by rectangular, flat capstones.

All the stones here came in groups from well-spread sources, which is something of a mystery, unless conjecture is correct that very small local 'communities' brought their own materials and labour.

Hougue means 'mound' or 'barrow', from the Old Norse *Haugr* (eminence), which also provided 'How' in northern England and Scotland. 'Bie' stems from *-by*, Old English and Scandinavian for a settlement.

LA LONGUE ROCQUE

*Les Paysans,
Guernsey*

MENHIR

WV 26527717

*In a field to the west of Les
Paysans. On private property,
so ask for permission to visit
the stone at the house opposite,
Val des Paysans.*

The largest menhir in Guernsey.

This is the largest menhir in Guernsey. Its total height is known because the site was excavated in 1894; the slim granite column measured 14ft 9in (4.5m) in length, of which 11ft 6in (3.5m) is visible above the ground today and has a circumference of 12ft 6in (3.8m). Although a Bronze Age burial was found under Britain's tallest standing stone (*see* PUNCHES-TOWN, Naas, Co Kildare), no burial was found beneath this menhir.

In a garden in St Stephen's Lane stands another smaller granite menhir which, according to the island's Ancient Monuments Committee, is probably La Petite Longue Rocque. It was recorded as long ago as 1793.

Mont Ubé

St. Clement,
Jersey

PASSAGE-GRAVE

WV 6769 4742

This somewhat mutilated grave was discovered in 1848, when W C Lukis, the father of archaeology in the Channel Islands, heard that an unusual group of stones was being quarried. He arrived too late to save the capstones.

The site was originally covered by an earth mound; the sad chamber we see today measures 24ft by 9ft 9in (7.3m by 3m). It is reached from the south-east through a tapering passage, which is 16ft 6in (5m) long and 6ft (1.8m) at its widest point. There is a small side chamber to the south and possibly there were others. A very small cist, or replica dolmen, has been found at the 'neck' of the passage, and objects found in Mont Ubé have included polished axes, stone rings and numerous pottery sherds.

This site has suffered for a long time because it is known to have been used almost continuously from late Neolithic to early Roman times. Possible fragments of the capstones lie around, but the drystone walling has all vanished.

Turn north off the A5 (La Grande Route de St Clement), on to La Blinerie. At the top of the hill a sign on the east side of the road indicates the path to the site.

The passage here is 16ft 6in (5m) long and 6ft (1.8m) at its widest.

LA ROCQUE QUI SONNE

Rue de l'Ecole,
St Sampson,
Guernsey

PASSAGE-GRAVE

WV 34978236

North of the harbour at St
Sampson, in the grounds of
Vale School.

The remains of this passage-grave lie in school grounds. This once substantial site was originally the largest chamber and passage-grave in the Channel Islands but was broken up in the last century so that the stone could be incorporated in a new house here; the sounds of the breakers' hammers could be heard many miles away – hence its name. Soon after, the newly completed house burnt down and its owner, who had dared to tamper with a prehistoric burial place, died horribly on board ship a few years later.

Today, the dead are honoured and left to rest in peace. After all, the old passage-graves were built to be secure.

Sufficient stone was removed from this site to load a 150-ton vessel. Other stones were used in doorposts and lintels.

Excavations in the 19th century revealed plain and decorated pottery beakers, a small bronze bracelet and a fragment of a jet band.

The passage-grave in school grounds.

LE TRÉPIED

Perelle Bay,
Guernsey

PASSAGE-GRAVE

WV 25987889

On the coastal road, north of
Perelle, overlooking Perelle
Bay at Le Catioroc Point.
Signposted between Saumarez
Fort and Richmond Fort.

A beautiful location, but one to be
avoided on Friday evenings.

Legend has it that Le Trépied is a place to avoid on Friday evenings, because witches had this day as their Sabbath and held covens among the stones. There are records of witch burning in the 17th century in this area of Guernsey; but elsewhere in the British Isles old practices have not died out entirely. It is reputed, but may not be true, that a stone circle in Oxfordshire can be rented for covens.

Perelle means 'rock'. The passage-grave here is 18ft (5.5m) long and has almost parallel walls, which is rare. Three times restored, there are modern supports in the chamber, which is 19ft 9in (6m) long, 6ft (2m) wide and 4ft 9in (1.3m) high. There are 12 uprights on this slightly raised site and its entrance faces north-east. Arrowheads, sherds of pottery and human bones have been found in this Late Bronze Age grave.

AVEBURY

A view of one of the majestic stone circles. Avebury is one of Britain's most important Neolithic sites; the outer circle of megaliths is probably the largest in the world.

Avebury,
Marlborough,
Wiltshire

STONE CIRCLES AND
EARTHWORKS

SU 103700

*The Avebury circles are
'among' a village. It is
therefore well signposted
6 miles (9.6km) west of
Marlborough, and 8 miles
(12.9km) north-east of
Devizes (where some artefacts
from and records of the Wessex
Group of megalithic
monuments can be seen in the
Museum, in Long Street). The
Alexander Keiller Museum in
Avebury is well worth a visit.*

*A stone outline with a familiar
shape: was that angled top surface a
foresight to the stars?*

Avebury has been called the 'metropolis of Britain' of 4600 years ago. Today it is the name of a Wessex village, but to prehistorians it is the nomenclature for an extraordinary array of monuments both in the village and nearby, including SILBURY HILL and WEST KENNET LONG BARROW.

The famous diarist and biographer John Aubrey is credited with 'discovering' Avebury on 7th January 1649, while he was out hunting foxes. He recorded that it 'does as much exceed in greatness the so renowned Stoneheng (*sic*) as a Cathedral doeth a parish Church' (*see* STONEHENGE, Wiltshire, and its Aubrey Holes). The first detailed account of the Avebury complex of Neolithic monuments was William Stukeley's *Abury, A Temple Of The British Druids* of 1743. In 1724 he attempted a reconstruction drawing, as would be seen obliquely looking northwards, of the area around Avebury. It depicts at its centre the majestic outer Great Circle of monoliths, which is the largest in the British Isles, and dates back to about 2600 BC. At that time Windmill Hill camp, also shown north-west of the Circle, was still in use. Within the stone ring, he shows two sets of concentric circles, parts of which remain today. Leading away from the circles were two avenues of stones, like great dragon features in the landscape, one curling away south-west, and the other to the south-east. The first he called Beckhampton Avenue, and the other Kennet Avenue, which swirled away to The Sanctuary and Overton Hill. South of the circles he showed Silbury Hill, and further south West Kennet Long Barrow.

Avebury lies on a mysterious alignment of sites. Taking Silbury Hill with its sighting notch as a centre point, a meridian line can be traced north through the churches at Avebury and Berwick Bassett; to the south, the same invisible straight line runs through the Milk Hill earthwork to Wilsford Church.

The most comprehensive account of this thrilling area is Aubrey Burl's *Prehistoric Avebury* (1979). The brief facts of the village circles are that they lie within a 28½ acre (11.5 hectare) site, enclosed by an outer bank, which is between 14ft and 18ft (4.2m and 5.4m) high. This was constructed from

The ditch inside the outer bank is up to 30ft (9m) deep.

RIGHT: *Avebury village, the ditch, bank and stones.*

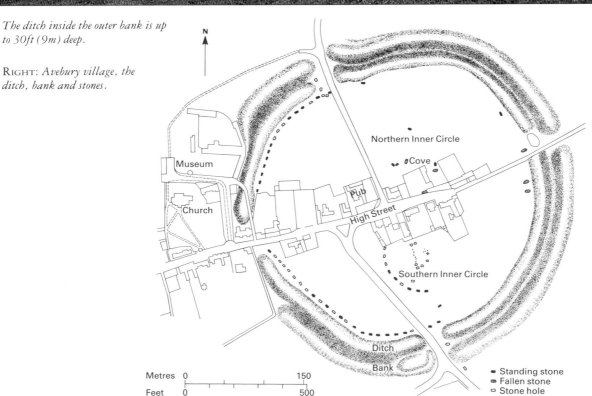

N

Northern Inner Circle

Cove

Museum

Church

Pub

High Street

Southern Inner Circle

Ditch

Bank

Metres 0 ⊢⊢⊢⊢⊢ 150
Feet 0 ⊢⊢⊢⊢⊢ 500

■ Standing stone
⬭ Fallen stone
▫ Stone hole
▫ Stone hole (probably)

the contents of a massive ditch; this was up to 30ft (9m) deep and an estimated 3,950,000 cu ft (111,864 cu m) of chalk and rubble was dug out from it. In Stukeley's 1724 engraving of the Great Circle, about 100 stones are shown, of which 27 stand today. The inner two stone circles were probably put up afterwards, though some question this; indeed a wooden structure and stone setting might have been constructed first, at the middle of the Great Circle. Avebury has suffered badly in the past, particularly at the hands of insensitive neighbours who seemed not to have appreciated its beauty and importance. In the 1930s, its condition greatly improved during the ownership of Alexander Keiller (of Dundee Marmalade fame);

his excavations of the western half between 1934 and 1939 revealed most of what we know of the circles and avenues today.

Like so many megalithic monuments, Avebury will probably conceal its secrets for a long time to come. Recently the earliest known drawing of the Great Circle (made by John Aubrey sometime between 1648 and 1663) was discovered in a library in London. It clearly shows four concentric circles within the outer bank, and also pairs of portal stones at entrances to the north, east, south and west. Thus the possibility is raised of there having once been not two avenues but four, leading away from the Avebury circles.

CASTLERIGG

*Keswick,
Cumbria*

STONE CIRCLE

NY 292236

The best time to visit Castlerigg is soon after dawn or at dusk, when the circle looks particularly imposing. However, its level site high on Chestnut Hill is accessible at all times and the views all around are stunning, but particularly to the north towards Skiddaw and Blencathra.

This Type A flattened circle has 38 stones, of which five have fallen, and is nearly complete in the form in which it was constructed in about 3000 BC. Its average diameter is 100ft (30m). Its entrance, towards the best view to the north, is marked with two fine portal stones.

Unique to this site is a rectangle of nine stones (known as The Cave) which are 'attached' to two more on the inside of the ring on the east side.

There are stones all around and in hedges, and one notable one is an outlier by the stile to the south-west, but it may have been moved there.

The late Professor Alexander Thom, who made a detailed survey of Castlerigg, concluded that it was a prehistoric observatory and capable of a number of calendrical functions. It is sometimes known as The Carles, apparently relating to a familiar old legend – that the stones are petrified men – but in fact, this is based on a mistaken reading of William Stukeley's word Carles (castle) in 1725.

Very clearly signposted by English Heritage east of Keswick, on the A66 and A591. Park at the field gate.

One of the most beautiful stone circles in Britain.

CHÛN QUOIT

*Morvah,
Cornwall*

BURIAL CHAMBER

SW 402339

*Take the B3306 west from St
Ives, turn left at Morvah,
towards Madron. Take the
lane on the right, leading to a
farm. The chamber is uphill
north-west of the farm.*

*A Cornish quoit, once covered by an
earth mound.*

This is a great and handsome monument. A quoit is a dolmen
or cromlech, and not always identifiable as a burial chamber.
Chûn Quoit is set high on a ridge, above Chûn Castle hillfort,
and was originally covered by an earth mound, of which much
evidence abounds.

It was a closed chamber. The mushroom-domed capstone
measures 11ft (3.3m) by 10ft (3m), with a maximum
thickness of 2ft 7ins (0.8m). It is supported about 7ft (2m)
from the ground by four substantial slabs. There is evidence of
an entrance passage to the south-east within the mound area.

This part of Cornwall is ideal for megalithic visits; in the
same vicinity there are Chûn Castle hillfort (very near, off the
same track), Lanyon Quoit (The Giant's Table), MEN-AN-TOL,
and Mulfra Quoit.

THE DEVIL'S ARROWS

*Boroughbridge,
Ripon,
North Yorkshire*

STANDING STONES

SE 391665

*Going north on the A1, take
the turning off (A6055) for
Boroughbridge. Immediately
cross over the road east and
carry straight on for
Boroughbridge. In the town,*

*turn left (after the Three
Arrows Hotel) up Roecliffe
Lane, passing Druids
Meadow. The Arrows are
either side, one on the left and
two in the field to the right.*

*One of the three remaining Arrows,
with the distinctive grooves at the
top.*

The famous line of three standing stones, intersected by a lane,
is 190yds (174m) in length. A fourth stone was pulled down
in the 16th century. Their heights are 22ft 6in (6.8m), 21ft
(6.4m), and 18ft (5.5m). The purpose for which they were
erected will probably never be known, although one theory
was that the unusual grooves running down the stones
provided a system of sight lines to the stars, since it was
considered unlikely that the millstone grit stones would have
weathered over millennia in such precise and matching ways.
But weathering marks on the stones are now confirmed. The
name of the stones comes from the story that the Devil aimed
and shot arrows at nearby Aldborough, but that they fell short
and landed on this site.

GRIMES GRAVES

PREHISTORIC
MINESHAFTS

TL 817898

Travel north on the A134 from Thetford to Mundford for 2 miles (3.2km), then turn left where the Graves are signposted. Park along the track on the left.

One of the galleries beneath the many mineshafts.

This is the best known source of flintstone in Britain. The Neolithic mineshafts were first worked between 3300 BC and 1650 BC, and it is estimated that nearly 4000 mines of different classes were dug. The origin of their group name is uncertain, since this was never a graveyard for human or animal remains, but may have Scandinavian roots. They were first discovered by a Reverend Greenwell in 1868 who, when exploring a circular depression, came across a gallery at a depth of 32ft (9.7m). Today you can climb 30ft (9m) down an iron ladder, and examine the elaborate gallery system below.

Shaped red-deer antlers were used as picks to dig a shaft and gallery, which took about six months. It has been estimated that one such mine would have yielded some 50 tons of flint. The stone was roughly shaped at the minehead into the required axe and arrow shapes, to save weight, and these implements were then 'exported' all over Britain.

At Grimes Graves which is a 34 acre (14 hectare) site, there are three flint layers, and the best material lies at the lowest. All these centuries later, hundreds of 'capped off' shallow craters can still be seen.

THE HURLERS

STONE CIRCLES

SX 258714

On Bodmin Moor. Travel south from Launceston towards Liskeard; take the right turning to Minions and park there.

A well-known group of Cornish circles on Bodmin Moor.

These three dressed, granite circles were set high on Bodmin Moor in about 1850 BC, close together, and so carefully that all their stones appear to be the same height. As with most circles, they are on a north-north-east/south-south-west alignment on a slope.

The northern circle is 115ft (35m) across; 15 stones remain, of which four have fallen, and there were probably a further nine there. A paved path led directly south to the slightly egg-shaped circle; its average diameter is 139ft (42.5m), and 14 stones are here, with 14 marker stones. The southernmost

circle has only nine stones left around its diameter, which measures 107ft 6in (32.8m).

The two 6ft 6in (2m) tall Pipers stand to the west, and there are doubts as to their authenticity. Petrification is part of a legend here. The famous historian William Camden, for example, recorded in his *Britannia Descriptio* (1610 edition) that: 'The neighbouring inhabitants terme them Hurlers, as being by devout and godly error perswaded that they had been men sometime transformed into stones, for profaning the Lord's Day with hurling the ball'.

KIT'S COTY HOUSE

Aylesford,
Kent

BURIAL CHAMBER

TQ 745608

Take the A229, going north
from the M20 to the M2

towards Blue Bell Hill. Turn
left for Burham, park at the
footpath on the right for the
short walk to the signposted
site.

One of the few megalithic monuments
discovered in Kent.

The close steel fencing around this burial chamber would not have amused Samuel Pepys, the famous 17th-century diarist, who saw it in happier times; he was, he recorded, 'mightily glad to see it'. Three upright stones topped by a capstone ('of great bigness') measuring some 13ft (4m) by 9ft (2.7m) are all that remain of this Neolithic burial chamber.

In Pepys' time and before, there was a long barrow here with an isolated recumbent stone at its western end; it was called 'The General's Tomb' but was destroyed by a farmer who wanted more acreage in 1867. There may also have been a forecourt façade at the eastern end. It has even suffered in name. Stow's 1580 *Chronicles of England* calls it 'Cits cotihous', and Camden's *Britannia* (1610 edition) mentions 'Keith-coty-house'.

To the south of the road leading north-west to Burham, about 500yds (457m) away, lie The Countless Stones. Now just a jumble of about 20 leaning or fallen stones, they once formed a burial chamber, sometimes called Little (or Lower) Kit's Coty House.

LITTLE MEG (MAUGHANBY)

Glassonby,
Penrith,
Cumbria

STONE CIRCLE WITH CARVINGS

NY 577375

Take the A686 from Penrith
to Alston. After about 4 miles
(6.4km), turn off to
Langwathby, then through
Little Salkeld. A little further
on towards Gamblesby, go
past the signposted track on the
left to Long Meg And Her
Daughters. This site is then
on the left in a field. Park at
the gate.

This Early Bronze Age site was once one of Cumbria's smallest circles, but today it is a half-hidden pile of disconsolate stones, with many of them aliens. An 1875 plan shows 11 stones in a ragged ring (enclosing a central cist in which a cremation was found), but there are many more now, including the largest stone, placed there in the relatively recent past. However, there are large early stones on the site, and one, lying just east of north, bears carvings of five concentric circles and a spiral.

Interestingly, among the 50 or so circles in Cumbria, LONG MEG, Little Meg, and the Glassonby stone circle, 1m (1.6km) away, are the only ones sporting carvings. The late Professor Alexander Thom proposed that Little Meg is on an alignment of considerable significance, involving his 16-month calendar.

Professor Thom proposed that, in the years 2000–1600 BC, megalithic man divided the year into 16 parts for the purposes of solar prediction.

Carvings on the remaining part of one of the stones in this small circle.

LONG MEG AND HER DAUGHTERS

*Hunsonby,
Penrith,
Cumbria*

STANDING STONE AND
STONE CIRCLE

NY 571373

Recent (1988) aerial photography has revealed a huge earthen enclosure, hitherto invisible, to the north of the circle, which meets with and fits exactly the flattened northern segment of the ring.

This was a large family! Originally there were about 70 stones, the Daughters, standing in a ring here; today 27 still stand, and 42 lie fallen. This is the third largest stone circle in Britain (the outer circles at AVEBURY, Wiltshire and Stanton Drew, Avon are bigger), and is a Type B flattened circle, set on ground which slopes to the north-east, and measuring 119yds (109m) by 102yds (93m). The stone is local granite, and the largest Daughter has a tremendous waist measurement of 10ft 9in (3.3m) and tips the scales at about 28 tons. Nothing of significance has been found at the centre of this unexcavated circle – any goods would have been easy to steal, because sadly a road runs right through it.

Long Meg, which is 12ft (3.6m) tall and of local sandstone, stands just outside the south-west entrance, 238ft (72.6m) from the circle's centre: this is the alignment of the midwinter sunset. Long Meg has a cup-and-ring, a spiral and an incomplete concentric circle carved on her 'best side', which faces north-east, back along that line.

Take the A686 from Penrith to Alston. After about 4 miles (6.5km), turn left to Langwathby, then through Little Salkeld. A little further on towards Gamblesby a signposted track to the left leads to the site.

A dramatic view of Britain's third largest stone circle.

MÊN-AN-TOL

Madron,
Penzance,
Cornwall

STANDING STONES

SW 427349

Take the B3306 west from St
Ives, turn left at Morvah, and
park after the next left
turning. Signposted.

The Stone with A Hole

The name of this group is Cornish for 'stone with a hole', and refers to the now central, circular stone. It is famous for its smooth hole, which is in the middle of the stone as it shows above the ground, and occupies about half its size. The stone is about 4ft 6in (1.3m) across its centre. The three stones are now aligned, but were once in a triangular formation, which makes certain astro-archaeological claims for it difficult to support.

Centuries ago, the holed stone was known as The Devil's Eye. Legends persist of strange rituals which involve crawling (often three times) through the carved-out aperture to conjure up cures, fertility, prophecies, etc. Cures for rickets in children were always a popular request. Elsewhere in Cornwall, in a private garden in Gweek, is a tall, triangular slab with a circular hole in it, 17¼ins (44cm) in diameter. These are two Bronze Age puzzles yet to be solved.

MERRIVALE

Princeton,
Tavistock,
Devonshire

STONE CIRCLE, STONE
ROWS AND CAIRNS

SX 555744

Not signposted. The hamlet of
Merrivale is midway between
Tavistock and Princeton
(Dartmoor Prison) on the
B3357; the rows are on the
right, about 400yds (365m)
to the east of the pub.

An exciting megalithic complex on
Dartmoor.

Mysteries abound at this bleak Bronze Age site. It is one of the most accessible among more than 70 or so stone rows on the vast area of Dartmoor, and features a multiplicity of megalithic remains. In this single respect it rivals the stone rows at KERMARIO and MÉNEC in Brittany.

Here there are two double rows and one single one. Both double ones are 'planted' east to west. The northernmost is 596ft (182m) long, and has some 170 stones. To the south of it is a 865ft (264m) long row, containing more than 200 stones. The third, single, row is only 140ft (43m) long, and is directed to the south-west.

At Merrivale there is also a fine standing stone, nearly 11ft (3.3m) high, a very incomplete stone circle oval in plan, and the remains of a small cairn-circle, which is located for some inexplicable reason about halfway along the second double stone row.

THE MERRY MAIDENS

*St Buryan,
Penzance,
Cornwall*

STONE CIRCLE

SW 432245

*Signposted. On the B3315,
4 miles (6.5km) south-
west of Penzance.*

This is Cornwall's prettiest stone circle. It is believed to be complete, which is rare, is 77ft 10in (23.7m) in diameter, and has 19 stones in its ring. They range in height from 4ft 6in (1.4m) in the south-west to 2ft 6in (0.8m) on the north-east side. The gap, exactly at the east, was either an entrance or the site of a missing stone. This delightful site has also been known as the Rosemodress circle, and as Dans Meyn, which is the Cornish for 'stone dance'.

According to legend, these Maidens were turned to stone for making merry on the Sabbath to the music of two Pipers – the two tall stones standing like naughty non-identical twins in another field to the north-east of the circle. The same legend attaches to THE PIPER'S STONES, Co Wicklow, Ireland. The north-east Piper is the tallest Bronze Age Cornish menhir, at 15ft (4.6m).

A peculiarity here is that when a line is drawn from this menhir through the second Piper, to its south-west, and continued onwards, it just touches the north-west edge of The Merry Maidens – forming yet another mysterious alignment of stones in Cornwall.

THE ROLLRIGHT STONES

*Little Rollright,
Chipping Norton,
Oxfordshire*

STONE CIRCLE,
STANDING STONE AND
BURIAL CHAMBER

SP 296308

*Travel north on the A34 from
Oxford. Pass the turning for
Chipping Norton and
Banbury. Turn left opposite
the second turning for Great
Rollright. Well signposted.*

This splendid and accessible group consists of a stone circle (The King's Men), a standing stone (The King Stone), and a burial chamber (The Whispering Knights). The King's Men is privately owned and a small fee is charged (which goes to animal causes) for a visit to stones which have distinctly anthropomorphic shapes. Dating back probably to 3000 BC, there are about 77 stones around the 103ft (31.4m) diameter. Early in the 17th century only 26 were standing; this captivating circle, tucked into its wooded glade, has been much tinkered with, and there was a major re-erection of stones in 1882.

The King Stone is across the road from the circle to the north-west; this twisted, pitted menhir is certainly prehistoric, but undated. It was probably once connected to a barrow to the west of it. Clearly visible from The King's Men, due east over rolling farmland, stands The Whispering Knights. This burial chamber was probably part of a long barrow in about 3750 BC. The steel fencing tightly encloses the mounded remains of a fallen capstone and four other stones leaning together around the south-south-east facing entrance.

The Rollright Stones have been popular for many centuries. The many legends attached to them involve Danish kings, druids, petrification, fairies, witches and covens, sacrifices and fertility. One such legend tells how the King's Men go down to a spring in Little Rollright spinney at midnight to drink; the King Stone goes to the spring too, but starts his journey only when he hears Long Compton church clock strike midnight (*see* FOUR STONES, Walton, Powys).

ROUGHTING LINN

*Doddington,
Berwick upon Tweed*

CARVED ROCK FACE

NT 984367

*South of Berwick-upon-
Tweed, leave the A1, after
Scremerston, on the right on to
the B6525. Do not turn left
at the crossroads for Lowick,
but continue, take the first
right turning signposted to
Milfield, and then park near
the track for Roughting Linn
Farm. The rock is tucked
away, just up the track, on
the right in a clearing.*

*One of over 60 mysterious carvings
on this natural stone outcrop.*

This important site can truly be called megalithic. The natural rock outcrop measures about 60ft by 40ft (18m by 12m), and is covered with over 60 cup-and-ring marks and other motifs. The grinding of holes in stone to produce these marks was an ancient, almost universal, practice in Neolithic times, commonly associated with funerary rites of some kind. They have been found all over Europe, Russia, Australia and America.

It could be argued that cups carved into horizontal slabs may have held oil, blood, or holy water but since they also occur on vertical stone faces, they may simply have been a form of exterior decoration, or fashion designs or paint boxes for 'the painted ones' (*see* SKARA BRAE). With megalithic mysteries such as these, one feels, surely, that a code, a Neolithic Linear B, is involved and will soon be deciphered.

RUDSTON MONOLITH

*All Saints Churchyard,
Rudston,
Bridlington,
Humberside*

STANDING STONE

TA 097677

*Rudston is about 5 miles
(8km) west of Bridlington
on the B1253.*

*The tallest standing stone in
Britain, measuring 25ft 9in (7.8m)
high, above ground.*

This is the tallest standing stone in the British Isles, and it is to be found only 12ft (3.6m) away from the north wall of one of the Church of England's places of worship, in its graveyard. It is therefore probable that the site of All Saints Church has been a sacred one for more than 4000 years continuously. The crumbling top of the 25ft 9ins (7.8m) high stone is possible evidence of an early attempt to 'christianize' it; this was common practice in Britain in the first centuries AD, and indeed elsewhere in Europe. As with so many monuments of this type, the source of its stone was not the nearest available, but gritstone known to have been quarried about 10m (16km) away on the coast south of Scarborough.

SILBURY HILL

*Beckhampton,
Marlborough,
Wiltshire*

EARTH MOUND

SU 100685

*5 miles (8km) west of
Marlborough on the A4. Park
in the lay-by at the base of the
mound.*

Silbury Hill is Europe's tallest prehistoric monument, and one of the world's largest man-made mounds. About 4600 years ago some 500 people slaved for approximately 15 years, under very sophisticated direction, to put 8.75 million cu ft (248,000 cu metres) of earth and aggregate on top of a 3.75 million cu ft (107,000 cu metres) natural hill. The base of the Hill is 550ft (167m) in diameter – and is perfectly round, like a bowl barrow. Its summit, 130ft (40m) high, is flat-topped and 100ft (30m) wide. It has a distinct notch, near the top, best seen from the east, and the whole is surrounded by a huge, causewayed moat.

What the Hill's significance, or purpose, was remains a mystery – for it is an undisputed fact that there is nothing and nobody buried inside Silbury Hill.

It may indeed be shaped like a bowl barrow, but the next highest of Wessex's bowl barrows (of which there are approximately 380) is only 25ft (8m) high; moreover, the Hill occupies 5½ acres (2.2 hectares) of chalky Wiltshire valley floor, unlike all the other barrows.

A large-scale excavation during 1967–70, led by Professor R.J.C. Atkinson, was televised by the BBC in the hope that dark secrets or a magnificent burial would be revealed. There were none. The writer Michael Dames has suggested that the mound and moat might be a sculpture of The Great Goddess, but he finally acknowledges that the monument remains 'a stupendous enigma'.

*An aerial view of one of the world's
largest man-made mounds; the
extraordinary crop circles in the corn
field behind it appeared overnight.*

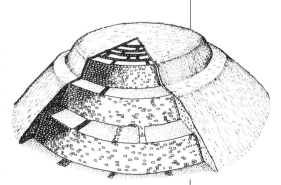

*The complex stepped construction of
Silbury Hill (towards the top),
which is one of the world's largest
man-made mounds and 'a
stupendous enigma'.*

STONEHENGE

*Amesbury,
Wiltshire*

STONE CIRCLES,
HENGE, AVENUE,
CURSUS AND STANDING
STONE

SU 123422

Stonehenge is the most complete, the most important, and the most famous prehistoric site in Europe. There is no single answer to the first and inevitable question 'what was it for?'. This is mainly because the complex was constructed in six broad phases; these have been very fully described at book length, and made the subject of commentaries literally for hundreds of years.

In about 3200 BC, the circular, non-defensive ditch was dug providing, over some 28,000 man-hours, about 3,500 cu yds (2,700 cu m) of chalk rubble for the bank inside; the 56 Aubrey Holes (white-painted markers today) were made, and (probably) the famous outlier, The Heel Stone, was put in place; the midsummer solstice sunrise occurs almost over this stone, an event celebrated by latter-day Druids since 1906. A

A familiar view of one of the most famous megalithic monuments in the world.

timber building may have been at the centre of the earth ring.

Around 2200 BC a double blue stone circle was erected (*see* GORS FAWR, Dyfed, for the amazing source of these stones). Then the Altar Stone arrived, a companion to The Heel Stone (a recent discovery), as well as two more entrance stones, and the first stage of The Avenue.

About 100 years later the main construction phase took place: the Altar Stone was moved, and the Sarsen Circle of 30 stones was put up (17 remain today), as probably were the four Station Stones and the five Great Trilithons which make up the Sarsen Horseshoe. Stone 56 stands alone in the middle of the Great Trilithons, its tenon visible on top, and is without doubt one of the most beautiful dressed stones in the world. In approximately 1800 BC, the Altar Stone was placed in its present position, the 29 Z Holes and 30 Y Holes were dug (the Aubrey Holes were once called the X Holes), and a bluestone setting of at least 19 stones was erected but then dismantled.

Take the A303 west from Amesbury, and then the A344 to the right. The stones are fenced off from the public. The site is open from 10.00am to 6.00pm in the summer, 10.00am to 4.00pm in the winter (1st October − 31st March). Kiosks at the entrance sell multi-lingual maps and guides to Stonehenge and other local Wessex prehistoric monuments. Toilets and parking. Admission charges (but free to English Heritage members).

A view towards one of the inner Sarsen Trilithons, of Stones 57 and 58. Note the tenons on the tall Stone 56 on the left.

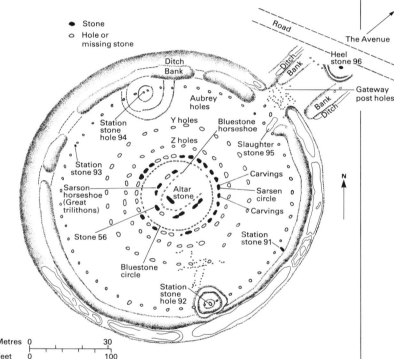

Stonehenge as it never was. Several construction phases, shown in one plan, from about 3100 BC to about 1550 BC. The Avenue was extended in about 1100 BC.

In about 1550 BC the Bluestone Circle (60 stones) and the Bluestone Horseshoe (19 stones) were raised into position, and, finally, in about 1100 BC The Avenue was extended south and then eastwards. This brief account necessarily omits many details which alone confirm that Stonehenge was mathematically an extremely sophisticated set of calendrical devices.

Stonehenge, the first stage of which predates the Great Pyramid at Giza, was first mentioned in literature by Geoffrey of Monmouth in his famous 'history' of 1135. His account of Merlin the wizard and the plan to 'fly' some great stones over from Naas, Co Kildare, was the first of a very long and often brilliant and entertaining collection of speculations about the origins of the stones and their settings. In summary, serious attempts have been made to prove that Stonehenge has been a sunrise, a moonrise, and an eclipse predictor.

Books such as Gerald Hawkins' *Stonehenge Decoded* enormously widened public interest in this extraordinary set of

A close-up view of the morticed and tenoned Trilithon comprising Stones 57, 58 and their lintel.

stones. But he was merely a recent entrant into the list of those who have felt personally involved with them, and a need to bring their own interpretations to the subject. Such a list would include Professor Richard Atkinson (the excavator and greatest authority on Stonehenge), John Aubrey (he of the Holes), William Blake, William Camden, Thomas Carlyle, William Caxton, Charles I and II, John Constable, Daniel Defoe, Ralph Waldo Emerson, John Evelyn, John Flamsteed, Jacquetta Hawkes, Henry VII and VIII, Henry of Huntingdon (who quoted Geoffrey of Monmouth's vanished history), Sir Fred Hoyle, Inigo Jones (who named The Altar Stone), Ben Jonson, Alexander Keiller (*see* AVEBURY, Wiltshire), the firm of Knight, Frank & Rutley, London (which auctioned off Stonehenge on 21st September 1915 as Lot 15 in a public sale; it went for £6600), Paul Nash, Samuel Pepys, Sir William Flinders Petrie, John Speed, John Stow, William Stukeley, Professor Alexander Thom (and probably every other serious archaeologist who has ever lived).

Countless times through its very long history, Stonehenge has been threatened by all kinds of authorities (even the Royal Air Force, which wanted to flatten it during World War I). Recently, there has been much public and professional controversy about how to cope with more than 700,000 annual visitors and all their needs. A new Visitors' Centre, much further away from the stones, is a welcome likelihood. To all newcomers, an unexpected warning: Stonehenge, at first sight, *always* appears much smaller than imagined. This is partly a trick of the landscape, and is a common impression.

The mighty Sarsen Stones (from the right) 29, 30, 1 and 2, with their three lintels, as seen from the Heel Stone. Stone 56, with its tenon, stands majestically in the background.

SWINSIDE (SUNKENKIRK)

*Broughton in Furness,
Millom,
Cumbria*

STONE CIRCLE

SD 172883

*32 stones survive in this beautiful
ring; 23 more have all fallen
inwards.*

*Travel west to Broughton in
Furness on the A595 past
Duddon Bridge. Take the
next road on the right, where
it is signposted; on foot, fork
left at Craig Hall up a
private track towards
Swinside Farm. The site is
about 1 mile (1.6km)
along on the right.*

This Late Neolithic circle has been called the most beautiful in England. Originally, there were a probable 55 stones, set closely together, almost like a defensive palisade, in stone rubble. Only 32 of them still stand, all of which have strangely fallen inwards. The palisade effect recalls CASTLE-RIGG, also in Cumbria.

The diameter of the ring is about 94ft (29m), and its entrance is at the south-east. This is guarded by two tall portal stones against the outside of the circle; this arrangement is also seen at LONG MEG AND HER DAUGHTERS, again in Cumbria, and far away at Ballynoe, County Down.

Swinside was excavated in 1901 and although little was found, there were fragments of red iron-stone which could have been used as pigment for body painting (*see* SKARA BRAE). The alternative name of Sunkenkirk derives from an old story that the local grey slate stones were foundation stones for a church under construction, and that the Devil came each night to re-bury them.

TRETHEVY QUOIT

*St Cleer,
Cornwall*

BURIAL CHAMBER WITH
PORT-HOLE IN
CAPSTONE

SX 259688

*Take the B3254 south from
Launceston to Liskeard. Pass
the right turn to Minions;
take the next right to the
hamlet of Darite and travel
1/2 mile (0.8km) south.
The Quoit is in a field behind
cottages on your right.*

*This dramatic burial chamber is
famed for the hole in its capstone.*

The wonder of this dramatic chamber (once known locally as The Giant's House) is not so much the size of the capstone, which is 12ft (3.7m) long and, in its half-fallen state, 15ft (4.6m) high in the air, but that the natural hole pierces it at its now highest point. It was probably chosen for this aperture.

The function of port-holes is a mystery; experts speculate that they were used for astronomical observation or, perhaps, to allow good or evil spirits to come and go. Whatever their purpose, they are rare in Britain. The rectangular chamber, which is 6ft 6in by 5ft (2m by 1.5m), is made of seven uprights, averaging 10ft (3m) in height, and is divided by a large doorstone at its eastern end. There is a puzzling 'doorway' cut out of the entrance stone, which may have been for the passage of bodies, but, curiously, the sloping angle of the top of this hole is reminiscent of many free-standing stones (for example, THE STONES OF STENNESS, Orkney Islands).

WEST KENNET AVENUE

*Avebury,
Marlborough,
Wiltshire*

STONE ROWS

From SU 103699
(Avebury) to SU
118679 (The
Sanctuary)

All through history, ceremonial avenues have been erected to someone's greater glory (in Paris over 100 years ago; in Bucharest in modern times) or for ritual of unknown origins. Some are literally straightforward; others have recently been shown to be astonishingly subtle astronomical instruments (*see* KERMARIO and MENEC, both in Morbihan, France).

West Kennet Avenue was originally almost 1½m (2.4km) long and connected the south-south-east entrance of the earthwork at Avebury with the concentric circles at The Sanctuary on Overton Hill. Some 30 pairs of stones in the northern section have been re-erected, and missing stones are indicated by markers.

There is a mysterious fact about this 'stone row'. In Late Neolithic times (as confirmed by grave goods and burials), it was decreed that the shapes of the 100 pairs of stones should alternate, both down each row and in their opposites, so that tall narrow pillars are followed by wide 'lozenge' shapes – thus suggesting male and female forms. They average 10ft (3m) in height, and stand, within their giant puzzle, about 80ft (24m) apart. Perhaps the raising of a form of energy, through coils and spirals, was involved.

The shapes of the 100 pairs of stones in the Avenue mysteriously alternate.

The Avenue runs roughly parallel to the B4003, going south-east from Avebury village towards West Kennet village.

WEST KENNET LONG BARROW

*Avebury,
Marlborough,
Wiltshire*

LONG CHAMBERED
BARROW

SU 104677

This is the most famous of Britain's 260 or so long barrows, of which 148 are to be found in the county of Wiltshire alone. In many parts of Europe long barrows have been given giants' names, as a reminder of their size and presence. But one of their puzzling aspects is that they are very long, for no apparent reason; the chambered tomb in West Kennet Long Barrow occupies just an eighth of the barrow's 340ft (104m) length. Nevertheless, it is the longest chambered tomb in England and Wales.

The Barrow is similar to many long, raised enclosures in Germany and Denmark, and particularly to GROENJAEGERS HOEJ ('The Green Hunter's Mountain'), Denmark. Construction commenced about 3600 BC, which surprisingly is some

Signposted about ½ mile (0.8km) west of West Kennet and 1 mile (1.6km) east of Beckhampton. Some parking space there. Then walk up path around fields for ½ mile (0.8km). Take torch.

The largest chambered tomb in England and Wales, and one of no less than 148 in Wiltshire.

A side chamber.

Earth barrow continues

Ditch

Ditch

Forecourt

Entrances

N

Metres 0   2

Feet   0   9

Drystone walling, which comes from 25m (40km) away.

West Kennet Long Barrow: the passage-grave occupies only one-eighth of the barrow's 340ft (104m) length. The side chambers were placed within an exact isosceles triangle.

400 years before the first stage of STONEHENGE. It was finally closed by the Beaker people in about 2500 BC.

As one looks along its green and bumpy spine, even the exterior presents an impression of design and effort on a scale which must tell us how important the site was in Neolithic times. Entering the tomb beyond the forecourt past the three massive upright sarsens (the biggest of which stands 12ft (3.7m) above the ground and weighs 16 tons), there are two burial chambers either side and a larger polygonal one at the end of the passage. The sarsen stones used for the interior uprights, capstones and corbelling are undecorated (unlike, for example, some of those at the mighty NEWGRANGE), and are local. However, the drystone walling is known to come from the Frome area, which is 25m (40km) away.

Why, therefore, was more than a ton of either Forest Marble or oolitic limestone purposefully hauled over such a distance? The probable answer does not involve magnetism, healing powers, or a false druidical significance, and is a surprisingly sophisticated one, given that it was spotted more than 5500 years ago: it was the right stone for the job, being comparatively easily worked and known to withstand weathering. Indeed, the stone is still used for house building today, as visitors to the Cotswold area can see.

The interior of West Kennet Long Barrow has an attractive geometry. Excavations in 1955–56 revealed that the side chambers occur inside an exact isosceles triangle, the height of which is twice the length of its base. Within were found the scattered remains of 40 to 50 people, although not all were buried at the same time. The chambers also contained relics and artefacts, some of which may be seen at the Devizes Museum, Devizes, Wiltshire. Those included later Neolithic Peterborough and grooved-ware, knives, scrapers, flint arrowheads, jewellery, and animal remains, such as a carefully sharpened boar's tusk, and a beaver's tooth.

The pottery was, as always, in pieces, and it is entirely reasonable to assume that a pot is totally unlikely to remain in its complete form for more than 5500 years. And yet the assumption may not be a sound one.

The destruction of pots over the dead in their place of burial used to be common all those years ago in very widely scattered cultures; the act was seen to symbolize the liberation of the spirits of the dead from perfect vessels, the former bodies, and it also provided sherds as utensils for the journeys thereafter. The burials at West Kennet Long Barrow, together with their magnificent housing, elucidate some mysteries but hide others.

I.33

BROWNE'S HILL

Kernanstown,
Carlow,
Co Carlow

PORTAL-TOMB

Map 3 (East) 275176

Very well signposted as you approach. Park by the signpost there, and then walk for 5 minutes around the fenced perimeter of the fields.

The capstone of this portal-tomb weighs about 100 tons, and is one of the heaviest in Europe.

The sight of this tomb, from the small car park looking south-west over fields, is magical. From this distance, the rough-hewn eastern vertical face of the capstone proclaims a sort of bullish majesty. It is named after a large local house, but must surely have been called The Giant's-something in the past. That stone reputedly weighs more than 100 tons, and is one of the heaviest capstones in Europe.

Browne's Hill (closely fenced in) is set on a slope, from west to east. Unusually, it was probably never covered in earth, as were almost all tombs of this type. Beyond the southern entrance, just to the west, there are three uprights, and two recumbents lie beneath the fallen western side of the capstone. A fourth upright stands nearby. From the west, up the slope, the capstone looks like a huge pudding, unsubtle in outline and yet smoothed to perfection all over; and its belly, the underside, a massive 41ft (12.5m) in girth, has been shaped to a completely flat surface. This must have been a tomb of an important figure, and in need of very secure protection.

I.34

CARROWMORE GROUP

Sligo,
Co Sligo

CEMETERY; PASSAGE-TOMBS, DOLMENS AND STONE WITH PORT-HOLE

Map 2 (West) 166333

Well signposted. In fields 2 miles (3.2km) south-west of Sligo.

An antler pin and a walrus bone ring were found in Grave 27.

Ireland's largest concentration of megaliths is at Carrowmore. The legendary Queen Maeve's Grave is in the far distance.

This huge site is 1 mile by 1½ mile (1.6km by 2.4km) in area, and possesses the largest concentration of megaliths in Ireland. It is possible that it was once the largest cemetery in Western Europe but, because tragic and scandalous quarrying has destroyed vital evidence, we will never know. One recent count produced 42 stone circles, 14 burial-chambers, and five other cists.

The necropolis is dominated by Queen Maeve's Grave (or Cairn or Lump) on Knocknarea. One of the largest tombs is Listoghil; the site is typical of the group, and of a type which spread west and north from the Boyne Valley, via LOUGHCREW

and Carrowkeel. The recently excavated Grave 27 is a very early version of the passage-tomb, in a cruciform shape; this is important because its probable construction date (before 3750 BC) controversially proposes that passage-tombs in western and eastern Ireland were not initiated by Brittany's megalith builders at all, but instead were developed independently by an already existing Neolithic population. Furthermore, Tomb 4, in the field on the Sligo side of the car park, contains the remains of a passage-tomb which may be the earliest in the country — pre-4500 BC. Diffusionist theories which suggest links between early cultures may yet be found wanting.

CREEVYKEEL

*Cliffony,
Co Sligo*

COURT-TOMB

Map 2 (West) 172354

*Signposted near the Creevykeel
crossroads. Up a path behind
a house east of the road from
Sligo to Bundoran.*

*Looking east across two burial
chambers to the huge oval open court.*

There are about 350 known court-tombs in the whole of
Ireland, but only five of them are in the south of the country.
Creevykeel is one of the most impressive, and has been finely
restored so is well worth a visit.

It is located within a clear wedge-shaped cairn, and was
originally about 200ft (61m) in length. The entrance is at the
eastern end through a small passage, which leads into the oval
forecourt; this has the extraordinary dimensions of 56ft by 33ft
(17m by 10m), and was, of course, originally paved. The tomb
continues on beneath a lintel stone through two successive
chambers, where four cremations have been found. Sealed off,
but even further on, are the remains of a possible three more
burial chambers, of which one plainly has a side entrance.

One of the most exciting discoveries at Creevykeel came in
1935; a chalk ball, similar to ones found in Brittany, provided
further confirmation that court-tombs, such as this, often
slightly pre-date passage-tombs. It also highlights fascinating questions about the migration of cultures. But much of
this history remains undiscovered.

DEERPARK (MAGHERAGHANRUSH)

*Sligo,
Co Sligo*

COURT-TOMB

Map 1 (North) 175336

*Signposted 'Leacht con Mhic
Ruis' 4 miles (6.5 km) east of
Sligo on the road from
Leckaun to Sligo; then a ten-
minute walk south on a
footpath.*

*The full length of one of Sligo's
many fine tombs.*

This is just one among many prehistoric sites in Sligo which
merit attention. It is situated on the top of a limestone ridge
with splendid views of Lough Gill. The 50ft (15m) long
central court lies within a cairn twice as long. One
two-chambered gallery is off the west end, and two more lie off
the eastern end of the court. They were originally roofed, of
course, and the line of the kerb indicates a trapezoidal
construction, dated at 3500–3000 BC.

DROMBEG

*Skibbereen,
Co Cork*

STONE CIRCLE, HUT
AND COOKING PLACE

Map 4 (South) 124035

*Signposted. 1 ½ miles
(2.4km) east of Glandore. To
the east of a side road, find the
400yd (366m) path.*

*Drombeg is noted for its prehistoric
cooking area.*

RIGHT: *The neat stone circle at this
megalithic complex.*

Drombeg was built around 1500 BC. It is full of interest as a collective site in reasonable condition.

Entering the site from the north, one comes to the stone circle 30ft (9.1m) in diameter on its natural rocky terrace. Of the original 17 stones, 13 remain in this well-ordered place. To the left of the entrance, one fine portal stone is 7ft 2in (2.2m) high; its opposite number is recumbent, measures 6ft 10in (1.9m), and has two egg-shaped cup-marks (one with a ring around it).

Excavations in 1957/58 revealed cremated bones in a deliberately broken pot near the centre of the circle. There is an additional interest for followers of Professor Thom, in that the axis of the circle points to the setting sun at the winter solstice.

A few yards to the west there are two adjoining huts; the smaller had a cooking place 5ft by 3ft 6in (1.5m by 1.1m), on the east side, which was still in use in the 5th century AD; this prehistoric kitchen had a trough in which water was boiled by dropping hot stones into it, and there was a well and a hearth for cooking. Drombeg has a functional but rather bleak feel about it.

FOURKNOCKS

A decorated lintel stone.

*Naul,
Co Meath*

PASSAGE-TOMB

Map 3 (East) 310262

*Signposted. 2 miles (3.2km)
north-west of Naul and 17
miles (27.2km) north of
Dublin. Obtain a key from the
first house on your left going
down the hill, going east from
the stile. Ten minutes' walk
up the path.*

This tomb with the puzzling name is only about 9 miles (14.5km) south-west of NEWGRANGE, the most famous of them all, and it has been dated to 1900 BC by the radiocarbon method but may well be 500 or more years older. The stretched oval main chamber is 21ft (6.4m) long – unusually long for an Irish tomb. Today it is covered and preserved by a concrete dome. It has some similarities to Portuguese passage-tombs, but most experts believe that it was the work of migrants and their successors from Brittany, and not from the Iberian peninsula.

Most unusually, the main chamber has probably never contained burials – although 60 or more of them were found during the 1950/52 excavations elsewhere on the site. It could have been a safe and protected meeting place for unknown ritual practices, celebrations of seasonal changes, and so on. It is notable also for its 12 decorated stones, one of which bears a crudely carved 'funny' face which is probably the earliest Irish portrait!

There are two other sites on this slate ridge: a crematorium, about 150yds (137m) east of the passage-tomb, with five cists containing infants, and two urn cremations; and there is a 50ft (15m) round barrow with a cremation and Bronze Age pots.

THE GREAT CIRCLE/LOUGH GUR

*Lough Gur,
Co Limerick*

STONE CIRCLE WITHIN
HENGE

Map 4 (South) 164140

*12½ miles (20km) south of
Limerick, east off the R512
near Kilmallock. Well
signposted.*

*Near the east-facing entrance to this
huge, elegant earth-banked circle of
contiguous stones at Lough Gur.*

Lough Gur, in terms of its location, is one of the most important prehistoric sites in Britain. Within the vicinity are more than 30 places of separate interest to anyone concerned with 'the way we lived then', and 15 of them make a full day out, with the assistance of the excellent Visitors' Centre.

Easily the most exciting of them is The Great Circle, a full orchestra of a place. The ring of contiguous orthostats (all stones touching) is 148ft (45m) in diameter, and is literally backed up by an earthen bank which averages nearly 33ft (10m) in its width. The flat, slightly raised area within this mighty, densely palisaded construction conveys prehistoric activities of high importance. On the north-east is a dressed stone of volcanic breccia which weighs about 50 tons. The impressive paved entrance to the circle, dated at about 2000 BC, is at the east.

Nearby and worth visiting is The Giant's Grave, a wedge-shaped gallery grave. Excavations in 1938 (preceding those at The Great Stone Circle by a year) revealed remains of at least four children and eight adults; Neolithic and Early Bronze Age pottery was also found. These are but two attractions in a huge area which was a major Stone Age dwelling place and was then used in parts right into early Christian times.

KILCLOONEY MORE

*Ardara,
Co Donegal*

PORTAL-TOMBS AND
COURT-TOMB

Map 1 (North) 172396

*¼ mile (0.4km) up the lane
behind Kilclooney Church, 4
miles (6.5km) north-west of
Ardara.*

*The 'flying' capstone of this fine Irish
portal-tomb presents a memorable
picture.*

Here are two portal-tombs within what remains of an 82ft (25m) long cairn. Both their chambers face eastwards and are about 29ft (9m) apart. The larger is visually impressive, and has a bird-like appearance to its capstone, which is some 13ft (4m) long and about 20ft (6m) across. It is supported by twin uprights 6ft (1.8m) high. The western chamber is almost identical but smaller.

About 66yds (60m) to the east of the road lies a corbelled court-tomb. It is well preserved, but very small, the maximum diameter of its mound being only 36ft (11m).

About 5½ miles (8.8km) to the north-east on the road to Trusklieve (near the northern tip of Toome Lough) is a long cairn containing two portal-tombs called Dermot and Grania's Bed; one wonders where such a cosy name came from, to come to rest on such flat and lonely moorland. About 160 portal-tombs are known to survive in Ireland; many are dramatically sited.

KNOWTH

*Slane,
Boyne Valley,
Co Meath*

DOUBLE PASSAGE-TOMB
TUMULUS WITH
CARVINGS

Map 3 (East) 299274

One of the carved kerbstones.

*Signposted, off the N51 Slane
to Drogheda road 2 miles
(3.2km) south-east of Slane.
NOTE: Knowth is closed to
the public while excavations
continue.*

A remarkable flint macehead,
probably a ritual object since
it is beautifully marked but
unused, was one of the finds
inside Knowth.

Knowth is one of the grandest of the 300 or so passage-tombs in Ireland (even though presently laid bare). About 25 tombs are in the Boyne Valley, the huge and impressive necropolis about which much has been written in recent years. Knowth is broadly contemporary with NEWGRANGE (middle of the fourth millennium BC). Excavations began here in 1962, and have gone on ever since under the direction of Professor George Eogan; interesting and valuable information continues to be published.

Site 1 is the great centre mound and covers an amazing 1½ acres (0.6 hectares). It is nearly oval in shape and measures between 262ft (80m) and 312ft (95m) across with its maximum height about 40ft (12m). Thrilling discoveries were made here in the late 1960s, revealing that this great mound contains two passage-tombs; they were probably built facing away from each other at the same time, on a precise east-west axis. These orientations have suggested to archaeologists that they had special functions at spring and autumn equinoxes and were designed to produce very accurate times for, among other activities, sowing and reaping.

The western undifferentiated tomb passage is 111ft (34m) long; outside its entrance lies a large kerbstone, 10ft 2ins (3.1m) long, decorated with concentric rectangles, and featuring a vertical groove carved into it. The slightly longer kerbstone at NEWGRANGE, which has more elaborate carvings, also has such a groove. A sill stone was placed where the passage widened into the chamber, and a carved stele was at one time there.

Its eastern counterpart is cruciform in shape, and is perhaps the longest tomb in north-west Europe: it measures just over 131ft (40m). Its right-hand recess is the largest of three and contains a heavily carved and decorated stone basin. Cremation remains have been found in all three recesses. Chamber stones at Knowth bear intricate carvings of familiar motifs, such as crescents, concentric circles, labyrinths, serpent shapes, spirals and zigzags. They constitute one of the great collections of passage-grave art in the world, and have been the subject of many theories.

Excavations at Knowth have continued since 1962.

LOUGHCREW

Oldcastle,
Co Meath

PASSAGE-TOMB
CEMETERY

Map 3 (East) 258278
(marked as Megalithic
Cemetery)

Loughcrew is part of the famed Boyne Valley group of megalithic tombs. The tombs here were probably, but not definitely, the work of Breton migrants as they passed west from their landing point at the mouth of the River Boyne, via the great sites of Dowth, KNOWTH and NEWGRANGE. The Loughcrew Hills have in the past been generally called Sliabh na Caillighe (The Hill of The Witch), but this is actually the name of a cairn in Carnbane East.

The sadly vandalized and neglected Carnbane sites are on two hill tops on a 3 mile (4.8km) east-to-west ridge. More than 30 tumuli are scattered about; a variety of tombs lie within them, and often their stones are decorated. The carved sunray motif occurs at Loughcrew, and is yet another piece of evidence of solar observation in Ireland. On Carnbane West, the decorated Cairn L (the third largest) contains a standing stone; it can be found to the left of the first left turning below the car park. Its purpose is still a matter of speculation.

LEFT: *Rayed, possibly solar,*
carvings in one of the Loughcrew
tombs.

BELOW: *Loughcrew passage-tomb*
cemetery.

Signposted. Marked as
Carnbane East and Carnbane
West in the Loughcrew Hills
3 miles (4.8km) south-east of
Oldcastle, and then up tracks.

The writer Martin Brennan found that the rising sun on November 8 (an important date in the ancient eight-fold year) had its light beam so narrowly sculpted by the entrance of Cairn L that it enters like a laser beam to illuminate just the top of the white standing stone.

NEWGRANGE

*Slane,
Boyne Valley,
Co Meath*

PASSAGE-TOMB

Map 3 (East) 301274

The entrance to Newgrange, showing the rectangular light entrance hole above it. A massive carved stone lies in front; it is famous for its unfathomable spirals and lozenges.

In three square miles (7.8sq km) overlooking the historic River Boyne there are 20 or more passage-graves; the great tombs of KNOWTH (to the north-west of Newgrange) and Dowth (north-east) are nearby, and there are standing stones, barrows and enclosures in abundance. Along with Carnac in Brittany, the Boyne Valley offers one of the greatest megalithic feasts in Europe.

In its much restored form, Newgrange is perhaps the most spectacular prehistoric cemetery in the world; detailed, comprehensive accounts of it are widely available. Here, it is sufficient to state that the monument took some 30 years to construct some time towards the end of the fourth millennium BC. It consists of a mound, containing a passage leading to a

About 28 miles (45km) north-west of Dublin. Travel 6 miles (9.6km) west from Drogheda on the N51; turn south 2 miles (3.2km) before Slane, following the signposts.

These linked spirals exemplify the great megalithic art at Newgrange.

RIGHT: *The covering mound at Newgrange was originally 40ft (12.2m) high; 12 of the surrounding circle of stones survive. (After M.J. O'Kelly)*

Newgrange, one of the great Boyne Valley tombs in section and plan. The dashed lines indicate the path of the midwinter sunrise rays for about 20 minutes through the unique roof box. {After a diagram in 'Midwinter sunrise at Newgrange', Nature, 249 (1974)}

The notable corbelled roofing.

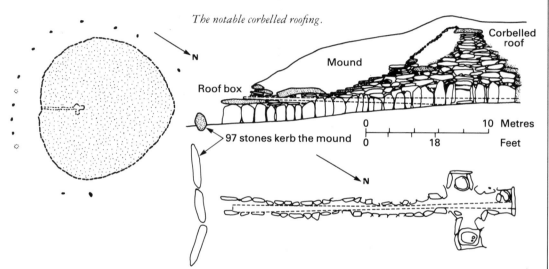

burial chamber, which has most of a circle of stones surrounding it; inside and out, some of the stones have been decorated with carved motifs of different kinds. But this simple description is misleading.

To begin outside, the ring of standing stones is almost unique in Great Britain and Ireland, with CLAVA CAIRNS, Culloden, being the other notable example (but also *see* LOANHEAD OF DAVIOT, Grampian). Though consisting today of only 12 stones, the Newgrange circle is one of the largest, with a diameter of about 340ft (104m). Inside it, the immense mound was originally 40ft (12.2m) high, made up of alternate layers of small stones and earth turves, rising to a formerly flat top with sloping sides, with the entire mound dome once covered in white quartz pebbles. The entrance façade was also walled with quartz, as it is again today. From far-off Tara, the ancient seat of Ireland's high kings, the monument must have presented a dazzling sight.

The huge covering mound is kerbed by no less than 97 stones; the largest and heaviest of them (up to 10 tons) are in the south-east entrance arc. The passage is 62ft (19m) long (not nearly as long as that at KNOWTH). Set above its entrance is a small rectangular hole, which is one of the best known

small stone holes in all Ireland. This is because it is precisely orientated to the midwinter sunrise; for about 20 minutes, one morning a year, eerie golden rays of light shine through and reach the very back of the chamber tomb. The corbelled roofing, the top flat slab of which stretches 20ft (6.1m) high above the floor, must be one of the most photographed megalithic interiors anywhere. The chamber itself measures 21ft 6in by 17ft (6.5m by 5.2m) across the three recesses; they have been badly looted over the centuries – but wonders remain.

The megalithic art at Newgrange is of a very high order indeed; here are cascades of arcs, chevrons, circles and half-circles (both single and concentric), cup marks, cup-and-ring marks, loops, lozenges, serpent shapes, spirals (single and double), triangles, wavy lines, and zig zags. About 40 per cent of the decorations at Newgrange are lozenges (much higher than at, for example, LOUGHCREW and KNOWTH nearby, or at GAVR'INIS, Morbihan). Zig zags were the next most constantly depicted motifs, followed by circles and (surprisingly low on the list) spirals.

There are a number of particularly fine decorated stones here. The roofstone of the right-hand recess, for example, has a beautifully precise spiral, that most challenging of motifs which to some represents the Mother Goddess of Earth. The entrance stone is justly famous for its five intertwining spirals and borders of lozenges. Knowth also⁻ has a magnificent entrance stone, and both have vertical grooves down them. At Newgrange the patterns cease above ground level, and so the stone was perhaps set into earth elsewhere, a prehistoric carver's studio, for the work to be done.

Many of the 97 kerbstones have carvings; K52 bears curious bordered rows of three holes. These are somewhat reminiscent of the rows of round protuberances, within borders, depicted on slate plaques, which have been found as far apart as ALTAMURA, Italy, TARXIEN, Malta, and FILITOSA, Corsica. Most oddly some of the kerbstones have carvings on their inside faces, against the mound and out of sight; K13 is a veritable sketch pad, of which all artists have need.

The much restored tomb today, with part of the ring of remaining huge kerbstones.

THE PIPER'S STONES

Hollywood,
Co Wicklow

STONE CIRCLE

Map 3 (East) 293203
(marked as Athgreany
Stone Circle)

Signposted as 'The Piper's
Stones'. 1½ miles (2.4km)
south of Hollywood, to the left
on the road to Baltinglass.
Park by the roadside.

The massive Piper, with a carved
cross on its back.

The outlying stone at this impressive megalithic site is a Falstaffian 25ft (7.6m) in circumference. This massive, smoothly-dressed, squat, grey granite boulder which lies down a steep slope 68yds (62m) to the north-east of the circle, must surely be the Piper, with the 18 stones in this Leinster-type ring being his players; 14 are large, and there are supporting pillars or erratics among them. Moreover, many large stones litter the banks and ditches of the meandering footpath that leads to the group. West of the circle, over a small valley, a probable burial group can be seen; a detailed survey of the whole area would perhaps reveal a prehistoric settlement.

Legend has it that The Piper's Stones were petrified for the sin of playing on the Sabbath. THE MERRY MAIDENS and The Two Pipers in Cornwall carry the same legend, which may be a reflection of puritanical thinking 350 years ago, but more likely there is a much older explanation. Perhaps our Piper here did indeed call a tune — one of great importance to his community — for he bears a giant cross all over his back, and one of the lines is deeply incised. This is a mystery worth looking into.

POULNABRONE

Ballyvaughan,
Co Clare

PORTAL-TOMB

Map 2 (West) 123200

Signposted. 5 miles (8km)
south of Ballyvaughan, on the
way to Corofin. The tomb is
clearly visible from the road,
where you park. The Burren
Visitor Centre is nearby.

The ever popular portal-tomb on The
Burren.

This is said to be the most photographed site in all Ireland. The Poulnabrone portal-tomb is a singularly dramatic site across the fissures of the stark, karstic limestone pavement of The Burren. The thin capstone has a somewhat insolent tilt to it as it sits protectively on two fine 6ft (1.8m) high portal stones (the eastern one is a replacement, following a discovery in 1985 that it was hopelessly cracked), to create a ragged chamber in a low cairn measuring 30ft (9m) across.

Excavations during the repairs showed that this was clearly a special burial place in about 2500 BC. Discoveries highlighted the importance in Neolithic times of precision in burial, and, most likely, timing, and the central role of the megalithic tombs as protectors against disturbance and robbery.

Uncremated remains were found in the chamber, its portico and in the grykes (crevices in the limestone floor). A detailed analysis of all the fragments of the disarticulated bones revealed exact planning — but for what purpose or reason we shall never know.

All the main body bones of one newborn baby, six juveniles, and probably 19 adults (of whom only one lived past 40) were discovered, as was the sex of eight adults; there were four of each. The bones indicated a hard physical life and a coarse diet. Ritual was obviously involved in their final journey, because the analysis further proved that the bones were naturally defleshed elsewhere, and only then moved, in a complete but disarticulated state, to be roughly scattered within the chamber at Poulnabrone.

Remarkably, visitors have made hundreds of miniature tombs nearby, perhaps in recognition of the burial and as unconscious votive offerings.

PROLEEK DOLMEN

*Ballymascanlon,
Co Louth*

PORTAL-TOMB

Map 3 (East) 308311

*Stone pebbles on top of the capstone
are evidence of an ancient belief.*

This modest but cheerful tomb is often known as 'The Giant's Load' – doubtless a reference to the massive capstone, which weighs 40 tons and is one of the heaviest in Ireland. It is supported by a tripod of uprights: two matching portals 7ft (2.1m) high and another upright of 6ft (1.8m), with the smaller one providing the ever-familiar slope to the capstone profile.

In this case, the pleasing slope has a legend attached to it. It has long been said that if you throw a small stone about 13ft (4m) up and on to the top of the capstone – and it remains there – then you will be married within the year.

If this fails to interest, take a walk 100yds (91m) to the south-east, and there on the flat pasture you can examine the few merits of the remains of a wedge-tomb.

Situated in the grounds of the Ballymascanlon House Hotel, from whence it is signposted – as it is also on the road from Dundalk, 3½ miles (5.6km) to the south-west.

PUNCHESTOWN

STANDING STONE

Map 3 (East) 291216
(not marked; find
racecourse)

Not signposted. Take the
R410 from Naas to Blessington
and turn right to
Punchestown. The stone is
clearly visible ½ mile
(0.8km) along the road to the
left, just before the racecourse
entrance. Park at the nearest
field-gate.

This is the second tallest standing stone in the British Isles (see
RUDSTON MONOLITH). The exact height of this beautiful
standing stone (the tallest in Ireland) is known, because it fell
down in 1931; it was measured to be 23ft (7m) high, and 9
tons in weight; three years later, 3ft 6in (1.1m) of the granite
were put back into the earth on its re-erection. The almost
square base is 11ft (3.3m) in circumference, and an identifica-
tion notice sits unhappily against its west face, spoiling an
otherwise elegant sculpture.

From the base it gradually turns wedge-shaped as it rises,
and towards the top it tapers finely to the south. Its function
was probably as a memorial stone to the Bronze Age burial
found beneath it; no role as a marker stone has yet been
ascribed to it, unlike some of the huge menhirs in Brittany.

The tallest and most beautiful
standing stone in Ireland, which
measures 23ft (7m) above and below
ground.

TEMPLEBRYAN

STONE CIRCLE; nearby ORATORY, WELL, STANDING STONE AND BULLAUN

Map 4 (South) 138044

Not signposted. 2½ miles
(4km) north of Clonakilty,
turn left (signpost:
Shannonvale 1 mile). At
crossroads (by Noel Phair
pub), turn left; the stone circle
is in a field about 300yds
(274m) up the hill on the
right, opposite modern houses.
Parking there and access by a
steep stile.

This marvellous megalithic site
includes a fine slender stone. The cow
has been drinking from a bullaun on
the ground beside it.

This is a very ancient site with an enticing variety of features,
although there is not a lot left of the sloping circle today. A
1743 survey shows nine stones and a central monolith but it is
thought that the original number of stones was 13; today five
flat-topped stones survive, of which one is recumbent, and the
old centre is now occupied by a unusual semi-embedded flat,
white quartz stone. White central stones occur in a number of
other Irish circles. The entrance to the circle was set at the
south, the internal diameter is 30ft (9m), and these impressive
stones are some of the very biggest in the area, suggesting an
important megalithic site.

Two fields away, to the north-west (on a working farm, so

remember the usual courtesies), is the ancient Teampull na
mBrienach, the now ruined church of the O'Briens, within a
ring fort (whose moat has now gone). At the south of the
enclosure lie the remains of a building, a well-head, and a
notable, slender standing stone. It is more than 11ft (3.3m)
tall, has faint ogham marks on its southern edge, and a pattee
cross on the west face, thus indicating use of the site through
to early Christian times.

Near it there lies a beautifully carved tri-cornered bullaun,
which resembles a pillarless font with a deep, smoothly dressed
bowl. Bullauns have been known as wart wells; this one seems
to work as a cow's drinking place.

I.49

The Dwarfie Stane

Hoy,
Orkney

Rock-cut Chamber
Tomb

HY 243005

Take the 9047 south from
Linksness, and then the road
on the right to Rackwick.
Before it bends westwards,
look for the sign on the left.

The only rock-cut tomb in Britain
outside Ireland.

This is probably one of only two chamber tombs in the British Isles ever to be hollowed out from solid rock (the other is at Glendalough, Co Wicklow). In fact, it most resembles a hermit's cell and has been called as much by travelling antiquaries; it even has a small spring near it. The Dwarfie Stane is of the late Neolithic or Early Bronze Age and is the only prehistoric site on the most hilly island in the Orkneys.

A vast rectangular block of local red sandstone from the nearby Dwarfie Hamars, it is 28ft (8.5m) long, a maximum of 14ft 9in (4.5m) wide, and 6ft 6in (2m) high. The narrow entrance is in its west face; inside, on either side, are two small recesses. The smaller is to the north and measures just 4ft 3in by 2ft (1.3m by 0.6m); the chamber to the south is 5ft by 3ft (1.5m by 0.9m). The roofing has been holed for centuries.

I.50

Maes Howe

Orkney,
Mainland

Chambered Cairn

HY 317127

Signposted. 5 miles (8km) east
of Stromness, just north of the
A965. A key is obtainable
from the local farmhouse
during normal hours.

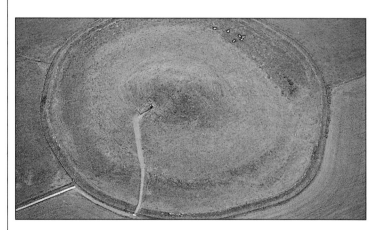

This fine cairn dates back to about 2100 BC. It stands on a levelled platform, and is covered by a huge mound 24ft (7.3m) high and 115ft (35m) in diameter. The 36ft (11m) long passage leads to a high 15ft (4.6m) square chamber, with a marvellous corbelled roof, at the centre of the mound. Ahead and on both sides lie small chambers, their square openings being just 3ft (1m) above the floor. Two huge fully dressed stones stand as supporting pillars for the corbelled roof.

The present appearance of the site was completed in the 10th century AD, when the low outer earth ring was added. Then, in the 12th century, Vikings broke into the tomb leaving 24 runic inscriptions and also pictorial carvings (including a splendid one of a dragon); they also referred to buried treasure, but alas none has been found so far!

The dressed 36ft (11m) long passage.

THE RING OF BRODGAR

Orkney,
Mainland

STONE CIRCLE and
HENGE

HY 294134

Fabulously situated, this is one of Britain's most majestic stone circles. Here, in about 2500 BC, 60 stones were originally set up on a slope facing east. Today, there are 27 left around the diameter of 113yds (103.3m), and the circle has two entrances, at the north-west and south-east.

Four of the stones bear different carvings — of an anvil, a cross, an ogham and a runic inscription. Between the ring and an outer earth bank lies a ditch which, in terms of man-hours devoted to its construction, rivals most in the British Isles. Quarried from solid sandstone bedrock, it was once no less than 12ft (3.6m) deep and 30ft (9m) wide.

To the south-east, 449ft (137m) away, stands the Comet Stone. The late Professor Thom believed The Ring of Brodgar to be a prehistoric observatory. Some 18th century antiquaries regarded Brodgar as the sun and STENNESS as the moon.

Travel east from Stromness on
the A965 for 4 miles
(6.5km), then turn left along
the B9055. The site is nearly
2 miles (3.2km) north-west
along the road on the left.

This impressive circle was probably a
prehistoric astronomical observatory.

SKARA BRAE

*Bay of Skaill,
Orkney,
Mainland*

NEOLITHIC SETTLEMENT

HY 230187

In the winter of 1850 a violent storm ripped off a covering sand dune at this site to reveal what had been covered by another terrible storm about 5000 years previously – a Neolithic hut settlement of nine dwellings in remarkably fine condition. Because the Orkney Islands have always been virtually treeless, the domestic 'fittings' were carved from stone, not wood – hence their excellent state of preservation. They included beds (also used as seats), hearths, shelves, storage compartments, and water tanks.

The important excavations at Skara Brae were begun by the eminent Professor Gordon Childe in 1926; he emphasised the importance of the flat-based grooved ware uncovered there. It linked this Late Neolithic site with Woodhenge (and later Durrington Walls) and other southern sites. This distinctive pottery is principally found, curiously, only in sites in

Travel north from Stromness on the B9056 for about 7 miles (11km), park at the signpost, and follow the path around the south of the bay.

This Neolithic hut settlement, overlooking the Bay of Skaill, was revealed by a storm in 1850.

Stone domestic 'furniture' at Skara Brae.

Curiously scratched stones with geometric lines have been noted at Skara Brae, and geometric stone balls uncovered.

The nine huts and alleyways at the Neolithic settlement at Skara Brae, overlooking the Bay of Skaill.

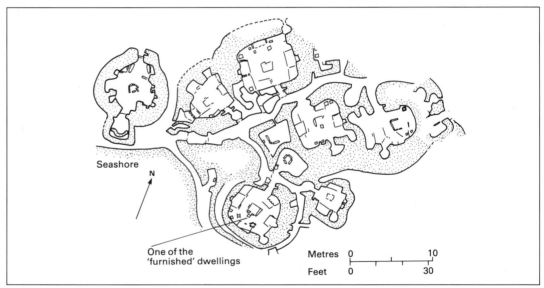

Seashore

N

One of the 'furnished' dwellings

Metres 0 ——————— 10
Feet 0 ——————— 30

Northern Scotland and the Orkneys in the north and in south and south-eastern England: little or none until recently was discovered in the hundreds of square miles in between. Its form and the 'spiral and lozenge' motifs link this settlement with the Irish Boyne Valley tombs (such as NEWGRANGE) and burial chambers in southern Spain and Portugal.

Among the domestic 'houseware' uncovered here were dishes, some of which contained traces of blue, red and yellow pigments. Now Julius Caesar recorded that 'all the Britons painted themselves'. Moreover, the Greek explorer Pytheas (as quoted by Strabo) referred, in the fourth century BC, to Britons as *Prettanoi*, ancient Greek for the Celtic word *Pritani* ('the painted ones'), from which comes the Latin *Britannia* ('land of the Britanni'), and so Britain. Evidently, ancient mainland Britons did not use vegetable dye (woad) at all, but a mixture of clay, metal carbonates and oxides, and the evidence is here at Skara Brae. Recent analysis of skin fragments from The Lindow Man (Pete Marsh) has provided scientific evidence of

this interesting habit of body painting, which is still practised by many tribal societies today.

The nine huts and alleyways that make up Skara Brae today probably formed the third settlement on the original site. Early Neolithic settlements such as this, which imply high degrees of intelligence and discipline in their leadership, are quite rare in Britain, but Skara Brae is one of the most complete, and has provided valuable information.

However, it is not as large a settlement as, for instance, Carn Brae in Cornwall, which held about 200 people and dates back to 3900 BC. Another fine and similar site, where most of the nine houses even had their own small gardens, is Chysauster, also in Cornwall.

These Neolithic villages perhaps housed the astronomer-priests of the day – a privileged class whose job it was to keep an eye on the heavens in order to predict the terrifying occurrence of an eclipse, or to maintain a constant watch on the 18.6 year cycle of the moon.

The Stones of Stenness

*Orkney,
Mainland*

Standing Stones and
Henge

HY 306125

The four stones left standing in this 104ft (31.7m) circle of originally 12 stones have most distinct slanted tops, each at a different angle; the tallest remaining one is 16ft 6in (5m) tall. It has been proposed that they were once part of a huge astronomical observatory, with Britons constantly stationed to look up along the smooth angles of sight in order to note movements in the night sky.

The site dates back to about 2970 BC, but the ditch and outer bank are now almost gone, and the three stones of the Cove were reconstructed early this century. Although the site today may seem a slight disappointment, in its time it was clearly very important. Thousands of man-hours must have been devoted to hewing the 3ft (1m) deep ditch from solid sandstone bedrock, as at the neighbouring RING OF BRODGAR.

To the north-west of The Stones stands the Watch Stone: 18ft 6in (5.6m) tall and with an interesting name.

About 4 miles (6.4km) east of Stromness, along the A965, on the left, just past the B9055 turning.

Two of the four remaining stones at this beautiful Orkney Islands site.

BANT'S CARN

Halangy Down,
St Mary's

ENTRANCE GRAVE

SV 911123

The kerbed mound of this impressive tomb is about 39ft (12m) in diameter, 6ft (1.8m) high, and has inner and outer rings of kerbstones. The cairn on top is some 26ft (8m) in diameter, and its existence indicates two periods of construction. The passage, just north of east, is 15ft (4.6m) long, and turns due east at the chamber which is handsomely roofed with four large capstones. Unhappily, a modern wall slices through the south-west section.

Excavation has given the tomb a construction date of around 2000 BC, after which it was continuously used for about another 500 years. Neolithic and Late Bronze Age pottery found at Bant's Carn indicates contact with Cornwall. Remains of a lower collar at this site also link it with Scillonian chamber tombs. There is a remarkable total of 50 or more such tombs in the Isles of Scilly.

The remains of an ancient settlement nearby, excavated in 1935 and 1964–70, revealed a site occupied from Bronze Age to Roman times.

Beside the coastal path at the northern end of the golf course on Halangy Down. Signposted from Macfarland Downs.

Four large capstones are prominent at this tranquil location. Remains of a lower 'collar' of stones can be seen to the right.

Innisidgen Carn and Lower Innisidgen

*Helvear Down,
St Mary's*

Entrance Graves

SV 921128 and
922127

*North-west of Block House
Bay, beside the coastal path,
between Bar Point and
Watermill Cove. Signposted.*

*Innisidgen Carn is the finest
mounded passage-grave in the Scilly
Isles.*

Innisidgen Carn, also known as The Giant's Grave, is the finest mound in these beautiful Isles. It is located at the top of a slope and has a diameter of about 27ft (8.2m). Remains of an outer ring of kerbstones can be seen to the north; within is a kerb of three courses of stones. It has one more capstone than its similar neighbour, BANT'S CARN, and they are most likely to be contemporary.

About 109yds (100m) along the path to the north-west lies Lower Innisidgen, below a slope and virtually at sea level, which is most unusual (although it is true to say that the level at the time of its construction, when most of the Isles were one land mass, was much lower). Its mound is a rough oval, and is slightly squeezed at its waist.

The chamber faces precisely due south, and has been dated at approximately 2095 BC. Deposits found in Scillonian graves indicate rituals involving both the living and dead.

Porth Hellick Down

*Porth Hellick,
St Mary's*

Entrance Grave

SV 928108

*Signposted on the A3110 at
Carn Friars to the north-east
of the Down.*

*The Down of Porth Hellick on the
island of St Mary's, with the
largest mound in the group clearly
visible.*

The 40ft (12.2m) diameter mound here, the biggest of five in this group, has a flattened appearance – but this is probably due to careless restoration, which has all but destroyed a lower, surrounding kerb or 'collar'. The three-course, high kerbstones contribute to the illusion. A roofless passage entrance is at the north-west, and approaches the chamber at a distinct angle; at the point where it turns, a protective upright slab stands guard. As with BANT'S CARN, the roof of the chamber consists of four capstones, with the edge of the first above the guardian slab. The site was excavated in 1899 and Late Bronze Age pottery was found; this indicates the ever-familiar re-use of the grave which is much older.

SCOTLAND

BALBIRNIE

1.57

*Markinch,
Fife*

STONE CIRCLE

NO 285030

*6 miles (9.6km) north of
Kirkcaldy off the A92; 1 mile
(1.6km) north-west of
Markinch. Park at the
Balbirnie Craft Centre.*

This site was excavated in 1970-71, prior to being moved 137yds (125m) to the south-east because of a road-widening scheme. The eight stones are accurately and cleanly reset, and the place, albeit shifted, is of unusual interest.

The stone circle of local sandstone is actually an ellipse, indicating that higher mathematics were used in the astronomical observations clearly conducted here, and is between 46ft and 49ft (14m and 15m) in diameter. The longer axis lies to the south-west.

Originally, a rough square of thin stone slabs was placed in the middle of the circle, but about 100 years later they were moved by another group of settlers, who used them for lining three new burial cists. There is also a paved rectangle there.

After that, cremations and burial goods, including already broken pottery (*see* WEST KENNET LONG BARROW, Wiltshire, for a possible explanation), were covered by a cairn (today removed). Cremated bones have been found beneath the four eastern stone holes; grooved ware in another hole gave a probable date for the circle of about 2000 BC.

After excavation in 1970–71, this elliptical setting of stones was moved 137yds (125m) south-east, due to a road-widening scheme.

CALLANISH

1.58

*Stornoway,
Lewis,
Western Isles*

STONE CIRCLE AND
ROWS

NB 213330

*Well signposted; 14 miles
(22.5km) west of Stornoway
on the A858. Turning on the
left after Garynahine.*

*'The Stonehenge of the North', as
Callanish is known.*

This is a visually satisfying site but a tantalising one archaeologically. It dates from about 1800 BC, but precise dates and proven functions have been hard to establish.

The site consists of a circle, 43ft by 37ft (13.1m by 11.3m) in diameter, of 13 tall slender undressed stones, with another at their centre which is the tallest of all at 15ft 6in (4.75m). Four incomplete avenues lead away, with single rows of stones to the east, south and west, and a double row just east of north. Had all the rows been completed the axial alignments of them would have converged at the centre stone. A second outer concentric circle was probably also intended.

The central standing stone is at the west of a later chambered tomb, the radius of which extends to the east of the circle. It has a short passage, and then two successive small chambers, now ruined. Professor Thom believed that Callanish was a lunar observatory. A popular legend says that marriage vows have been taken there — and yet it is also known as Tursachan, meaning a place of pilgrimage or mourning!

*Camster,
Lybster,
Caithness*

CHAMBERED CAIRNS

ND 260442

Take the A9 south-west from Wick. At Lybster turn directly north on the minor road; after Camster, the cairns are on the left.

RIGHT: *Camster Round, with Camster Long to the north-west.*
BELOW: *One of the two entrance passages in Camster Long.*

There are two quite different outlines in plan to these tombs (also known as The Grey Cairns of Camster). Camster Round is roughly oval, but flattened at the south-east where the entrance lies. It is about 11ft 9in (3.6m) in height, and some 60ft (18.3m) in diameter. Here is yet another entrance passage which, at just over 2ft 6in (0.8m) along its eight-slabbed 19ft 9in (6m) length, is very low. Its central chamber, reached through a small antechamber, is more agreeable for the megalith hunter with a height of 9ft 9in (3m) to its corbelled roof; it contains three compartments, separated by slabs.

Camster Long lies 220yds (200m) to the north-west. It shares a similar ground plan to the Tulloch of Assery cairn not far away in Halkirk. Both are double-horned. At Camster Long, the two entrances and chambers have very different shapes. They were constructed quite separately, and covered by their own unconnected mounds.

Later, today's distinctive, long, double-horned cairn was put over both of them. The cairn is now over 200ft (61m) at its longest, and a maximum of 65ft 6in (20m) across its horns.

CLAVA CAIRNS

*Culloden battlefield and
area,
Inverness,
Highland Region*
CHAMBERED CAIRNS
NH 757444

This group is one of the most notable in Scotland, and has some unique features; they, and the battlefield nearby, combine to offer a fascinating visit. The tomb group as a whole consists of about 30 cairns in three main areas. Six of them, some of which are described here, are around the Beauly Firth, north of the River Ness; 17 are on riversides in Strath Dores and Strath Nairn, and at least seven are to be found in Strath Spey.

Three tombs at Balnuaran, Clava, in the first group, provide the chief interest, because the heavily-kerbed ring-cairn and passage-graves are surrounded by stone monoliths in a formation nearly unique in the British Isles (but *see* LOANHEAD OF DAVIOT, Grampian, and NEWGRANGE, Co Meath). More-

*5½ miles (8.8km) east of
Inverness, and ½ mile
(0.8km) south-east of
Culloden battlefield, by a lane
between Clava Lodge and
Balnuaran Farm. Signposted.*

*A view along the megalithic
alignment at Clava Cairns.*

LEFT: *Balnuaran North-East*
passage-grave at Clava Cairns.

The unusual oriention of the
passage-grave entrances point to a
midwinter sunset at CLAVA CAIRNS.
There are cup marks at all four
constructions.

over, they all contained cremations and have cup marks.

The northernmost is Balnuaran North-East; this passage-grave is in a stone-covered and egg-shaped cairn, with large kerbstones measuring 103ft 6in by 97ft 6in (31.6m by 29.7m). One of the kerbstones, which are largest at the south and west, is heavily indented with cup and cup-and-ring marks, and grooves. A cup-marked stone in the passage can be spotted on the north-west side. The central and roofless chamber is 13ft (4.0m) in diameter; the passage to it is orientated to the south-south-west, in contrast to most other chamber tombs in the British Isles which face in an easterly direction. The ring of stones surrounding the cairn is not completely circular, as Professor Thom has shown; they too have cup marks.

Balnuaran Central is a circular ring-cairn, 104ft (31.6m) in diameter, and again kerbed. It has nine stones in its circle, one of them cup marked, and three of them are mysteriously attached to the cairn by thin earthen banks, like spokes to a hub. The remains of a cist were found in the middle during Stuart Piggott's excavations in 1952/53.

Balnuaran South-West is the other passage-grave here, and also now roofless. Twelve cup marks can be seen on the boulder at the west side of the chamber entrance which, also unusually, faces south-south-west. It had a diameter of 104ft 6in (31.8m).

On the western perimeter of the Clava Cairns site, at the foot of a tree, there is a small Late Bronze Age 12ft (3.7m) stone circle. Its stones are fallen or recumbent, and contiguous, and they bear cup and cup-and-ring marks. Scattered fragments of white quartz have been found inside the circle here, as they have at the well-preserved, huge, kerbed Corrimony passage-grave 25 miles (40.2km) away at the west end of Glen Urquhart. It has been proposed that the Clava Cairns represent a fine flowering of a type of tomb which originated in south-western France or Iberia, then migrated north-west to Ireland, east across the Irish Sea to the Firth of Lorne, up the Great Glen here, and thence onwards to Denmark.

Dr Johnson and his amanuensis James Boswell visited one of the Clava Cairns in 1773. Boswell wrote: 'About three miles

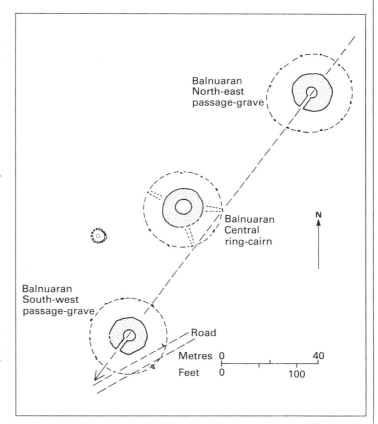

beyond Inverness, we saw, just by the road, a very complete specimen of what is called a Druid's temple. There was a double circle, one of very large, the other of smaller stones. Dr Johnson justly observed "to go and see one druidical temple is only to see that it is nothing, for there is neither art nor power in it; and seeing one is quite enough"'. Dr Johnson clearly did not do enough 'seeing'; if he had, 'believing' would surely have followed. This is a remarkably moving place.

The three chambered cairns at Clava have bequeathed puzzles. There were cremations in each tomb, but no pottery has been found. They were evidently not family mausolea, but were used for favoured individuals of both sexes.

CROFT MORAIG

Aberfeldy,
Tayside

STONE CIRCLE

NN 797472

Although somewhat hidden away, Croft Moraig is a very important site. Like STONEHENGE, Wiltshire, and The Sanctuary, Wiltshire, it has seen a succession of constructional phases, and like them the first, in about 2850 BC, involved wooden posts – in this instance, a horseshoe-shaped setting of 14 posts.

After subsequent repair, the site was levelled and 'planted' with a horseshoe setting of eight undressed stones. A bank of earth and huge stones was then erected behind it. No less than 23 cup marks are to be seen on the top of a supine stone, lying along the line of the midsummer full moon at the south-west; it may have been a decorated entrance stone, in the manner of the magnificent one at NEWGRANGE in the Boyne Valley, Ireland.

At a third stage, more than 800 years after the first, 12 huge stones encircled the horseshoe, but within the bank, and two more formed an entrance at the east. As elsewhere in Britain, quartz pebbles and fragments have been found here; they are a true minilithic mystery.

Just south of the A827, 4 miles (6.5km) west of Aberfeldy on the way to Kenmore, at the north-eastern head of the Tay Valley.

The complex henge and circles at Croft Moraig evolved through several phases.

FORTINGALL

Fortingall,
Aberfeldy,
Tayside

STONE CIRCLES

NN 745469

There were once three stone circles at this Early Bronze Age site. They were then virtually destroyed, although three stones were left standing — apparently — in each. However, when two of the three (Fortingall East and West) were excavated by Aubrey Burl in 1970, it was discovered that deep inside each five more stones had been buried. The original settings had been rough rectangles of eight stones each; an unusual arrangement in this region. The third circle, Fortingall South, could possibly have been a recumbent stone circle in the Aberdeenshire tradition.

Ten stones, remnants of three stone circles on the eastern edge of Fortingall village, above the River Lyon.

Travel west from Aberfeldy on the A846; take the second road on the left, signposted to Fortingall.

GARYNAHINE

Stornoway,
Lewis,
Western Isles

STONE CIRCLE

NB 230303

12 miles (19.3km) west of Stornoway on the A858, at the junction with the A8011.

The supine rectangular centre stone within this ovular setting is located on the left.

This circle is very near the majestic CALLANISH complex, and serious megalith hunters should allow for a three-day visit to this endlessly fascinating island. Here is a compact oval setting measuring 42ft 3in by 30ft 3in (12.9m by 9.2m); the five remaining stones in it surround a low rectangular central one. This was placed in a cairn, which was not always the case.

The establishment of a focal point in a circular stone setting seems a perfectly natural idea from a design point of view. Much taller central pillars have an obviously totemistic role (*see* BRYN CELLI DDU, Anglesey, Ty-ar-Boudiquet, Brittany, and LOS MILLARES, Almeria, Spain). Ritual and celebration

around maypoles and sacred trees are very ancient occurrences. It is possible that central stones which were not associated with burials (as is the case at Garynahine) were command posts, or positions for the conduct of rituals, religious or otherwise, like preachers' crosses (*see* HAROLD'S STONES, Gwent).

Notable sites with centre stones in their circles are at nearby CALLANISH and at TEMPLEBRYAN in Co Cork. The most famous supine centre stone of all is The Altar Stone at STONEHENGE, and the mystery about it is that this blueish-grey micaceous sandstone, heavy with quartz grains, does not occur anywhere else at the monument.

THE HILL O' MANY STANES

Lybster,
Wick,
Caithness,
Highland Region

STONE ROWS

ND 294384

Leave Lybster on the A9;
before Wick take the farm lane
going north-west. The rows,
about 650yds (600m) from
the A9, are to the south-west
of it. Signposted.

The site of 22 fan-shaped stone
rows, perhaps an observatory.

This famous and unusual site consists of 22 or more splayed rows of more than 200 stones. Unlike those in the Carnac alignments (*see* KERMARIO and MENEC, Morbihan, France), these stones are small, less than 3ft 3in (1m) high, and mostly only a few inches wide. They are set on a south-facing slope, below a cairn lying on top of it. The stones are in fact set in a slight fan shape, and were analysed meticulously by Professor Alexander Thom.

He showed that the stones at the site (which he designated Mid Clyth) must have been set up in about 1900 BC for the purpose of identifying the exact maximum moonrise in summer and winter by plotting the movement of certain stars. A standing stone, now fallen, 147ft (45m) to the west of the cairn, might well have been associated with this prehistoric observatory.

KINTRAW

Kintraw,
Argyll,
Strathclyde

CIRCLE, CAIRN AND
MENHIR

NM 830050

Near Kintraw Farm. On a
plateau off the road from
Craignish to Bealach,
Kilmartin and Lochgilphead.

The standing stone, viewed from the
large kerb cairn, looking towards
the Jura hills.

Kintraw is an important and exciting site, and its place in the history of megaliths is assured as a result of Professor Thom's survey of the site in the early 1960s. In 1967 he wrote that Kintraw ' . . .may be another solstitial observatory capable of giving a very accurate value of the obliquity of the ecliptic' (that is, the sun's declination down through the sky). From his detailed survey, he was able to date the site at about 1800 BC.

Kintraw consists of a ring cairn, a menhir 12ft (3.7m) high, then (on the same north-easterly alignment) a large ruined cairn 48ft (14.6m) in diameter, a further large stone and, finally (across a gorge and stream), a ledge.

In 1970/71, excavations proved that Thom's deduction was probably correct. The ledge was likely to have been a Late Neolithic observation platform of stones which provided a line of sight 26¾ miles (43km) long over the gorge, cairn, menhir and circle to the col between Beinn Shiantaidh (one of the Paps or hill peaks of the island of Jura) and Beinn a' Chaolais. Air and eyesight were much clearer in Neolithic times.

LOANHEAD OF DAVIOT

*Daviot,
Inverurie,
Grampian*

RECUMBENT STONE
CIRCLE AND CEMETERY

NJ 747288

This circle is in line with New Craig stone circle (visible from Loanhead of Daviot) and the site of a former stone circle in the churchyard of nearby Daviot.

This elegant grouping is set on ground which slopes to the north-east between two rivers; it is one of more than 15 megalithic sites in this lovely area. The circle has a diameter of 67ft (20.5m), and is dated at approximately 2500 BC. A strange feature recurs here; the huge recumbent stone and its flankers were set just inside the line of the circle (*see* MIDMAR KIRK, also in Grampian).

Professor Thom, who surveyed his native country in his long retirement years, was able to show that the distance from the circle's exact centre to the edge of the inner cairn is precisely 20 megalithic yards, and, further, on to the circle edge was another five megalithic yards. Two outliers to the south-east confirm a probable role in the prediction of midwinter sunrises.

During 1934 excavations, broken pottery sherds were found around the bases of most of the monoliths, indicating single burial cairns at each. In the middle of the low Bronze Age cairn within the circle lay a rectangular mortuary pit, which might be the oldest part of the site. The recumbent stone and its pair of flankers stand in great state at south-south-west, watching over eight further equally spaced uprights at this fine prehistoric place.

The nearby circular-banked cemetery, of about the same age, consists of a 950sq ft (88sq m) cremation site. There is one prominent central burial, and several burials with grave goods in urns.

Inverurie is 13 miles (20.8km) north-west of Aberdeen on the A96. Leave the town north-west on the B9001; take the fourth turning on the right for Daviot, and the first left. The circle is signposted on the right.

The huge recumbent stone in the circle near Daviot.

MIDMAR KIRK

Midmar,
Aberdeen,
Grampian

RECUMBENT STONE
CIRCLE

NJ 699064

The church in tiny Midmar is 15 miles (24km) west of Aberdeen on the B9119, beyond Echt.

Part of the recumbent stone circle at Midmar Kirk; modern graves can be seen behind, to the left.

In 1914 a graveyard was established around this 57ft (17.4m) diameter stone circle and today it is a most manicured place, with a neat disc of grass within the circle, and a gravel path between and around the ring of stones. This is clearly saying that it was here first, and the cheerleader in the matter is without doubt the massive recumbent stone, lying, as it always has done, between two tall portals.

Recumbent stone circles are peculiar to the Aberdeen area (though there are others in the south-west of Ireland), and in many cases, as at Midmar, the recumbent stone is placed a little inside the circle; their top surfaces are almost always horizontal.

Professor Thom has pointed out that the left-hand portal stone, looking from the centre, is almost always about 1ft 6in (0.46m) nearer the centre. Such odd facts define this circle as having been a delicate instrument of some kind – another monument to the wonders of prehistoric engineering.

TEMPLE WOOD

Kilmartin,
Strathclyde

STONE CIRCLE AND
STANDING STONES

NR 826979

Travel south from Oban on the A816, past Kilmartin and the turnings for Slockavullin. The signposted circles are now on the right. The standing stones are not generally accessible.

The central cist and its kerb within a boulder-strewn stone circle.

This is a small, somewhat lonely, but beautiful circle, with 20 stones in its setting among trees. Its diameter is 44ft (13.4m), and boulders, small and various in shape, are strewn over the inside. Excavations in 1928 and 1974–76 revealed a much smaller inner ring, 11ft 6in (3.5m) in diameter, and, inside this at the centre, a large open cist. There were several burials in the cairn, which dates back to about 1750 BC. A second small cist, with a burial and goods, was located just outside it.

The standing stones to the east were, according to Alexander Thom, set in such a position as to make the Temple Wood site a lunar observatory using a notch in a nearby ridge; his exhaustive and highly accurate surveys confirm that the stone circle's dimensions can be expressed in terms of round figure megalithic yards (*see* 'Measuring the Megaliths'). The several 'temple' or 'teampull' sites in the British Isles are each held by archaeo-astronomers to be of special significance.

A notable feature at this one is the circle stone exactly to the north of the cist. In 1973 a large though faint double spiral was discovered on it by Aubrey Burl; what is more, this most mysterious of motifs continues down into the ground below the packed stone surface. This means, of course, that it was carved before the monolith was erected, and therefore could have been used before elsewhere.

Other decorated stones are to be found in the Kilmartin Valley, at Nether Largie cairns, and among the standing stones at Kilmartin and Ballymeanoch, all close to Temple Wood. The 'Bally' prefix to the latter place name implies an Irish connection: the incredible megalithic art in the Boyne Valley tombs (*see* KNOWTH and NEWGRANGE, Co Meath) is not far away across the sea.

TORHOUSEKIE

*Wigtown,
Dumfries and Galloway*

STONE CIRCLE

NX 383565

One of the cairns near this circle was opened in the 19th century. Soon after, locals observed a mysterious light repeatedly emerging from the open cist. Such light phenomena have been reported in other copper-rich areas.

This unusual circle is all nicely fenced and neat, when you get there, but it also feels a little lonely. It is supposed to be the nearest stone circle to Ireland, and it does have affinities with sites across the North Channel.

Its 19 stones are set on a gently raised platform of stones and earth, and they are carefully graded towards the south-east in height. The tops of the now lichen-covered boulders were mostly hammered into smooth, round shapes; this could indicate former funerary rites in their midst, rather than astronomical observation of some kind. The circle probably stands on an artificial earth platform. There are three outliers 1094 yds (1000 m) to the east of it. On the other side of the road, west of the circle, lies a curious circular stone structure.

Two large stones and one small one (of local granite, like the rest) are aligned in the centre of this circle, which is 60ft (18m) in diameter, and Aubrey Burl has suggested that such a grouping may possibly indicate a variant of a recumbent stone circle. These are mostly concentrated in north-east Scotland and south-west Ireland (Torhousekie lies in between) and associated with copper and gold mining, together with ritual celebration. Copper mining goes on today near Wigtown which is about 4 miles (6.4km) away from this site.

3 miles (4.8km) west of Wigtown, on the B733; on the left and signposted.

The 19 graded boulders which make up this beautiful circle, with its central setting of three further stones.

WALES

ARTHUR'S STONE

I.70

*Llanrhidian,
West Glamorgan*

STONE CIRCLE WITH
BURIAL CHAMBER

SS 491905

The burial chamber and part of the circle.

*On the Gower Peninsula.
Take the A4118 west from
Swansea. At Upper Killey,
take the right fork on to the
B4271. At the village of
Crickton, turn left at the
signpost and go along the
trackway. Park and walk as
directed.*

According to the ancient Welsh texts, *The Welsh Triads*, this site is one of Britain's 'three wonderful things'. The other two were SILBURY HILL and STONEHENGE. Inspired by this tribute, travellers and antiquarians have for many centuries subjected it to the indignities of false reportage. Legends have grown up around it including the familiar one about how the stones go down to the sea nearby to drink at midnight. Indeed, a new one appeared in print as recently as 1973!

The facts are that the ring cairn here is 75ft 6in (23m) in diameter. Unusually, a burial chamber lies at its centre, and it is in two sections. The capstone is supported by four of the 10 uprights, and is part of the original 30-ton stone: today it measures 13ft (4m) long, and 6ft 6in (2m) wide, and 7ft (2.2m) thick. There are very many erratic stones spread all around this famous group which is perhaps the most in Wales. It is also called Maen Ceti and The Big Stone of Sketty.

BRIDELL

I.71

*St David's Church,
Bridell,
Cardigan,
Dyfed*

STANDING STONE WITH
OGHAM NOTCHES AND
CROSS

SN 176420

RIGHT: *The remarkable stone at Bridell.*

FAR RIGHT: *A detail showing the circled cross with ogham marks visible down the left edge.*

*3 miles (4.8km) south of
Cardigan on the A478. On
the right, at a junction where
you can park. Church
generally locked.*

This is a strange and fascinating site. For a start, the porch and door (the only one) into the church are placed, unusually, on the north side. And the most likely reason is to be found within a few feet of the south side: a standing stone, a prehistoric relic from pagan days which might have offended newly converted Christians arriving at their place of worship.

Its cup marks give a broad Bronze Age date although the ogham notches on the north-east edge of this 7ft 3ins (2.2m) tall stone, opposite the smooth, dressed side, date from AD 5-6. They read as *Nettasagru Maqui Mucoi Breci*, and translate as 'Nettasagus son of the descendants of Breci'.

Soon after, the Christians incised a big, broad cross within a circle on the side facing their church. Thus thousands of years of worship are manifest in this one single spot.

CARREG SAMSON

*Abercastle,
Fishguard,
Dyfed*

BURIAL CHAMBER

SM 848335

*Take the A487 south from
Goodwick (north-west of
Fishguard). At the junction
with the B4331, turn off
north-west, through Mathry
and Abercastle. The drive to
Longhouse Farm is on the
right, and the chamber is
signposted. It is 200yds
(180m) into a private field.*

*A handsome burial chamber,
overlooking Strumble Head. Carreg
is Welsh for rock: St Samson was
born in South Wales in about AD
490.*

This handsome Neolithic chamber occupies a wonderful site overlooking Strumble Head. Three of its seven remaining uprights support a large chunky capstone — all of which were once covered by an earth mound. It is a fine burial place, although little is known about it.

What it does have is an ancient and interesting name. *Carreg* is Welsh for 'rock'. Samson refers to the remarkable saint of that name who was born in South Wales in about AD 490 and became successively a monk, an abbot, a hermit, and finally a bishop in what today is Dol de Bretagne, Ille-et-Vilaine (*see* DOL). He ministered in Cornwall, The Isles of Scilly, Ireland, Jersey, Guernsey and Brittany (where he died in AD 565). Such was his fame, and reputation for miraculous deeds and his ability to communicate with birds, that his biography was written soon after his death. Some Arthurian experts have proposed that he was the original Sir Galahad.

THE DRUIDS' CIRCLE (MEINI HIRION)

I.73

*Penmaenmawr,
Dwygyfylchi,
Gwynedd*

STONE CIRCLE

SH 722746

*The hillside site, near Cefn
Coch, is reached by a
signposted footpath which starts
on Graiglwyd Road, south of
Penmaenmawr and the A55.*

*Only 10 of about 30 large dressed
stones survive here.*

This circle, containing some of the largest dressed stones in Wales, stands on a rocky bank about 85ft (26m) in diameter. According to one authority, there were originally 30 stones; 10 have survived and they are almost 6ft (1.8m) high. One of them has been called The Deity Stone, and another is still called The Stone of Sacrifice. The entrance to the stone circle is at the south-west, and is marked with two big portals. The circle is sited beside a Bronze Age trackway; northwards along it, at Graig Lwyd 765yds (700m) away, was once a well-known axe factory.

There are remains of many other circles and cairns in this area, and a number of cremations. Three cremations of children have been found in The Druids' Circle; two were close to the centre, and the other to the west where the cremation was found in an enlarged food vessel, with a bronze knife. Another cremation and pot has been found about 164yds (150m) south-west in a ring cairn. Evidence for the sacrifice of children within several circles in North Wales and Anglesey, and directly across the water in Co Down, is plentiful. A macabre feature is that children's ear bones frequently occur.

FOUR STONES

Walton,
Presteigne,
Powys

FOUR-POSTER

SO 245608

Travel west from Kington on the A44. Take the next road on the right after the B4357 to Walton. Park at the first trackway (which completes a crossway) on the left. The Stones, which cannot be seen from the road, are in the field to the left of the field gate.

This 'four-poster' is a rough, rectangular setting of surprising attraction.

This rough rectangle of stones lies on ground which slopes sharply to the east; each of the four is precisely placed on an axial line of a quadrant. The internal circumference is about 15ft (4.6m), and the distances between the stones varies between 8ft 10ins (2.7m), from the tallest stone at north-west to the smallest at north-east, to 5ft 8ins (1.75m); the largest stone has a well-fed girth of 15ft (4.6m). Though apparently not part of a circle, the stones have 'presence'; 76 similar examples occur in Scotland, and at least eight in England.

An ancient legend relates that the stones go down to Hindwell Pool, 200yds (183m) to the east, to drink at night, perhaps to the sounds of the bells of Old Radnor Church, which is located on a high and ancient site nearby; similar legends are attached to many stones around the British Isles.

In a great, flat field 300yds (274m) east-north-east of the Four Stones lies the Walton Stone. This attractive little stone is 2ft 7ins (0.84m) high and is visible to the north-west of the field gate there (one of a pair), about 100ft (30m) in.

GORS FAWR

Mynachlog-ddu,
Cardigan,
Dyfed

STONE CIRCLE AND
STANDING STONES

SN 134294

The circle and two standing stones have a wonderful setting; the dark Preseli Mountains can be seen to the right in the distance.

Going south from Cardigan on the A478, take the first road on the right (unnumbered), signposted to Mynachlog-ddu. Go straight through the village, ignoring the right turn. The signposted stones are over 1 mile (1.6m) south, on open moorland on the right. Park at the sign there.

This is one of the most beautiful megalithic sites in the British Isles: it is on gorse-covered moorland where sheep and cattle graze and is watched over by the dark Preseli Mountains to the north. Here there are square miles strewn with prehistoric circles, stones, chambers, and doubtless sight and ley lines. From the Mountains, 'bluestones' (as they appear in the rain) were apparently hewn, shaped and then transported 240m (386km) to STONEHENGE (though some experts disagree).

The delightful stone circle here is a perfect ring 73ft (22.3m) across, and its 16 stones have been designed to rise gradually in height towards the south. The entrance looks away to the south. Two standing stones, 7ft (2.1m) tall and 15yds (13.7m) apart, have been placed 109yds (100m) to the north-east. Their purpose has yet to be divined although they were perhaps outliers in some giant scheme, which may yet be revealed at this magical site.

HAROLD'S STONES

Trellech (variously spelt) is 6 miles (9.6km) south of Monmouth, on the B4293. There is an excellent framed map of the village and its prehistoric attractions in the main street.

The stone table, or outside altar, in the churchyard at Trellech. The three Harold's Stones are nearby.

Trellech takes its name from these three huge stones which are set on a slope in a line 34ft 6in (10.5m) long, and have stood there for about 3500 years. They were first recorded in 1689, in stone, on a remarkable sundial which is now in St Nicholas' Church there. They are depicted on one face and mysteriously bear the numbers 7, 10, 14, which may well be their former height in feet; today the two upright stones measure 15ft (4.6m) and 9ft (2.7m); the leaning stone is 12ft (3.7m).

Nearby, in the grounds of Court Farm, sits Tump Terret, a three-tiered earth mound. The notice there states that it 'dates back to the thirteenth century', but very probably it is pre-Christian. So, most certainly, is a stone table in the two-acre Churchyard of St Nicholas nearby, set in front of a medieval preaching cross. This enthralling little village holds yet more secrets. Over the crossroads from Harold's Stones there is a holy well; it is now labelled The Virtuous Well, but it has been appropriately called The Red Pool, and, very long ago, St Anne's Well, implying the place of a beacon fire.

PENTRE IFAN

Clearly signposted, on the right going east from Newport on the A487. Turn off it southwards at Temple Bar. Park at the footpath.

The famous Welsh burial chamber, perhaps part of a larger setting.

This is one of the most popular tomb sites in Wales; it is easy to find yet in remote countryside, and well-presented with a storyboard at the gate into the area. The lasting impression that one carries away is without doubt of the huge, almost flying capstone, most delicately poised on its three uprights. The quality of the engineering feat is plain to see. The stone, which is dressed on its south face, weighs over 16 tons; it is 16ft 6in (5m) long and 8ft (2.4m) high off the ground.

This chamber, which dates back to about 3500 BC, was once covered and at the end of a long barrow about 120ft (36m) long. The recessed south-facing forecourt once had stones closely packed between the portals, and these would have been laboriously removed every time there was a fresh burial. The north-south axis is rare. Some of the original kerbstones around the barrow can still be seen. Excavations took place at Pentre Ifan in 1936–37 and in 1958–59.

All around the area there are large stones which pose unanswered questions. Were the stones at the gate in the field to the east once associated with the tomb? What of the enormous dressed stone against the drystone wall in the field 140yds (128m) directly to the west? Was there perhaps an enormous circle of stones around the site, enclosing a settlement? Possibly, since *pentre* means 'village'.

St Lythan's (Maes-Y-Felin)

Duffryn,
Barry,
South Glamorgan

CHAMBER TOMB

ST 101723

This chamber's name translates as
The Mill in the Meadow.

West of Cardiff. Turn off the
A48 at St Nicholas, at the
sign to Duffryn Conference
Centre and Gardens; pass the
entrance and continue to the
road junction. Turn left, and
it is signposted on the right.
Park there.

lithic monuments gradually acquire 'a sense of place'.

The chamber, which faces almost due east away from the downward slope, measures 8ft (2.4m) by 6ft (1.8m) and is 6ft (1.8m) high. The insides of the two portal stones have been smoothed, and the back stone has a port-hole near its top. Externally, the brown stones are very heavily pitted; huge they are, and eminently sited, but as nothing compared with the neighbouring TINKINSWOOD in general attraction.

St Lythan's capstone is 14ft (4m) long, 10ft (3m) wide, and 2ft 6in (0.7m) thick: it is said that on Midsummer's Eve it spins around three times, which must be an awesome sight! This story fits with the chamber tomb's Welsh name, which translates as 'The Mill in the Meadow'.

There is a tradition that the field in which the remnants of this tomb stand is cursed, and that nothing will grow there. The site certainly feels uncomfortable; constant visitors to mega-

TINKINSWOOD

*St Nicholas,
Barry,
South Glamorgan*

HORNED BURIAL
CHAMBER

ST 092733

West of Cardiff. Turn off the A48 at St Nicholas, at the signs to Tinkinswood and the Duffryn Conference Centre and Gardens. The site is shortly before the Centre, on the right. Walk south across a field, and then over the signposted small wooden footbridge.

RIGHT: *The horned forecourt of Tinkinswood, which is a rare feature in Britain.*

The 40 ton capstone here is like a giant slice of home-made brown bread, and has suffered only one crack since 4000 BC when it was first placed here to shelter burials. The horned entrance beneath it faces north-east, and indeed towards a radio transmitter (which will interest fans of quartz at ancient sites). The earth mound either side and to the south-west of the chamber is 130ft (40m) long and is 60ft (18m) wide. On it, on the west side, there is a pile of stones beside a pit.

Following excavations in 1914, the whole site was greatly restored; the horned entrance is most impressive, though spoiled a little by the close fencing. A depression exactly at the south-east marks the site of a possible side entrance. There are standing and fallen stones all around, including two uprights south-east of the chamber, just inside the entrance gate.

More than 50 burials have been found at Tinkinswood, which has attracted the attention of archaeologists ever since the first excavations. In 1925, Sir Mortimer Wheeler recorded the old legend that anyone who spent a night in the chamber on a pagan spirit night (such as Beltane or Hallowe'en) would die, go raving mad or become a poet.

YSBYTY CYNFYN

*St John's Church,
Ysbyty Cynfyn,
Devil's Bridge,
Dyfed*

STONE CIRCLE AND
CHURCHYARD

SN 752791

2½ miles (4km) north of Devil's Bridge on the A4120, as it leads up to the A44.

Two standing stones in the wall of St John's Church.

Early Christian missionaries in Britain, Europe and elsewhere, soon learnt that their aims were best served if they did not destroy the pagans' ancient places of worship, but converted them. Here there is a circular churchyard with a circle built into part of its wall. Five stones remain of the circle that previously tenanted the site; two serve as gateposts (perhaps they were formerly portals) at the church's east entrance, two are incorporated in its churchyard wall, and one, the tallest at 11ft (3.3m), is in its original position among the graves.

Other churches with standing stones in their graveyards include Ste Marie du Câtel, Guernsey (*see* LE CÂTEL, Jersey); St Gwrthwl's Church, Llanwrthwl, Powys; St Brynach's Church, Nevern, Dyfed (with ogham markings); and St David's Church, Bridell (*see* BRIDELL, also with ogham markings, and others). The largest British example of the overt Christianisation of a site is the huge ditched earthwork at Knowlton, Dorset, where a Norman church now stands right in the middle of it.

Raised circular or oval-shaped churchyards (but not those with deeply sunk church foundations) often indicate a probable prehistoric place of worship. Old Radnor Church, Powys (*see* FOUR STONES, Walton, Powys) is a fine example. Such church sites are very often found on leys (invisible straight lines which criss-cross the landscape, with ancient sites occurring along their ways). A single piece of stone lying in a churchyard can, in fact, be the remaining stump of a standing stone, and a clue to a ley. There is one at Lenham, Kent — and they are quite common all over the country.

II

France

France is a megalithic wonderland. There are literally thousands of stone structures in most parts of this huge country, and the study of passages of its successive prehistoric cultures among them can be relied upon to provide both popular and academic controversy for many years to come. The 33 sites described here offer a cross-section of megalithic sites; many of them are located in Brittany which is easily the most popular area of the country (and probably in Europe) for their enjoyment and study. Less accessible areas are also rich in monuments; for example, the southern *département* of Aveyron has more of them than are found in England and Wales together.

There are some outstanding sites therefore to be explored. For megalithic art, GAVR'INIS, Morbihan, rivals NEWGRANGE, Ireland, with mysterious, detailed carvings on 23 of its uprights; they have similarities with those on stones in Malta and Spain as well as Ireland. The broken colossus LE GRAND MENHIR BRISÉ, Morbihan, may never have stood; KERLOAS, Finistère, is Europe's tallest standing stone, at 31ft (9.5m) above ground. The stone rows at KERMARIO and MÉNEC, both in Morbihan, each offer a long walk among more than 1000 stones, standing in serried ranks and posing some very difficult questions. Down in the south, the Neolithic camp at VILLENEUVE-TOLOSANE, just outside Toulouse, Hâute Garonne, is a sophisticated works site.

The language of stones

The word dolmen was invented by a French archaeologist, Carnet, in 1796. He put together the Old Breton words *tôl*, *taol* or *dol* (table) and *maen*, *mên* or *men* (stone) to describe the archetypal megalithic monument which occurs over many parts of France. About two hundred years of commentary have produced terminological confusion! Consider the following.

A dolmen in France, three or more uprights supporting a capstone, is the same as a cromlech in parts of Britain; TRETHEVY QUOIT, Cornwall, and CARREG SAMSON, Dyfed, Wales, are generally marked as cromlechs on maps. But the word cromlech also occurs in France. It comes from the Breton word Kroumlec'h derived from *kromm* or *kroumm* (curved) and *lec'h*, *leac'h* or *liac'h* (sacred stone or circle of stones), and means stone circle (of which, incidentally, there are remarkably few in the whole country). The Cornish and Breton languages were very similar, and it is possible that in fact Carnet derived the word dolmen from the Cornish word *tôlven*, which unfortunately refers to one natural boulder supported by others, without human intervention. A *dolmen*

simple in France is not, when translated into English, a simple dolmen, but a open-ended rectangle of stone slabs probably featuring false corbelling over its passage or chamber. It is an odd fact that the first published reference to a French chamber tomb was by Rabelais (c.1494–1553) in his Pantagruel, Book V; he was referring to La Pierre Levée, St Saturnin, Poitiers, one of many dolmens bearing this name.

The French term *allée-couverte* is in many ways preferable to the English gallery grave (which 50 years ago was called a long stone cist) because it more precisely defines the absence of a distinct chamber (as at La Chaussée-Tirancourt, Somme). A chamber tomb in France may be covered by an earth mound or cairn (like the many-chambered LES MOUSSEAUX, Loire-Atlantique), and is unconnected with the non-megalithic British tumulus. The lone vertical stone in Britain is a standing stone; in France it is a menhir. Legrand d'Aussy coined the word in 1796 from the Breton *méan* or *men* (stone) and *hîr* (long or tall). In the British Isles, Cornish has supplied MÊN-AN-TOL, Cornwall, but this is a group of standing stones; Welsh has contributed to THE DRUIDS' CIRCLE (MEINI HIRION), Gwynedd, where there are stone circles and cairns. One of the great menhirs of France is the 31ft (9.5m) DOL (though KERLOAS was once higher) in Ille-et-Vilaine – but, as previously mentioned, the Breton words *tôl*, *taol* and *dol* mean table which it manifestly is not (unlike, for example, the Minorcan *taula*). But then DOL might not even be a true menhir in any case; there is a controversial record that about a century ago a large area of ground around it was stripped of its top soil, revealing that the stone is in fact carved directly out of the broad granite plateau which lies beneath the soil. This is an entertaining tale, but the plateau is schist, and the menhir was probably quarried (and dressed) about 2¾m (4km) away.

Even apparent facts can confuse. The massive BAGNEUX, Maine-et-Loire, is widely referred to as an 'Angevin' chamber tomb, but it is very doubtful that it ever received a burial. Adding to the language problems, guide books sometimes resort to idiosyncratic nomenclature; for example, the English Michelin green guide to Brittany goes to the trouble of translating LES PIERRES PLATES, Morbihan, as Dolmen of Flat Stones!

The first monuments

The 5000 or so burial chambers and other megalithic monuments in France are mostly grouped in a few large areas. They are dense in the Paris basin, northern Normandy, west of Caen, the north-west peninsula of Brittany, from St Malo west

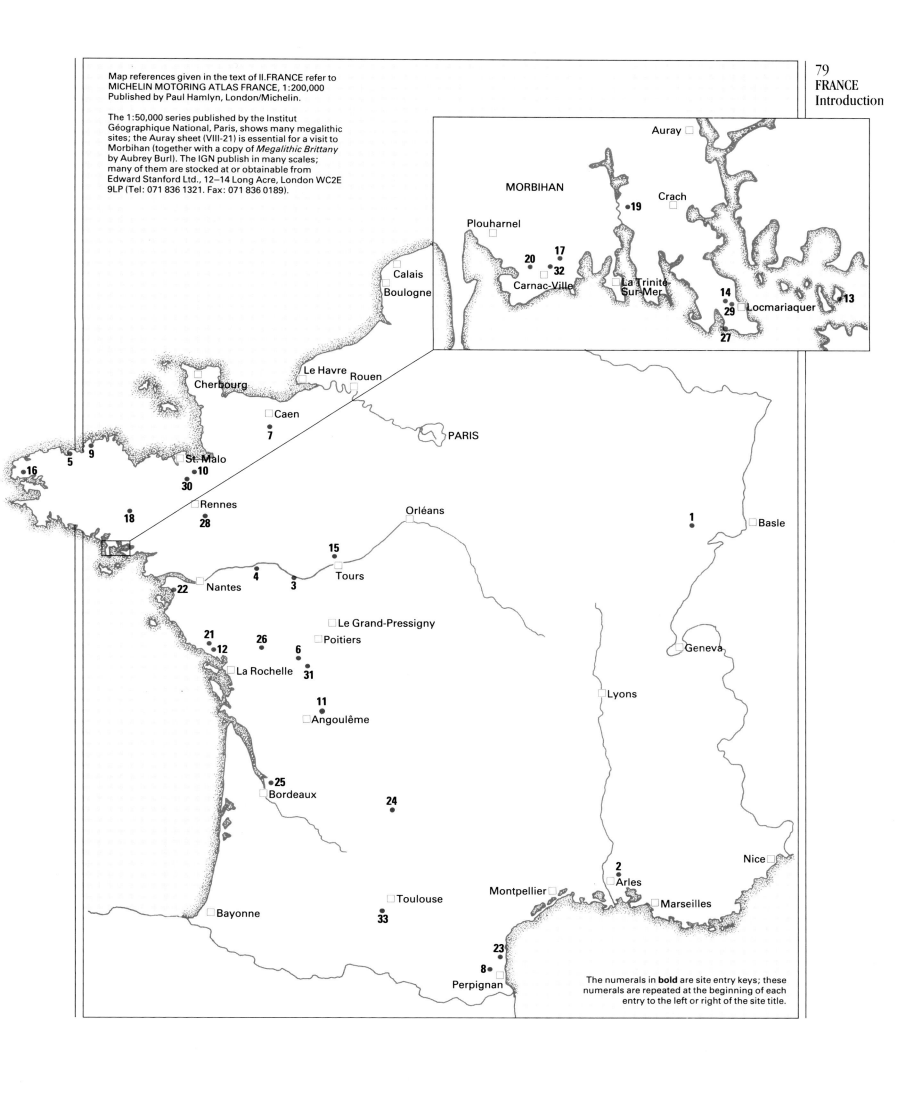

Map references given in the text of II.FRANCE refer to
MICHELIN MOTORING ATLAS FRANCE, 1:200,000
Published by Paul Hamlyn, London/Michelin.

The 1:50,000 series published by the Institut
Géographique National, Paris, shows many megalithic
sites; the Auray sheet (VIII-21) is essential for a visit to
Morbihan (together with a copy of *Megalithic Brittany*
by Aubrey Burl). The IGN publish in many scales;
many of them are stocked at or obtainable from
Edward Stanford Ltd., 12–14 Long Acre, London WC2E
9LP (Tel: 071 836 1321. Fax: 071 836 0189).

MORBIHAN

Auray

Crach

19

Plouharnel

20   **17**
         32
Carnac-Ville   La Trinité-
                Sur-Mer
                          14   **13**
                          29 Locmariaquer
                             27

Calais
Boulogne

Cherbourg   Le Havre   Rouen

Caen

7

PARIS

5   **9**
16
         St. Malo
         10
         30

Rennes
18   **28**

Orléans

15

Tours

4   **3**
Nantes

22

Le Grand-Pressigny

21   **26**   Poitiers
   12
      6
La Rochelle   **31**

11
Angoulême

1   Basle

Geneva

Lyons

25
Bordeaux

24

Nice

2
Arles

Montpellier   Marseilles

Toulouse

Bayonne   **33**

23

8
Perpignan

The numerals in **bold** are site entry keys; these
numerals are repeated at the beginning of each
entry to the left or right of the site title.

ABOVE: *The 25-ton entrance lintel stone is a dramatic feature of* LA ROCHE AUX FÉES, *Ille-et-Vilaine, one of France's finest chamber tombs.*

RIGHT: *Two of the four pairs of 'breasts' at* TRESSÉ, *Ille-et-Vilaine. Both are in the end cell. Together these measure 13ins (33cm) across; traces of necklaces can be seen beneath each pair.*

LEFT: *A café in Montguyon, Charente-Maritime, celebrates in its name the local prehistoric attraction,* LA PIERRE FOLLE. *Note the 'M'.*

and south down the Atlantic seaboard as far as Chârente Maritime, and from there in a broad belt across central southern France, through Aveyron towards Montpellier. There are further concentrations west of Cannes over to the east of the French side of the Pyrenees.

In the north, the earliest farming communities appeared on the left bank of the Rhine in about the middle of the fifth millennium (the cemetery at Rixheim, Alsace, for example). The old and difficult question of indigenous spontaneous tomb construction in several parts of France (indeed, in different countries) is highlighted by a date of 4600 BC obtained from Tomb G at BARNENEZ, far to the west in Finistère. A very similar date (4675 BC) has come from Kercado in Morbihan; this is a fine, mounded burial chamber with a menhir on top. So here is a funerary construction in Brittany which predates STONEHENGE, Knossos and the Great Pyramid at Giza.

The early Neolithic Bandkeramik culture (named after the swirling patterns on its pottery) came to north-east France, and even as far as the Channel Islands, from east of the Danube, also spreading all over Germany and the Low Countries. Its people were not intense farmers however, and it is likely that the practice of agriculture reached Brittany from south-west France.

From about 3400 BC to 1800 BC the Paris Basin culture held sway. It was clumsily named Seine-Oise-Marne (SOM), after the rivers, in 1926 by two Spanish archaeologists, P. Bosch-Gimpera and J. de C. Serra Raffols. Its collective chamber tombs, mostly *allées-couvertes*, are generally distributed north of Paris and on river sites. Some have port-hole slabs, and most are sunk in trenches with their capstones showing just above ground level; they were rarely covered by earth. Though probably of local origin, some have argued that the origin of the *allée-couverte* may well lie in southern Spain, following north the routes of the earliest farmers on the way; these tombs are earlier than the somewhat similar versions found to the north, in Germany, Denmark and Sweden.

In the south

The first Neolithic farmers settled in south-western France in the century or so before 5000 BC. A date of 4830 ± 200 bc has been obtained from one of the deepest hearths in the Grotte

Gazel, Sallèles-Cabardès, Aude, where Impressed Ware occurred. This is also called Cardial Ware; *cardium* is Latin for cockle, the shell of which, once it contents were consumed, was used to effect a serrated style of pottery decoration. This pottery probably originated in Yugoslavia, spread west to Italy, across to Sicily, and thence by way of Provence, to Spain.

Early Impressed Ware sites in Provence include Châteauneuf-les-Martigues, Bouches-du-Rhône, where Hearth 5 produced the date of 5570 ± 240 bc, which is very much earlier than other Midi sites. The succeeding culture, that of France's first intense farmers, has left the date of 3810 ± 140 bc in Level 8B in the upper network of Grotte de l'Eglise, Baudinard, Var. It is found in many different types of burial sites and settlements, including, for instance, La Grotte des Fées, in the ARLES-FONTVIEILLE GROUP, Bouches-du-Rhône, which dates back to about 3100 BC.

The Chasséen culture reached the Paris basin just before the start of the third millennium BC, leaving behind few satisfactory dates in western and central France for a tracking exercise. On the other hand, this could indicate broadly contemporary indigenous tomb development – but some pottery assemblages go against this argument. The Chasséen culture was named by the eminent Australian archaeologist Gordon Childe (1892–1957) after the fortified hill site of Chassey-le-Camp, near Chagny, which is south-west of Beaune, Burgundy's wine capital.

Brittany

All around the Breton *départements* of Finistère, Côtes-d'Armor, Morbihan (where Carnac is), Ille-et-Vilaine and Loire-Atlantique lie many hundreds of megalithic structures: dolmens, menhirs, chamber tombs within and without stone cairns and mounds of earth, passageless or otherwise – with entrances frequently facing the midwinter sunrise.

And then there are the oddly disturbing stone rows (*alignments*); at KERMARIO, Morbihan, over 1000 menhirs are set up in seven main rows over a distance of 1230 yds (1125m). The site's name means Village of the Dead, but the Scottish surveyor Professor Alexander Thom has, less prosaically, concluded that the stone rows constituted a giant eclipse predictor.

FRANCE

AILLEVANS GROUP

Aillevans,
Villersexel,
Vesoul,
Haute-Saône

HORNED CHAMBER
TOMBS

76 C 2

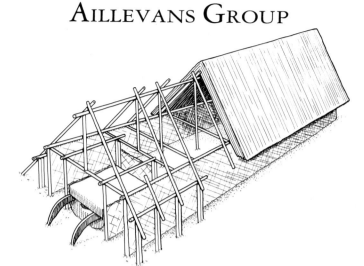

Take the D9 south-east from
Vesoul towards Belfort. After
16 miles (26 km), turn
north, through Villersexel, on
the D486. Aillevans is
signposted on the left.

A conjectural reconstruction of Tomb
I, one of three horned chamber-tombs
forming the Aillevans Group.
(After P. Pétrequin and J.-F.
Piningre, 1976)

The three monuments here date, through successive use, from the Late Neolithic to the Early Bronze Ages. Each of them is small, about 6½ft (2m) square, set east to west precisely, with the antechamber and horned entrance at the east.

In Tomb I, at least 23 bodies were deposited; the tomb's mound was circular at first but, in a second stage, the tomb was covered by a long wooden trapezoidal hut about 65½ft

(20m) long, and partly paved. In Tomb II, at least 100 burials took place; animal bones, flint arrowheads and a dagger blade have also been uncovered there.

Tombs I and II were re-used a number of times, and on occasions the bodies were placed complete, and not in the more familiar foetal position, with the heads facing west, away from the entrances.

ARLES-FONTVIEILLE GROUP

Sainte Croix,
Fontvieille,
Bouches-du-Rhône

ROCK-CUT TOMBS
(HYPOGÉES)

158 A 2

Among the finds at Castelet were arrowheads, beads, axes and pottery; at Bounias, a copper dagger was found.

Leave Arles northwards on the
N570; turn right on to the
D17 towards Fontvieille. The
group is at Sainte Croix and
beyond the ruined L'Abbaye de
Montmajour, on the right of
the road. Somewhat
inaccessible.

The smoothly dressed interior of La
Grotte Arnaud-Castelet.

There are five tombs at this important site, and, in the general Provençal tradition, they are all orientated to the setting sun. Within their earth mounds, they are beautifully carved (with the exception of the drystone walled Coutignargues) and smoothly finished, and each is covered by a large capstone. Other rock-cut tombs or *hypogées* such as these are found in Mediterranean regions such as Malta, Sardinia and Sicily.

The largest here, with a length of 141ft (43m) in a mound 230 ft by 165 ft (70 m by 50.3 m) is La Grotte des Fées on the north side of Montagne de Cordes, which dates back to about 3500BC (human remains and radiocarbon dateable artifacts have been found in most of these tombs). Carved stone stairs lead 11ft (3.3m) down to an antechamber, with one small

chamber on each side, and then on through a doorway to the main chamber. This is 80ft (24.4m) long, about 11ft (3.3m) high, but only 9ft (2.7m) wide; it gradually tapers like a hilted sword, from which fact the tomb's alternative name, L'Epée de Roland, might have been derived.

La Grotte Arnaud-Castelet (the only site on the other side of the road) is somewhat similar to La Grotte des Fées, but smaller; over 100 skeletons were found here during excavations. La Grotte Bounias and La Grotte de la Source share similar findings, including arrowheads, axes, beads and pottery sherds. The tomb of Coutignargues, on the Plateau de Castelet, is not a true *hypogée*, since it is constructed of drystone walling.

BAGNEUX

*Bagneux,
Saumur,
Maine-et-Loire*

'ANGEVIN' CHAMBER
TOMB

81 D 1

*The massive 'Angevin' chamber tomb
in the café courtyard in Bagneux.
Locally it is called Le Grand
Dolmen.*

This tomb belongs in any book of records; it is the largest
tomb of its kind in France – alas it cannot be used as a dance
hall (floodlighting already installed). 'Angevin' graves are
often found grouped together in this area, and they are not
generally set on high or prominent places; even among them
this monster is unique.

At almost 65ft (19.8m) long, and 25ft (7.6m) wide, it bears
some resemblance to LA ROCHE AUX FÉES, Ille-et-Vilaine,
which is a little longer but otherwise smaller. The entrance,
which faces just south-south-east, leads into a veritable hall of
stone; four massive capstones cover the entire length of the
tomb, and the largest of them is 25ft (7.6m) long. They
support four opposing pairs of massive flat slabs, square or

*Leave Saumur south-west on
the N147. The tomb is in a
café courtyard in Bagneux (a
suburb of Saumur), nearly 1
mile (1.6km) along on the
left.*

rectangular and leaning slightly inwards. The largest capstone weighs no less than 86 tons, as compared with the weight of an unladen red double-decker London bus which is a meagre 9¾ tons.

First excavated in 1775, Bagneux was never covered by an earth mound on its slight slope in the entrance direction, and nothing is known with certainty to have been found inside it, though there are reports of some finds in 1849. Called a tomb, perhaps it never was one.

Inside, its ceiling height is 10ft (3.1m) – just the place for a prehistoric party, for celebration, for rituals of unknown significance, then as now.

This 'Grand Dolmen' is located in the gravel courtyard of a modest family-owned café/bar/tabac, and is probably the largest private megalithic monument in the world. Entrance is free only if you spend in the café!

The interior of the Bagneux tomb – 'a veritable hall of stone'.

LA BAJOULIÈRE

*Saint-Rémy-la-Varenne,
Angers,
Maine-et-Loire*

'ANGEVIN' CHAMBER
TOMB

66 B 4

This is one of the most impressive tombs of its type in France, and in terms of its sheer size can be compared with BAGNEUX, Saumur, which is not far away. In plan it is similar to the sole of a man's shoe, with a trapezoidal surrounding mound.

Inside lies a simple, most elegant and almost completely symmetrical chamber. Two square boulders stand guard at its south-east facing entrance. An antechamber leads to an enormous square chamber, measuring no less than 23ft by 23ft (7m by 7m). This 58½ sq yds (49sq m) area is covered by a single capstone; like many Angevin chamber-tombs, it is divided inside by a curtain wall of six stepped uprights with a door space left in the middle. This Late Neolithic grave appears 'younger' than it is because of the neat squared-off finish given to the capstone and chamber uprights.

Leave Angers south-east on the D952, along the River Loire. After about 12½ miles (20 km), at St. Mathurin-sur-Loire, turn right, southwards, over the bridge on the D55. Immediately turn left to St. Rémy-la-Varenne, then right on to the D21. Now take the first left, and then fork right towards La Roche. The tomb is on the left, before the small village.

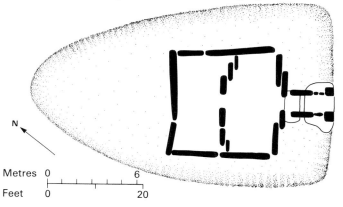

The peaceful setting of La Bajoulière. There may be remains of further tombs in the nearby wood.

Metres 0   6

Feet 0   20

La Bajoulière is famed for its size and symmetry; two ditches reach out from the entrance like horns. (After Gruet)

BARNENEZ

*Plouézoc'h,
Morlaix,
Finistère*

CAIRN WITH MULTIPLE
PASSAGE-GRAVES

27 E 2

This is one of many magnificent monuments in Brittany, the land of megalithic superlatives. Here there are an incredible eleven passage-graves, and they demonstrate almost all the forms of grave construction in Neolithic times.

The massive stepped cairn, aligned north-east/south-west atop its dramatic hilltop site, was built in two distinct stages, and using different stone (green dolorite to the east, granite to the west). The first, at the north-east, is dated at about 4600 BC; it is 115ft (35m) along its north-east/south-west axis, and 26ft (8m) at its widest. In its south-east flank there are five passage-graves, with their entrances in a row. From south to north-east, they are labelled today as Tombs G, Gi, H, I and J. A few centuries later, another cairn was literally attached to

Take the D76 north from Morlaix along the estuary. Go through Plouézoc'h. At the next fork, take the lane on the left to Kernelehen. Ticket office, exhibition and bookstall. Closed in the winter, midweek, and, of course, lunchtime. Only two of the graves (C and D) can be visited. Take a torch.

RIGHT: *This impressive complex at Barnenez of 11 passage-graves was built in two stages, and discovered as recently as 1954 (when excavators were seeking stone aggregate behind tombs A, B, C and D). (After P.-R. Giot and Y. Lecerf)*

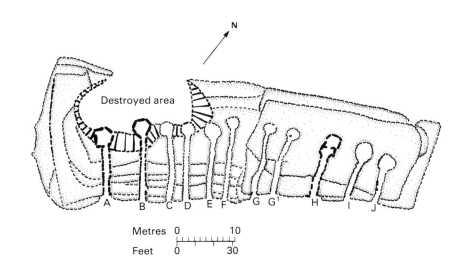

Destroyed area

Barnenez from the air. The dark area to the left, at the back of the passage-graves, is where 'stone' was taken for road building.

Looking north-east along the restored cairns at Barnenez. Some entrances can be seen.

A legend has it that this site was built by fairies and that an underground passage led out from the cairns to the sea.

it to the south-west, together with another six passage-graves joining the row. From the south they are called Tombs A, B, C, D, E and F. In its entirety, the present cairn measures 230ft (70m) long and 82ft (25m) deep.

The whole site was only discovered in 1954, when contractors seeking stone aggregate for a new road in the area tore the backs off Tombs A, B, C and D, exposing the splendid chambers to the elements. Quarrying was immediately halted and in 1955 P.R. Giot commenced a two-year excavation of the site.

The Barnenez passage-graves were without doubt just that, even though there were few human remains among the amazing finds. Tomb A is dated at about 4400 BC; its corbelled roof was partly destroyed in 1954, its passage is lined with orthostats and broken pottery, indicating burial, was unearthed. Of interest are seven carved wavy lines on one of the uprights.

Tomb B has a megalithic chamber, now partly ruined, in which human bones were found, as well as pottery sherds.

Tomb C, in contrast with its southerly neighbour, has a passage of drystone walling. The partly destroyed corbelled roof is topped, not with corbelling, but with a capstone, in keeping with the capstones roofing the passage. Among the

finds here have been a copper dagger and flint arrowheads.

Tomb D is constructed like C, but has drystone walling in between orthostats; burnt human bones, Beaker sherds and flint arrowheads have been discovered in this tomb. E is constructed in the same way as C.

Tomb F is the longest at the site, with a passage and chamber stretching 46ft (14m); it has two small stelae at its entrance, and has been dated at about 4500 BC.

Like C, Tomb G is of drystone walling and has the oldest date here at about 4700 BC. Tomb Gi is likewise similar to C except that a thin rectangle of granite stands near the entrance to its chamber.

Of all the tombs, H proved to be the archaeological treasure house. It is the most elaborate and important megalithic structure, with a huge capstone over its back chamber. Stones inside bear carvings of axes, triangles, wavy lines and zigzags, and small stelae in its antechamber are very similar to those at LOS MILLARES, Almeria.

A further variation in passage construction is seen in Tomb I, which is half uprights and half drystone walling. The chamber is exclusively drystone with a corbelled roof. Finally, Tomb J is notable for the rough carving, which probably represents a female form, beneath the capstone.

*Bougon,
St. Maixent-L'Ecole,
Niort,
Deux-Sèvres*

CEMETERY

94 C 2

In Tomb C four skeletons were found seated along the wall, and attached to it with stone brackets.

Archaeologist Jean-Pierre Mohen considers that some of the stone chambers at this site were not used for burials.

This very important Neolithic site was first discovered as long ago as 1840. It consists of six tombs in a tight cluster. Serious excavations commenced in 1968, and then in 1972, under the direction of Jean-Pierre Mohen.

Tomb A is enclosed in a circular mound which is 130ft (40m) in diameter, and dates back to about 3750BC. The passage leads to a divided rectangular chamber measuring 24½ft by 16½ft (7.5m by 5m); in the 1840 excavations, some 200 skeletons were uncovered in three distinct, separated layers. Complete pots were also found, which is unusual.

Tomb B contains two small stone cists in a 115ft (35m) long mound, which is dated at approximately 4250BC; later two passage graves with four-sided chambers, and two others, were constructed. Tomb C has a diameter of 185ft (56m), and a height of 13ft (4m); inside the mound is a squarish chamber at the west end. Tomb D is not in any way prehistoric but is a 275ft (84m) long mound.

Tomb E, which had a round, corbelled-roofed chamber when first constructed, shows two virtually parallel passage-graves to the east.

The final Tomb F is notable for its substantial capstone over a rectangular chamber tomb at the north; it weighs 32 tons and measures 19¾ft by 11½ft (6m by 3.5m); at the other end of the extended mound there is a second, round corbelled chamber.

In July 1979 the Tomb F capstone was the object of a famous experiment by Jean-Pierre Mohen. With a team of 200 able-bodied men, a 32 ton replica of the stone was pulled along by 170 men, with the help of the other 30 levering the slab along over 30 rounded oak trunks on 'railway lines'. As a result, Mohen estimated that it would have taken one and a half months to bring the stone about 2½miles (4km) from its original source to the Bougon site. In those prehistoric times, the disciplines involved in this exercise alone must have been of an amazingly high order.

St. Maixent is about 15 miles (24km) north-east of Niort on the N11. After the town turn right on to the D737. After 6¾ miles (11km), at La Mothe, turn left on to the D5, then take the second turning on the right for Bougon. Marked 'tumulus' on the map, just north of the village.

One of the six tombs, after excavation and restoration by Jean-Pierre Mohen.

CAIRN DE LA HOGUE AND CAIRN DE LA HOGUETTE

Fontenay-le-Marmion,
Caen,
Calvados

CAIRNS WITH MULTIPLE PASSAGE-GRAVES

32 A 2

There are 12 entrances to passages in Cairn De La Hogue

Leave Caen southwards on the D562. After 6¼ miles (10km), at May-sur-Orne, turn left on to the minor D41b. Cairn de la Hogue is soon seen on the left.

This type of cairn was invariably placed on a prominent, high site, and from the time of construction always incorporated passage-graves. These two are roughly contemporary, late Neolithic, and are not strictly megalithic in that they are made of drystone walling.

De La Hogue is almost rectangular — 140ft (42.7m) long, 102ft (31.1m) wide, and some 30ft (9.1m) high. There are no less than 12 entrances to passages leading to small round chambers at the end of each; six disarticulated skeletons were uncovered here and, in 1829, a small primitive altar, made of chalk, and a perfect miniature dolmen, were found in one of the chambers.

De La Hoguette is 650 yds (595m) away, dates back to about 2300BC, and is almost 98½ft (30m) long by 65½ft (20m) wide. Its excavation, begun in 1964, has revealed an interesting find. It contains seven round chambers (there was once an eighth); in six of them, remains of 56 complete skeletons have been identified, and there are, unusually in late Neolithic tombs, almost exactly equal numbers of men, women and children.

LA CLAPE GROUP

Laroque-de-Fâ,
Aude

CEMETERY

172 B 3

Eight chamber tombs make up this site, which dates from about 2000BC. Tomb 1 is a passage-grave within an oval mound; the teeth of 15 people have been found there in the two side chambers. Tomb 2 is a three-sided burial cist. Tomb 3 is a rectangular grave, which contained the remains of two people (a child and a young adult), and a flint knife; it is in the same mound as Tomb 5, nearer the centre. This is an open-ended passage-grave, where 24 people were buried. Only one was a man. Tomb 4 is a simple passage-grave.

Tombs 6 and 7 lie within the same kidney-shaped mound, the longer 6 to the south, and 7 to its north, where another 24 people, mainly youngsters, were laid to rest. Tomb 8, the most symmetrical, has an unusual, almost circular chamber with two well-placed portal stones without, and all inside a round mound 16½ft (5m) in diameter.

Laroque-de-Fâ is a mountain village on the D212, which runs south from the A61 autoroute between Narbonne and Carcassonne. The tombs are just south of the tunnel through Col de Bedos.

CRECH-QUILLÉ

2½ miles (4km) north of
Lannion on the D788, turn
right to Crech-Quillé.

*Saint-Quay-Perros,
Côtes-d'Armor*

ALLÉE-COUVERTE WITH
SIDE ENTRANCE

28 A 1

This passage-grave was discovered only in 1955, and it was excavated in 1963-64. The late Neolithic long mound is aligned almost east-west, measures 98ft by 36ft (30m by 11m) and the large kerbstones around it are in-filled with drystone walling. On the south side of the grave towards the eastern end, the short side entrance passage is set, and a single stone stands there.

The chamber is 53ft by 6ft (16.2m by 1.8m), and contains a Breton mystery in the form of a large stele, facing the passage entrance, like a sort of guardian; upon it are carved two breasts, in relief, with a necklace or collar looped below them. Perhaps it was a string of token beads, an indication of wealth, and thus of power.

Such an image has been found elsewhere in passage-graves in France, and also at CÂTEL, Guernsey. Graves of this type are similar to the *hunebedden* in The Netherlands and passage-graves in northern Germany.

The side entrance of Crech-Quillé, looking towards the carved stele.

Excavators found a stone cist containing five pots and some pendants in the passage.

Metres 0   1

Feet 0   5

N

DOL

II.10

*Champ Dolent,
Dol de Bretagne,
Ille-et-Vilaine*

MENHIR

48 B 1

Take the D155 coastal road from St Malo south-east to Le Vivier-sur-Mer, and then south to Dol de Bretagne. Leave the town southwards on the D795, and then, after about 1 mile (1.5km), turn right, as signposted. The menhir is now visible on the right.

Champ Dolent means 'Field of Sorrow', recalling a legend of a great battle here between good and evil. Today however this is a most pleasing spot with no air of sadness about it.

The splendid menhir is 31ft (9.5m) high; and almost square (unlike KERLOAS, Morbihan, although the faces of the stones are similarly aligned, east-north-east/west-south-west). Dol's surface has been dressed to a smooth finish (doubtless at its quarry source to lose weight), so that, in ever-changing weather, it would be less likely to fragment and crumble (like the top of RUDSTON, England, for example, though of granite, a different stone). It has two strange holes at shoulder height.

St Samson, whose name is attached to two menhirs in Côtes-d'Armor, died in Dol de Bretagne, and the cathedral there is dedicated to him (*see* CARREG SAMSON, Wales).

The giant menhir standing in the 'Field of Sorrow'; there are now picnic tables all round it and a storyboard of the area.

DOLMEN DE LA MOTTE DE ST. JACQUILLE

Chateaurenaud,
Mansle,
Angoulême,
Charente

PASSAGE-GRAVE

108 B 1

Travel northwards from Angoulême on the N10 for 16 miles (26km), then turn left for Mansle. In the town, turn north over the River Charente and then left along the river to Chateaurenaud. Then turn north-west towards Villesoubis on the D61. After about ½ mile (1km), at La Motte, the site can be seen on the left.

The remarkable 'swinging door'.

'Too little too late' was probably the sad verdict of the 1981/82 excavators at this unique site. The tomb had been much robbed, and just a few bones, flint arrowheads and pottery were found. On the other hand, they were able to report a quite remarkable feature in the tomb – what may have been the world's oldest known swinging door.

A circular mound, 98½ft (30m) in diameter covered the now roofless chamber. The long passage bends to the right just before the chamber entrance, which consists of an inner, two piece port-hole, and is closed off on the passage side by a stone door, 4ft high by 3¼ft (1.2m high by 1.0m). It swung by means of the tenons at the top and bottom which still survive, fitting mortices set in the lintel and threshold. Close by this Late Neolithic doorway is La Motte de la Garde, with a polygonal chamber, just to the south-west towards Luxe.

LA FRÉBOUCHÈRE

Le Bernard,
Avrillé,
Les Sables d'Olonne,
Vendée

'ANGEVIN' CHAMBER TOMB

92 B 2

Le Bernard is a hamlet, 15 miles (24km) south-east of Les Sables d'Olonne. Take the D949 eastwards out of Les Sables d'Olonne. After 17 miles (27km), after Avrillé, turn right on the D91 towards Le Bernard; the site is on the right.

The almost complete 'Angevin' chamber tomb, with its immense capstone, which is now split into two.

This 'Angevin' chamber tomb (sometimes called Le Bernard), about 3 miles (4.8km) from the Atlantic, was once used as a sheepfold, which seems perfectly sensible. After all the 2½ft (0.75m) thick and handsome capstone (which was split in two by lightning in the 19th century) is 27½ft (8.5m) long and 10½ft (3.2m) wide.

Supporting this huge megalithic covering are nine uprights: one great endstone, three pairs of opposing ones (though one has now fallen inwards) and two doorway stones. The capstone also has the help of two fine portal stones at the south-east. Most of the monoliths have rounded tops. A little mystery exists inside La Frébouchère: a betyl (a small stone pillar, probably of sacred significance) stands in the chamber, and no-one knows exactly why.

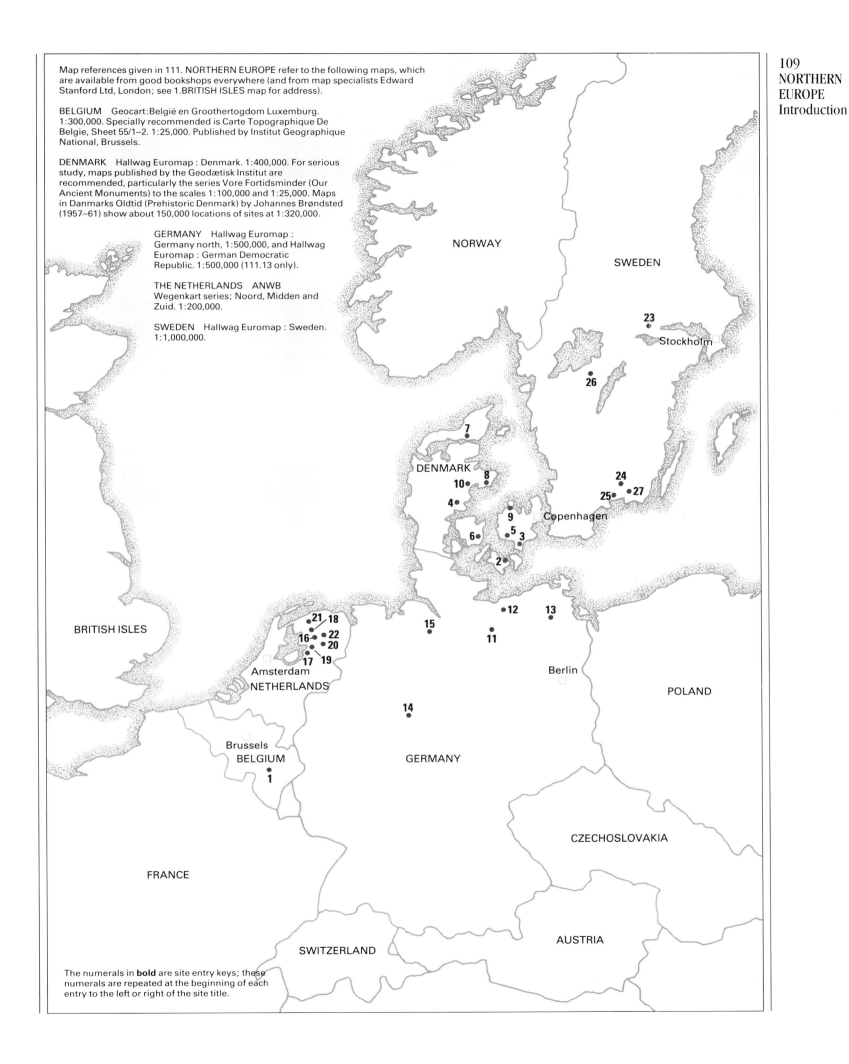

Map references given in 111. NORTHERN EUROPE refer to the following maps, which are available from good bookshops everywhere (and from map specialists Edward Stanford Ltd, London; see 1.BRITISH ISLES map for address).

BELGIUM   Geocart:België en Groothertogdom Luxemburg. 1:300,000. Specially recommended is Carte Topographique De Belgie, Sheet 55/1–2. 1:25,000. Published by Institut Geographique National, Brussels.

DENMARK   Hallwag Euromap : Denmark. 1:400,000. For serious study, maps published by the Geodætisk Institut are recommended, particularly the series Vore Fortidsminder (Our Ancient Monuments) to the scales 1:100,000 and 1:25,000. Maps in Danmarks Oldtid (Prehistoric Denmark) by Johannes Brøndsted (1957–61) show about 150,000 locations of sites at 1:320,000.

GERMANY   Hallwag Euromap : Germany north, 1:500,000, and Hallwag Euromap : German Democratic Republic. 1:500,000 (111.13 only).

THE NETHERLANDS   ANWB Wegenkart series; Noord, Midden and Zuid. 1:200,000.

SWEDEN   Hallwag Euromap : Sweden. 1:1,000,000.

NORWAY

SWEDEN

Stockholm

DENMARK

Copenhagen

BRITISH ISLES

Amsterdam
NETHERLANDS

Berlin

POLAND

Brussels
BELGIUM

GERMANY

FRANCE

CZECHOSLOVAKIA

SWITZERLAND

AUSTRIA

The numerals in **bold** are site entry keys; these numerals are repeated at the beginning of each entry to the left or right of the site title.

ABOVE LEFT: *The restored* ganggraf *HAVELTE WEST, Drenthe, in The Netherlands. It has been dated at about 2750 BC.*

LEFT: *A deplorable though amusing defacement of a standing stone at Süntelstein, near Osnabruck, Germany.*

ABOVE: *The much visited Dutch* hunebed *PAPELOZE KERK ('Priestless Church').*

RIGHT: *The massive front capstone of* DE STEENBARG. *This is the only* hunebed *in the Dutch province of Groningen.*

Bremen. It was originally kerbed by no less than 105 upright carefully selected natural boulders, which were graded in size along the grave's axis, from north-east to south-west. This Bride of Visbek has an even longer Groom 2½ miles (4km) away. This truly enormous *hünengrab* measures 354ft by 33ft (108m by 10m), and is testimony to the abilities of that remarkable culture.

A *steinkist* (stone burial chamber) in Germany (treated as united in this book) often has distinct similarities with the SOM culture's *allée-couverte*. LOHNE-ZÜSCHEN, Hesse, is, in the typical manner, sunk in a trench so that the tops of its 24 uprights show above ground level, along its north-east/south-west alignment. Its entrance vestibule is separated from the main gallery chamber by another typical feature, a port-hole slab (*seelenloch*). Another form of German passage grave is the *einteilige galeriegräber*, a long rectangular megalithic chamber sunk in a trench, with access through the top, via a wooden covering or opened stone slab. There is a surprisingly large number of standing stones in Germany; a concentration of them is within a broad circle drawn through Luxembourg,

Bonn, Koblenz, Frankfurt-a-M, Mannheim, Karlsruhe and Saarbrücken.

The Netherlands

The Funnel Beaker (TRB) people spread all over The Netherlands and flourished during about 4000–2800 BC. Their predominant megalithic bequest is however confined to the north-eastern province of Drenthe and, in fact, only three monuments are known to have been outside it. The reason is simple. Glacial moraines are plentiful down through Drenthe; big round erratic boulders were everywhere. A brief account of the unique and remarkable Dutch megalithic chamber tombs, which are called *hunebedden* (Hun's Beds), and their different types and characteristics are given below under NOORDLO and elsewhere in this part.

A drive southwards from Groningen to Emmen on the N92 provides an excellent introduction to Dutch archaeology. The *hunebedden* mostly date from about 3300–2800 BC (a date for HAVELTE WEST, for instance). This produces a puzzle, because the earliest of them predate the oldest Danish passage graves to

the north; SCHIMMERES has been placed early in the fourth millennium. Another odd fact is that there is not a single French-type dolmen in all The Netherlands, *Hunebedden* were constructed for collective burials, although single burials did occur. Because their total number is so small (only 53 still exist today, out of 76 recorded), and through the exhaustive efforts of Professor Albert E. van Giffen from the beginning of this century for some 40 years, all of the tombs have been carefully accounted for. and most excavated. Generally the grave goods were the usual flint flakes, broken tools and pottery sherds (with very simple decoration). After the Beaker period, megalithic construction all but ceased – although, strangely, this was certainly not the case in northern France and Britain, where great monuments were going up.

Sweden

The Slate Culture, named after some of its tools, arrived in northern Sweden in about 4000 BC, probably from the far east. About 1500 of their sites have so far been identified in Norrland, where rock carvings and cave paintings also occur,

in very inaccessible locations. One amazing site, and not remote, is at Nämforsen, Ådals-Liden, Ångermanland; here there are some 1500 naturalistic stone carvings all around the river bank, rapids and islets.

The Funnel Beaker people probably arrived in Sweden in about 3350 BC; traces of their early farming practices have been found on the west coast and in Västgotland. The first megalithic structures were simple four-sided dolmens – in Swedish *dosar* (singular *dos*). This is the first of the three classes of Swedish tomb pronounced by the famous Oscar Montelius (1843–1921) in 1898; the other two were *grafvar med gang* (or *gänggrift*) and *hallkistor*.

In the Middle Neolithic period, passage-graves (almost always with collective burials) were being built, and often in clusters. Some 234 of the country's 330 or so occur on the high plain of Falbygden, in the east of Västgotland. Others are found, in descending order of numbers, in Skåne, Bohuslän, Halland and Oland. In these, and the other 4500 or so megalithic tombs in Sweden, very few grave goods have been found, apart from broken votive pottery at their entrances.

BELGIUM

WÉRIS GROUP

Wéris,
Erezée and Oppagne,
Marche-en-Famenne,
Luxembourg

ALLÉE-COUVERTE,
GALLERY GRAVE AND
STANDING STONES

20 I

Belgium occupies 11,778 sq m (30,513 sq km) of Europe but only three megalithic tombs are known to exist today in the whole country (compared with 2067 in Denmark out of a total of 23,774 known prehistoric monuments). Two more are known to have existed, and for some strange reason, they are all in the neighbouring provinces of Namur and Luxembourg. This group in the Ardennes has been thoroughly explored and written about by Sigfried J. De Laet; he has also drawn attention to two unexplored long mounds in Brabant. The Wéris group of graves share the Seine-Oise-Marne (SOM)

Leave Liege southwards on the A26 autobahn. Take Exit 49, then take the N651 westwards, and continue to Erezée on the N807. Beyond the village take the minor road north to Wéris.

Two of the stones at Bouchaimont.

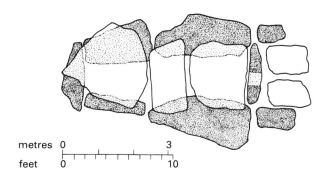

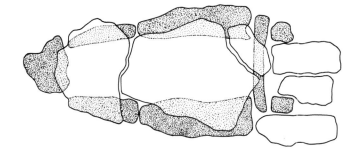

*Two graves in the Wéris Group,
Dolmen d'Oppagne (left), a
sunken* allée-couverte *was
discovered in 1888 and restored in*

*1906. Dolmen de Wéris
(right), an above ground gallery
grave, was discovered in the same
year. (After De Laet).*

metres 0   3

feet 0   10

culture (2400–1600 BC), and are connected with the *allées-
couvertes* of the Paris basin through the West German *einteilige
galeriegräber* (sunken gallery graves without compartments).

In the same area a group of three menhirs and a single one
also occur – and the remarkable fact is that the tombs and
menhirs, all made from the same local puddingstone, are
placed in a straight line. The 5000–4500-year-old Wéris
alignment commences at Tour, Heyd, north of Wéris, where a
standing stone is known to have existed (and to have been
broken up about 100 years ago); the total length of the
alignment, which extends south-west from this point, is about
3 miles (5 km).

The next monument is the Dolmen de Wéris (known as Le
Grand Dolmen). This above-ground gallery-grave was restored
in 1906, with virtually no finds. Now fenced off and among
trees, it was once covered by an earthen mound and measured
36ft (11m); its internal chamber length is 18ft (5.5m), and its
width is 5ft 6in (1.7m). The larger of its two capstones is badly
cracked; there may have been a third, consisting of the three
present substantial paving slabs at the entrance. The chamber
is walled with two pairs of uprights and an endstone, and in
separated from its antechamber by a slab which has a doorway
hole carved out of it.

Next in the alignment is an unnamed, 10ft (3m) tall
standing stone, which was found buried in a field and clumsily
re-erected beside the road in 1947. The rather ugly, lower part
of the stone which was once below ground is now visible.

Approximately 1 mile (1.6km) away from the Dolmen de
Wéris, among trees, lies the Dolmen d'Oppagne (known as Le
Petit Dolmen). This one is an *allée-couverte* of the SOM type, in
a trench, so that only the three capstones are above ground
level. It was discovered in 1888, and excavated in the same
year by A. Charneux; all his finds have now sadly vanished,
but reportedly included human and animal bones. This
dolmen was restored in 1906, a great year of activity in
Belgian archaeology, following these monuments' acquisition
by the nation. The internal chamber length is 15ft (4.6m), the
width 4ft (1.2m) and internal height 2ft (0.6m). It has two
pairs of uprights and an endstone, with the interstices being
filled with drystone walling. There is an antechamber, of
which two uprights survive. Again, the two paving slabs
might have formed part of a fourth capstone over it. As at the
Dolmen de Wéris, a septal slab, this time with a large
port-hole, separates the chambers.

At the end of the line, about 650 yds (600m) away, at

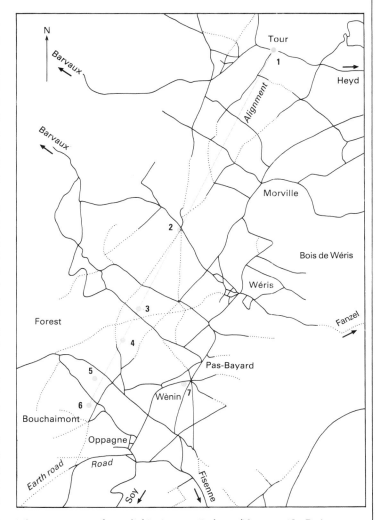

*The Wéris group of megalithic sites.
1 Standing stone, destroyed about
100 years ago. 2 Dolmen de Wéris
(Le Grand Dolmen); gallery grave. 3
Standing stone, beside road. 4
Dolmen d'Oppagne (Le Grand*

*Dolmen d'Oppagne (Le Petit
Standing stone; just west of
alignment. 6 Bouchaimont group of
three standing stones (not shown in
IGN map no. 55/1-2; 1:25,000).
7 Puddingstone fragment.*

Bouchaimont near Oppagne, is a tight group of three standing
stones; they are visible from the road. The tallest of these
Belgian stones, beneath the tree, stands about 8ft (2.4m)
above the ground. They too were found buried, and erected
again in 1906.

Although not in the Wéris alignment and some distance

away, remains of a third megalithic burial chamber were identified in 1976, near Jemelle, Namur; two now-destroyed graves were also located: Bois des Lusce, a gallery grave at Jemeppe-Hargimont, Luxembourg; and La Pierre du Diable (The Devil's Stone) at Velaine-sur-Sambre, Jambes, Namur. At the latter site there is also a standing stone called La Pierre Qui Tourne which, according to local legend, spins three times during nights of the new moon. There is another Pierre Qui Tourne at Baileux, and two more standing stones complete the list of Belgian megaliths; Pierre Brunehaut (between Bléharies and Hollain) and Zeupîre (at Gozée).

A visit to the Wéris area could be completed with an inspection of the large piece of puddingstone which lies beside a street in the hamlet of Pas Bayard, just south-west of Wéris. It has the approximate shape of a capstone, thus presenting another megalithic mystery.

The Bouchaimont group of standing stones, at the south-western end of the alignment of the main Belgian megalithic sites.

——— DENMARK ———

Frejlev Skov Group

*Nysted,
Lolland*

NEOLITHIC BURIAL
COMPLEX

J 9

*Leave Nykøbing west, take the
first left and then the minor
road south, just before
Kettinge, to Nysted.*
*One of the four round dolmens, with
a passage-grave capstone behind.*

Denmark has more prehistoric monuments than any other country in the world. The smallest village has 'something', whether part of a standing stone, the remnants of a barrow or a complete long dolmen; pride in the preservation of monuments is shared with visitors, with the well-stocked museums, guide books and signposting.

This forest site on the island of Lolland possibly offers a greater variety of so-called monuments than any other in this

book. The area faces Guldborge Sund, and is roughly 2½m (4km) long and 1m (1.5km) wide. Among the trees are four round dolmens, five passage-graves (dated at about 3000 BC), nine long dolmens, more than 100 Bronze Age barrows (most of them fairly small), and a somewhat spoiled stone circle with a tall monolith beside it. The greatest concentration of monuments is the middle section of this huge site, among fields and either side of a lane, which is good for parking.

Grøn Jaegers Høj *This long dolmen is 335ft (102m) in length.*

*Fanefjord,
Stege,
Møn*

LONG DOLMEN
(LANGDYSSE)

K 8

*The dolmen is about 8m
(13km) south-west of Stege,
and ⅓ mile (0.5km) south of
the church at Fanefjord. Car
park beside a farm barn.*

The name of this delightful Neolithic dolmen on the west of Møn island, translates as 'the Green Huntsman's Mound', and it reflects its still sylvan setting. It is one of Denmark's finest long dolmens (*langdysser*), and the second longest. The rectangular mound measures 335ft by 33ft (102m by 10m). It is bounded by no less than 134 huge kerbstones up to 6ft (1.8m) tall, with drystone walling between them. It lies on an east-west axis, and beyond the western end three large stones are set, for some unknown purpose (unless as a triumvirate guard representation). Inside the mound there are three burial chambers; today only the westernmost retains its capstone.

Long dolmens, mounds, tumuli or barrows, containing megalithic chamber tombs, either in a primary or secondary

context, are found all over Northern Europe (*see*, for example, WEST KENNET LONG BARROW, Wiltshire, England, and LISCUIS, Côtes-d'Armor, France). Not a single long mound has ever been found on the Iberian peninsula.

Nearer Denmark, famous similar tombs are VISBEKER BRAUT, Visbeck, Bremen, Germany, and SCHIMMERES, Emmen, Netherlands. In the north-east of England, there are nearly 40 trapezoidal-shaped long barrows. The same shape of long mound is found in Denmark with chambers; Bygholm Nørremark, Jutland, for instance, which is dated at about 4000 BC, is 197ft (60m) long, and only much later acquired a megalithic burial chamber inside an extension. However, most Danish long dolmens are rectangular.

GRØNHØJ

Bygholm Park,
Horsens,
Jutland

PASSAGE-GRAVE

E 6

The grave is situated in a
hedged enclosure about 330ft
(100m) south of Lake
Bygholm, in Bygholm Park,
just west of Horsens (finds are
in the Museum there).

The well-worn entrance to the 'green
mound'.

Grønhøj means 'green mound', and this is a large one: 10ft (3m) high and 82ft (25m) in diameter. Its revetment has 60 kerbstones, mostly about 3ft 3in (1m) high, with drystone walling between them. The passage to the chamber is a very narrow 3ft (0.9m) and 13ft (4m) long. The chamber at its end measures 11ft 6in by 8ft 9in (3.5m by 2.7m) and is formed by seven uprights and two capstones.

Grønhøj was excavated in 1940 by Knud Thorvildsen, and subsequently repaired. Two levels of burial were found. In and around the grave Thorvildsen discovered 7,000 Middle Neolithic sherds of pottery in a 1ft (0.3m) deep pile, and also 20 complete vessels, dated at about 3000 BC. These pots had been carefully placed upside down, together with some serving ladles, outside the grave entrance. There was evidence that they had originally been positioned in rows on top of the forecourt uprights, or just behind them.

GUNDERSLEVHOLM

Gunderslevholm,
Zealand

LONG DOLMEN
(LANGDYSSE)

J7

Leave Naestved northwards on
road 14; fork left soon on to
the 239, and left again at
Skelby to the site.

One of about 1200 long dolmens in
Denmark.

About 2000 long dolmens or mounds have been recorded in Denmark, the country where methodical cataloguing of megalithic remains began earlier than in any other country in the world. About 1200 remain to be seen today. Round dolmens (*runddysse*) (see MOLS GROUP, East Jutland) invariably have a single burial at their centre, whereas long dolmens may have up to five in their extended rectangular confines.

Here, 61 kerbstones have survived, packed with drystone walling, as is almost always the case. The stones were probably local erratics, carefully selected for rounded shapes. The largest of them, as usual, are at one end only. There was probably a vestibule at the opposite end. Inside the grave there are three chambers, two side by side, and each of a size to accommodate one adult flexed burial.

Similar long dolmens are sometimes found in pairs, such as the remarkable group at Blommeskobbel, Mommark, on the island of Als in the south of the country, and at Steneng, Bredebro, Tønder. A pair of long dolmens actually joined down a long side can be seen in the woods on the coastline at Oleskoppel, near Blommeskobbel, on Als.

LINDESKOV

*Lindeskov,
Ørbaek,
Funen*

LONG DOLMEN
(LANGDYSSE)

G 7

*On the Ørbaek to Ringe road,
1¼ miles (2km) west of
Ørbaek. North of the small
village of Lindeskov a minor
road leads off to the north,
over a railway, to the site.*

Denmark's longest dolmen.

The island of Funen is often called the Garden of Denmark. Its city of Odense is the country's third largest and attracts tourists as the birthplace of Hans Christian Andersen.

Funen is also host to Denmark's longest Neolithic dolmen. It is 551ft (168m) long, and is kerbed with 126 boulders. At the north end there is a small roofless chamber, and there is speculation that more may lie within the huge length of raised earth. Perhaps this is because at nearby Ellested, north-west of Lindeskov on the main road south-east of Funen, there is another long dolmen, which, most unusually, contains five megalithic chambers, over four of which capstones survive as do many of the kerbstones.

Lindeskov Hestehave, about 655ft (200m) away, also has dolmens, but they are mostly in poor condition.

LINDHOLM HØJE

*Nørresundby,
Aalborg,
Vendsyssel,
Jutland*

CEMETERY WITH STONE
SHIPS AND MOUNDS

E 3

*A large site beside the
Limfjord on an undulating
hill overlooking farmland.
Leave Aalborg north on the
bridge over Limfjord. Take
the A17 north-west for 1¼
miles (2km), turn right into
Viaductrej, left at the traffic
signals and then right at the
next site signpost.*

*There are about 200 'stone ships'
here, among more than 700 tombs.*

This is the most impressive of Denmark's early historic sites, created in the early years of the Christian era, and therefore not megalithic in this book's sense. In about 1100 AD it was covered by sand, which accounts for its fine state of preservation (as at SKARA BRAE, Orkney Islands).

It is largely Viking (about 700–1100 AD), but, during excavations in 1952–59, parts of an associated earlier settlement were uncovered, including a square-shaped house and courtyard. There was also evidence of metal working. Lindholm is justly famed for the extraordinary sight of more than 700 stone-kerbed tombs, of which some 200 are shaped like ships in plan, recalling the ancient concept of death as the start of a journey.

The oldest burials date back to the 6th century AD, and they were almost all cremation burials, marked by mounds. Further burials, over 300 years later, were inhumations and bounded by stones; they are in various shapes, such as triangles (the earliest), circles, ovals, pointed ovals and squares.

The ship-shaped burials came later in the Viking period. At the end of it about 30 more inhumation graves marked by mounds were grouped in the south-east of the site. The cremation graves also contained burnt burial goods such as glass beads, knives, personal ornaments, counters for playing games, and also animal bones – everything needed for a safe trip to the Great Beyond.

Finds are in Aalborg Museum.

MOLS GROUP

Knebel,
Mols,
Djursland,
Jutland

ROUND DOLMEN
(RUNDDYSSE)

F 5

The huge round dolmen near Knebel.

Take road 15 north-east out of Aarhus as far as Tastrap. The village of Knebel, overlooking Knebel Vig, is about 6 miles (9.6km) to the south-west.

Porskjaers Stenhus is a magnificent round dolmen (*runddysse*), which is often called 'Knebel', after the village of that name, just over ½m (1km) to the south-west. It is one of the largest of its class in Denmark among the 300 or so remaining; they represent the earliest type of passage-grave, with a passage as here of just two portal stones.

On top of a natural hillock, 23 huge roughly (and probably naturally) rounded boulders are set in a circle measuring

65ft 6in (20m) in diameter. Originally an earth mound covered two chamber tombs. The surviving one is positioned off-centre in the northern part of the round enclosure; its five uprights, 7ft (2.1m) high, are topped with an enormous capstone which is perfectly flat underneath.

By the road to Agri, 1¼m (2km) to the north of Porskjaers Stenhus there are three more burial chambers. The one with the polygonal chamber has nine Bronze Age cup marks on its capstone. In the vicinity there is another fine polygonal tomb with a large capstone; it is called Stenhuset (the Stone House) and lies to the north of the road between the villages of Strands and Torup. A cup-marked capstone is also to be found on the square chamber tomb just west of Torup.

To the north-west of Agri lie the Stabelhøje group of Bronze Age barrows, dramatically sited on two neighbouring chalky hilltops overlooking Kalø Cove. Shaped and close together, they are known (like all such pairs) as 'maiden mounds'.

The Julingshøje group of ten barrows is 1¼m (2km) north-east of Agri, and the three Trehøje are just to the south, by the road to Vistoft. These barrow sites are all worth visiting for the views from them alone.

TROLDSTUEN

Stenstrup,
Ods Hundred,
Nykøbing,
Zealand

DOUBLE PASSAGE-
GRAVE

J 6

Nykøbing is on the road 21 in the north Odsherred, over-looking Isefjord. The site is signposted.

Inside one of the 'Siamese twin' chambers.

These prehistoric Siamese twins (the Trolls' Chambers) were excavated as early as 1909, and are among the finest of the many passage-graves in Zealand. They are joined at the broadest ends of their chambers beneath their shared mound.

The northern grave has its entrance at the east, and the southern one at the south-east. The dimensions of each are the same. The separate passages are 23ft (7m) long, with massive uprights leaning slightly inwards and gradually increasing in height; as usual they are packed with drystone walling. They give on to very broad chambers, measuring 23ft by 6½ft (7m

by 2m). Even the dimensions are shared.

Each chamber has four capstones, including a contiguous pair, which is why the chambers are most unusual; they come from the same boulder, which was split in two by fire and water, and the halves placed with their internal flat face downwards. All the capstones rest on a single course of flattish boulders running along the tops of the leaning uprights. The chambers look like vaults, which is what they are; remains of more than 100 skeletons were found here. Other finds here included Late Neolithic pots and flint daggers.

Tustrup Group

*Tustrup,
Aarhus,
North Djursland,
Jutland*

Burial Chamber,
Round Dolmen
(runddysee), Passage-
Grave, and 'Temple'

F 4

The burial chamber in the Tustrup complex.

This famous complex was discovered in 1954 by Poul Kjaerum, and excavated by him over the next three years. The site is broadly semi-circular, measuring about 164ft (50m) across. Within this area a burial chamber, a round dolmen (*runddysse*), and a passage-grave were identified, forming an isosceles triangle; north of its base lies a so-called temple.

The burial chamber is polygonal in shape, and now without a capstone (which may, however, be the large slab lying not far away). The remaining uprights lean inwards and are 6ft (1.8m) high. The round dolmen is a very hefty affair; its mound (if there was one) has gone, as has the capstone; what is left is a set of two concentric circles of rough and ready boulders. The outer ring was, of course, a revetment. The

Park at the sign Stendyssene (Stone Dolmens), which is on the southward road between Fjellerup and Vivild, nearly 1 mile (1½km) west of the village of Tustrup. A few minutes' walk on the footpath, down through a wooded valley and on to open heathery heath, leads to the site.

The round dolmen.

Burial chamber

Temple

Possible fallen
capstone

Round dolmen

N

Passage grave

*The Tustrup Group, in a broadly
semi-circular setting, about 164ft
(50m) across.*

interior five uprights forming the polygonal chamber lean inwards, and are some 6ft (1.8m) high, making the construction as a whole a squat one. A single stone stands just outside the outer ring.

The passage-grave (in Danish *jaettestue* meaning 'Giant's Tomb) is within a round, grass-covered, earth mound, today partly revetted around its passage entrance at the south-east. Part of the once covered passage lies open. The rectangular chamber opens out to left and right, giving dimensions of 32ft 9in (10m) by 6ft (1.8m). A second, much smaller rectangular chamber is joined by a deep stone passage to the other longer side of the first chamber. Votive pottery has been found, as is usual, around the entrance. Finds are now in the local Aarhus Moesgaard Museum.

The fourth structure in this wonderful place, to the east of the others, is variously described as a temple, sanctuary ossuary, mortuary house, and 'house of the dead' (or funeral parlour). It is roughly horse-shoe shaped, with a very wide gap at the north-east, the direction of the midsummer sunrise. It had a revetment of contiguous small blocks which stretched 16ft 6in (5m) along each side, and was about 2ft 6in (0.8m)

high, of which many are now missing. Against them, on the inside, is a line of piled stones up to 5ft (1.5m) thick, like an embankment, surrounding an area 18ft by 16ft (5.5m by 4.9m). A small shallow depression can be seen in the middle of the enclosed space. This was an oval pit of sand which could have been the location of an altar or shrine, or the penultimate resting-place of a great tribal chieftain before he was buried in one of the tombs. Around this spot Poul Kjaerum's excavations uncovered 28 attractive clay pots of different shapes and designs, together with eight spoons or ladles, of the Middle Neolithic period.

In the middle of the open end there is a block of stone, which might have been the support, originally 5ft 3in (1.6m) high, for a wooden roof, which was destroyed by fire, probably deliberately, after one great funerary ceremony. It is unlikely that cremations were involved, as the place is too early for this practice (as the charred timbers have proved).

What is so interesting is that here was a wooden-roofed building in use at the same early date of about 3200 BC as the nearby megalithic burial tombs. Other such compounds have been found more recently at Ferslev, Herrup and Foulum.

The remarkable 'temple' at Tustrup.

The passage-grave.

122
NORTHERN
EUROPE
Germany

GERMANY

III.11

EVERSTORFER FORST GROUP

*Barendorf,
Kr. Grevesmühlen,
Schwerin,
Mecklenburg*

TOMB COMPLEX

M 3

One of the ten urdolmen *in the forest.*

Leave Lübeck eastwards on the 105. Grevesmühlen is about 19 miles (30 km) along the road, near the forest.

This astonishing group of monuments is mainly located in the northern part of a beautiful forest in the far north of what was East Germany; it lies half-way between Lübeck and Rostock. There are ten *urdolmen* (simple burial chambers), three *erweiterte* dolmens (extended burial chambers), one *grossdolmen* (large burial chamber, rectangular or trapezoidal in plan), five *rechteckig* (rectangular) graves, two trapezoidal mound graves, one *ganggrab* (gallery grave), and one *steinkreis* (stone circle) – making a veritable megalithic academy! No dates have been calibrated for this site, but, for guidance, one can note that of 2216 ± 120 bc (c.2900BC) for the complicated ringed *erweiterter* dolmen, Serrahn, Kr. Güstrow, about 40m (64km) to the west.

As usual, none of the tombs is complete but, oddly, stones are generally missing from either one end or the other of the long compartmented graves. The burial chambers within the long rectangular or trapezoidal above-ground or entrenched earth mounds are rarely centrally placed and are now open in most cases; some of them are set on earth mounds as well, and, like KATELBOGEN, Kr. Bützow, situated upon a hillock.

One *erweiterte* dolmen near Naschendorf in Everstorfer Forst is especially impressive; 14 of the original 24 boulders set in a ring around it are still to be seen. Another strange fact about this site is that although it is quite compact, there is no consistency in the entrance directions at all. The peaceful sylvan setting for these stone chambers and arrangements, in their mostly excavated clearings, provides a memorable megalithic outing.

KATELBOGEN

*Kr. Bützow,
Güstrow,
Mecklenburg*

GANGGRAB IM
HÜNENBETT (GALLERY
TOMB IN MEGALITHIC
GRAVE)

N 3

Leave Güstrow, northwestwards. Immediately after Bützow turn directly west; the site is soon on the left of the road, before the windmill on the left.

III.12

This splendid site is one of several monuments in what is known as the 'Mecklenburg Group'; it is on a hillock, isolated in ploughed farmland, with trees growing on and around it. Set amid the trees is a long domed mound containing an almost complete burial chamber. The rectangular mound has a north-east/south-west axis. Surrounding the rectangle of earth there were once 36 upright boulders, including five at each end; 22 remain today, of which all five at the north-east have gone. Inside, the rectangular burial chamber shares the same alignment. Its length is 26ft 3in (8m), width 7ft 6in (2.3m) and height 6ft (1.8m); its condition is very good.

Originally, above earth level there were five capstones across five pairs of opposing uprights, packed in between with much smaller stones. One capstone, the south-westerly one, is now missing; this allows daylight into some clearly delineated burial compartments which were continually re-used. Over the short 9ft 9in (3m) passage on the southernmost long side, there are two more smaller capstones over three more uprights. Finds here, including 127 potsherds, helped to establish the tomb's date as Late Middle Neolithic.

KRUCKOW

*Kruckow,
Demmin,
Mecklenburg*

GROSSDOLMEN
(CHAMBER TOMB)

H 3 (Hallwag GDR
Map)

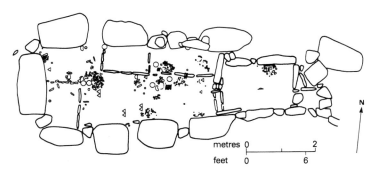

metres 0 — 2
feet 0 — 6

N

*Leave Neubrandenburg north
on road 96. After 25 miles
(40km), turn left at Völsehow
for Kruckow. Fork left on to
the 110; go past the turning
on the left to Vro Marienfelde.
The site is signposted on the
right past the woods.*

This trapezoidal site, another in the Mecklenburg Group, is 82ft (25m) long, and is aligned north-south, with its internal chamber entrance facing east. In the course of its length it narrows from 37ft 9in (11.5m) wide at the south, before the vestibule, to 21ft 3in (6.5m) at the north.

The kerbstone boulders retain a flat earth platform, and they originally numbered 40, of which only five are missing (two were once at the north, within another small vestibule only one pair of stones deep). Two vestibules in a *grossdolmen* is most unusual. The chamber here is in remarkably good condition. It has four pairs of uprights each supporting a capstone; the westernmost also has the endstone beneath it and is the biggest, measuring 9ft 3in by 5ft 6in (2.8m by 1.7m) and over 3ft 3in (1m) thick.

This *grossdolmen* has a short passage in the long side, giving a total tomb length of 37ft 9in (11.5m), which is comparatively large. It also shows a number of compartments inside, separated with thin upright very low slabs.

LOHNE-ZÜSCHEN

III.14

*Fritzlar Züschen,
Hesse*

STEINKIST (BURIAL
CHAMBER) WITH PORT-
HOLE SLAB

H 8

*Leave Kassel (north of
Frankfurt-a-M)
southwestwards on the 231;
after 2½ miles (4km) turn
south onto the 450, and take
the second right to Züschen 14
miles (23km) down the road
to Fritzlar.*

*The handsome port-hole is sometimes
called a spirit hole.*

This is a handsome and unusual *steinkist*. The 62ft (19m) long rectangular trench is sunk in earth to the level of the tops of its 24 boulders. The axis is north-east/south-west. At the north-east there is an entrance vestibule (thus it is also known as a *portikusdolmen*); separating it from the main gallery stands a slab with a large smoothed, round access hole. These are sometimes known as spirit holes, although this one is rather large merely for escaping vapours!

Towards the south-west lies an internal chamber, and beyond it, a single huge endstone at the end of the rectangle; it is the biggest stone at the site. No capstones have survived at a grave which has many similarities with SOM tombs.

Remains of 45 people were uncovered here, along with bone, stone and flint tools, ornaments and Neolithic vessels. Another point of interest at this site are its 'decorated' stones which depict interlinked, broken horizontal lines, and one possible and another definite oxen outline. The mystery of why 'spirit holes' are not more common remains.

VISBEKER BRAUT

*Wildeshausen,
Visbek,
Oldenburg*

HÜNENGRAB
(MEGALITHIC GRAVE)

F 5

The Visbeker Braut (bride of Visbek) was constructed by the Funnel Beaker people (in German *Trichterbecher*; thus the common abbreviation TRB for them), who represented the earliest Neolithic culture in Northern Europe.

This stretched rectangle of stones measures 262ft by 23ft (80m by 7m). It was originally kerbed by 105 upright boulders, which increase in size from the north-east to the south-west end of the axis. It does, in fact, narrow slightly at the north-east end where the three middle endstones are missing. Altogether 23 stones are gone, including a line of eight directly south-west of its chamber, and two to the north of it (perhaps evidence of tomb robbers). Others have fallen outwards. The passageless chamber towards the south-west end of the kerbed mound is 19ft 9in by 5ft 3in (6m by 1.6m); the capstone is missing, and the tops of the upright stones forming the burial chamber are level with the earth inside the long monument.

Visbeker Bräutigam (the bridegroom) lies 2½m (4km) to the south-west of his bride. It is longer and wider along its almost east-west alignment, being 354ft by 33ft (108m by 10m). The earth platform inside the kerbstones, which are higher – up to 8ft (2.4m) – at the east, has gone, but five great capstones still reside on the ground towards the western end.

There are many other dolmens in this beautiful wooded area, including notably the Pestruper Gräberfeld, a few miles directly south of Wildeshausen. But the bride and her groom should be at the start of a day's German megalith hunting.

5 miles (8km) north of Visbek. Take the 213 west from Wildeshausen, which is 30 miles (48km) south-west of Bremen, towards Cloppenburg. Turn left at the sign to the site, pass beneath the E37 Bremen-Osnabrück autobahn, and park at the sign by the woods on the right.

Visbeker Braut (the bride).

Visbeker Bräutigam (the bridegroom).

III.16

——— **THE NETHERLANDS** ———

125
NORTHERN
EUROPE
The
Netherlands

BORGER

*Hunebedstraat,
Borger,
Emmen,
Drenthe*

RIJKSHUNEBED (D.27)
Noord Nederland B.7

*All hunebedden in The
Netherlands are numbered. D.27 at
Borger is one of eleven in and
around the village.*

There are no simple 'French dolmen' burial chambers at all in The Netherlands. The country is however renowned for its *hunebedden* (see NOORDLO, Drenthe). This *hunebed*, D.27, is one of 11 in and around the village of Borger. Although hugely impressive in size, it is in a very dilapidated condition. An 1833 drawing shows it as it is today – all traces of an earthern covering gone, forlorn, but immensely climbable for children! It is, in fact, quite a moving experience to wander in and out and beneath this massive megalithic skeleton, along the enormous 80ft (24.4m) length, set in a charming clearing among trees.

The axis of this *rijkshunebed* lies, as most do, north-east/ south-west. It consists of 26 uprights (*draagstenen*) and two endstones (*sluitstenen*); above them at now odd angles lie nine capstones (*dekstenen*) of huge size, their top surfaces some 12ft (3.7m) from the ground and their underbellies levelled to a flat smooth surface, to form what must have been a formidable internal long chamber.

The chamber's entrance, at the south-east, now has four portal stones (*poortzijstenen*) and one remaining entrance capstone (*portal dekstenen*). To the north-west of the tomb, two kerbstones (*kransstenen*) reside, indicating a long gone earth covering mound, which must have been one of the most substantial one in The Netherlands.

Travel northwards from Emmen on the N34; 5 miles (8km) north of Odoorn turn right on the road towards Stadskanaal. Turn left immediately for the village of Borger on the minor road towards Gasselte. Follow the signposts to Bronneger round to the east. Continue straight on to Hunebedstraat (and not north-east to Bronneger). The monument is signposted on the left.

126
NORTHERN
EUROPE
The
Netherlands

III.17

HAVELTE WEST

*Havelterberg,
Havelte,
Drenthe*

RIJKSHUNEBED
(GANGGRAF)
(D.53)

Noord Nederland B.5

This ganggraf dates back to about 2750BC, and is covered with nine large capstones; only their undersides were roughly dressed.

Though now in a somewhat dilapidated state, this megalithic monument has been admired since at least 1732. It was excavated by Professor van Giffen in 1918 and restored to its present appearance in 1954. It is dated at about 2750 BC.

At least five stones survive from a former revetment around a broadly ovular mound. The entrance to the central long chamber is at south-south-east; either side and all around it there was once an ovular circle of 48 stones, of which 23 remain today. A capstone resting on two uprights form the passage.

The central chamber, lying about north-east/south-west like its surroundings, consists of 23 uprights along its sides, which lean inwards over once paved flooring. Most of the inside faces have been dressed to present flat smooth walling, with drystone packing; there are also stone slabs at each end. They support nine very thick capstones.

This D.53 *hunebed* is almost identical in plan to the German *grosssteingräber* of Gross Bersen, Emsland, just over the border, and Thuine, Emsland; the latter has an extra ovular ring of stones inserted between the outer and inner ones. All three *hunebedden* share the same axial direction. Two more remarkably similar *grosssteingräber*, but with entrances at the south-west instead, are Gross Stavern, also in Emsland, and Gandersee, Oldenburg, a little further to the east in the former West Germany.

Leave Meppel northwards on the N.32 motorway; at the Havelte exit turn off north-eastwards on to the N371. After 2½ miles (4km), at Overcinge, turn left north-west towards Tuinbouwschool. Turn right at the Café Hunebed and park where indicated. Walk past the next field on the right and then turn right, as signposted, to the site.

The chamber lies on a north-east/south-west axis and is lined with 23 uprights.

NOORDLO

*Annen,
Groningen,
Drenthe*

PROVINCIAAL HUNEBED
(D.9)
Noord Nederland A.7

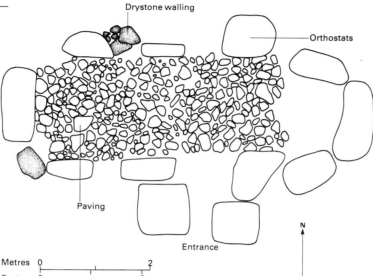

Drystone walling

Orthostats

Paving

Entrance

N

Metres	0		2
Feet	0		6

*Leave Groningen southwards
on the E232 motorway. After
7½ miles (12km) leave at the
Zuidlaren exit, and take the
N34 to the south-east. After 3
miles (5km) the monument is
on the left, just before the
crossroad connecting Annen
with Anloo.*

**In 1878 reports reached
London of over-zealous
excavation and restoration of**
hunebedden **in The Netherlands.
As a result, the leading
British archaeologists
William C. Lukis and Sir
Henry Dryden were
despatched to the country to
investigate by The Society of
Antiquaries. They visited and
recorded this site – which is
how finds from D.9 come to
reside in the British Museum,
London.**

Hunebedden (Hun's beds) are typical of the northern part of The Netherlands, and are megalithic tombs of the Funnel Beaker (TRB) culture which flourished about 3400–2200 BC. They have round or oval kerbed earth mounds which cover rectangular burial chambers; these have entrances on one of the long sides, sometimes accompanied by a very short passage-, which relates them to Danish passage graves (*jaettestuer*). The burial chambers are normally long, and lie on a north-east/south-west axis (though not always). Sometimes the chambers are below ground in a shallow trench, with pairs of opposing uprights carrying capstones (above ground) like a succession of trilithons. They can be as long as 80ft (24.4m), like *hunebed* D.27 at BORGER, which sports ten capstones. They were often placed on a slope, with taller uprights above ground, and were used for multiple collective burials.

There are 53 *hunebedden* still existing (in 1990) in The Netherlands (all but one of which are in the province of Drenthe), from a total recorded of 76. The first *hunebed* to be recorded in about 1570 was called Duvels Kutle, which means 'Devil's Cot' or 'C**t'. It is thought to be D.6-Tinaarloo. The first complete list of these tombs was drawn up in 1818–20 and in 1925 the famous Dutch archaeologist Professor Albert E. van Giffen gave all extant *hunebedden* a letter for its province (D is for Drenthe) and a serial number. Van Giffen, by design or chance, was the excavator of D.6-Tinaarloo in 1928, a year after it was re-discovered.

This partly destroyed Neolithic *hunebed* (D.9) is totally accessible, on a surburban village roadside next to a modest bungalow. It lies in flat countryside in a province which is easily the richest in *hunebedden*. It was excavated in 1952 by Professor A. E. van Giffen, very much the father of Dutch 20th-century archaeology. It looked then much as it did in that first depiction of it in about 1570: two pairs of uprights,

an endstone at the west side, with partial drystone walling in between the megaliths. The capstones were at one time taken down by villagers of Annen because they were considered unsafe but they are now back in place. Since then this monument has been thoroughly researched by D. J. Groot and his findings published. *See* BORGER, Drenthe, for the main 'megalithic words' in Dutch; they are useful for reading the details of site notices.

The eastern end of the grave is now destroyed, but it once consisted of a further five uprights placed in a semi-circle to the east, and two more to the south, in the style of two portals. It is thought that there may have been an upper floor; this would have been most unusual, and the evidence for it is not fully accepted. More dependable are the distinct traces of an earthen mound which most likely once covered the whole long chamber.

Most of the finds at Noordlo are now to be found in the Provinciaal Museum at Assen 20½m (33km) up the N371 to the north-east. They included 870 potsherds, of which 810 are TRB and the others Early Bronze Age ware. At least 101 vessels were identified after laborious examination and partial reconstruction. There were 41 funnel beakers (naturally), 23 bowls, ten tureens, six amphorae, one pail, five collared flasks and 15 others. There was no sign of any cremation at the site, or indeed of any funerary practices. There could of course have been burials, articulated or otherwise, but the acidity of the soil here would have destroyed the bones. In any case, no soil stains were noted.

To the west of this *hunebed*, on the other side of the road, north of Anloo, there are *hunebedden* D.8 -Anlo-N (Kniphorstbos) and then D.7 (Schipborg), roughly equidistant, and worth visiting. These would be two more to add to the list of 53 *hunebedden* which could be visited in a fortnight's holiday.

Papeloze Kerk

Schoonoord,
Sleen,
Emmen,
Drenthe

RIJKSHUNEBED
(GANGGRAF)
(D.49)
Noord Nederland B.7

RIGHT: *The roofed entrance to the*
'Priestless Church'.

A view of the chamber showing the
undersides of some of the six
capstones.

The name of this interesting burial chamber means 'priestless church'; it is a kidney-shaped *ganggraf* (similar to a *portaalgraf*, but with its entrance passage roofed). Professor van Giffen's excavation and restoration here was on a large scale.

About a third of the earth mound at the south-eastern end is open to the sky, and so some of the replaced uprights can be examined. Giffen restored 24 missing kerbstones; at the beginning of this century there were only four, and there were no portal stones or capstones on top of them.

The central chamber tomb lies along a north-west/south-east axis, which is most unusual; it is lined with 12 uprights and six enormous capstones (the biggest is the one just past the entrance, and weighs 25 tons). In addition, there are two endstones, and two pairs of portal stones with a capstone over them make the entrance at the south-west. Such a thoroughly complete restoration has much to demonstrate to megalith hunters, and its woodland setting has been left in such a way that the site's name gains a mysterious significance.

Take the main road west from
Emmen's centre. After 5 miles
(8km), turn right north-
westwards towards
Schoonoord; the site is only
1¼ miles (2km) along on the
left, down a pathway.

SCHIMMERES

*Emmen,
Drenthe*

MOUND WITH TWO
BURIAL CHAMBERS AND
SIDE ENTRANCES
(*LANGGRAF*) (D. 43)
Noord Nederland B.7

This is one of ten *hunebedden* in and around Emmen, but it is the only *langgraf* in The Netherlands. It was partly restored in 1870 and boulders from the demolished *hunebed* D.43a nearby were incorporated into it. It was again excavated in 1913 by J.H. Holwerda, and in 1960 by Professor van Giffen, who dated the site to the early fourth millennium.

The 131ft (40m) long grave is set in sparse, tranquil woodland on a north-north-east/south-south-west alignment, nearly a direct north/south one though. It is shaped like a huge longboat; around a raised earth platform 52 uprights remain, with drystone walling in the wide gaps between them. The larger stones, up to 6ft (1.8m) high above the ground, are at the northern end. The triangular boulder at the southern pointed end has a slightly raised 'spine' on its outward facing back. There are several free-standing stones west of the grave.

This unique *langgraf* contains two burial chambers. One is at the northern end, with an entrance at the east-south-east beneath a flat earth covering. Its rectangular chamber has six uprights at its sides, two endstones and three capstones; the entrance consists of a pair of portal stones supporting two smaller capstones, which now lie close by. To the south, near the centre of the enclosure, lies the second, longer chamber. Strangely, there is no outer sign of a passage connecting the inner tomb with the outer kerb, and so perhaps it was entered from above after the entrance was blocked. Above the now slightly domed earth cover, lie nine uprights, two endstones, and just two of a probable seven. There is cobbled paving, both in and around both chambers, and more to the south-west near a fallen internal slab, possibly once the capstone of a third chamber in a logical position.

There are two burial chambers inside this unique langgraf *in the Dutch* hunebedden *province of Drenthe.*

From Emmen's market place and main cross roads, take the Grongingen road to the north. Pass Weerdingestraat and then Walstraat on the right; the site is then signposted to the left, down a path. This is the only megalithic site in this book which is within a few minutes' walk from a railway station!

De Steenbarg

*Noordlaren,
Haren,
Groningen*

Rijkhunebed (G.1)

Noord Nederland A.7

The front capstone of this monument, the only *hunebed* in Groningen province, looks preposterously large, and must surely be the largest natural boulder ever to be heaved on to supporting stones for funerary purposes in The Netherlands. It covers a very wide opening and is supported, along with a much smaller stone behind it (they both have small, round holes drilled through them), by two pairs of uprights and an endstone.

Professor van Giffen and others thoroughly explored the eastern part of De Steenbarg in 1957; they established that originally there were ten uprights, five capstones, two endstones, and two portal stones with their own capstone. There is an unattractive small replica of the monument on Zuidlaarerweg in Noordlaren, which is to be found south-east of the real thing.

The stones were already missing by 1768, according to a Petrus Camper drawing. Early in the next century the two capstone holes were drilled; they were to receive gunpowder, in preparation for the demolition of the already partly ruined monument. Fortunately for posterity, this foul plan was halted at the last moment.

The interesting part of this near-tragedy is that it is fully recorded by the contemporary historian J. Boeles, in the *Groninger Volks-Almanak* for 1845. He did this in order that, in his own words 'over time people will not fill their heads with conjectures as to the origin and meaning of these stones. After all, people already fool the small children with the story that giants put their thumbs in the holes so that they could throw the stones at each other'. The moral of this true tale should be noted by propagators of legends 'from the old days'. Facts are usually more interesting.

The same historian also noted a recollection from his clergyman father of an excavation at the beginning of the 19th century. Between two layers of pebbles under the grave was a layer of sand, into which had been placed urns containing human ashes and small bones.

Leave Groningen southwards on the E232 motorway. After 6 miles (10km) take the Eelde Airport Exit east and then southwards towards Zuidlaren. After 2 miles (3km), past the windmill, just to the south of Noordlaren, the signposted site is on the right at a crossroads about 550yds (500m) down a lane.

De Tweeling van Bronneger

*Bronneger,
Borger,
Emmen,
Drenthe*

Rijkshunebedden (D.21 and D.22)

Noord Nederland B.7

These two *hunebedden*, only yards from each other, translate as 'the twins of Bronneger'; D.21 is sometimes called simply Bronneger-W, and D.22 Bronneger-O (East). The site is beside a road, and trees there, no doubt self-seeded, stand very close to both graves, rather spoiling their appearance.

The first is much the more complete today, and is a *portaalgraf*. It has seven uprights (one of the pairs is missing), two endstones, and three immense, craggy capstones. One portal stone survives at its south-east entrance. Inside, the boulders are smoothly dressed, and the floor is paved with small loose stones; among them 600 potsherds of the Funnel Beaker culture have been found. This monument seems to have had successive periods of use.

D.22, a moment's walk to the south-west and set among trees, is a miserable thing today. Only three uprights are still standing, together with two endstones and two capstones, one of them huge and uneven in shape. Clearly, the twins are not identical!

North of Emmen join the N34 towards Borger. In the village turn north-east to the signposted site.

SWEDEN

ANUNDSHÖGEN

Badelunda,
Västerås,
Västmanland

STONE SHIPS, MOUND AND RUNE STONE

F 5

The site is only 3¾ miles (6km) from Västerås. Leave the town north-east on the minor road towards Tortuna following the signs. Instead of turning left for Badelunda, turn right; the site is immediately on the right. Local guides.

A 174ft (53m) long stone burial 'ship', with the 'stern' in the foreground.

This marvellous wooded site, on the shores of Lake Mälaren, compares not unfavourably with the more famous stone ship cemetery of Gamla (Old) Uppsala but lacks its historical associations. Here is one of Sweden's longest stone ships: stone bounded, ship-shaped graves, often containing a wooden boat and burial. It is 174ft (53m) long, with a large triangular stone lying at the prow, and a tall rectangular one marking the stern. Either side of them, forming the sides of the boat, lie matching lines of smaller boulders, 11 in each, with gaps between them. The majestic Late Bronze Age ship at Boge, Gotland, has its lining of stones placed in a contiguous fashion. Other stone ships can be seen at Anundshögen, and a further group of eight at nearby Tuna Alsike, where one excavated Viking boat revealed a large wooden boat, bearing what probably were the remains of a chieftain's wife. Very few

such grand burials have been discovered. Close to the mound there is a fine standing rune stone.

Anundshögen means 'Anund's mound', and it is one of Sweden's largest, being 49ft (15m) high. It is dated at about 600–700 AD and was the location of a court (*thing*), as found all over Europe. This is why 'court' appears so frequently in house and place names near prehistoric raised earth mounds.

This mound is 16ft 6in (5m) higher than any of the three famous mounds at Gamla (Old) Uppsala, north of today's city. Gamla evidently flourished as a centre of pagan worship and ritual from about 500 AD until the end of the 11th century. *Beowulf*, the Anglo-Saxon epic, relates the story of the three Swedish kings buried there beneath the mounds – Adils, Aun and Egil of the Ynglinga family, as does the famous chronicle *Ynglingatal* in the eleventh century.

CARLSHÖGEN

The entrance to this burial chamber is unusually placed off-centre, to the south-east.

*Hagestad,
Löderup,
Skåne*

BURIAL CHAMBER WITH
PASSAGE ENTRANCE

D 1

Leave the south coastal Skåne town of Ystad travelling east. After 5 miles (8km), take the first right fork to Hagestad. Not signposted.

Högen means 'mound', and this site was named after Carl Wulferona, a local landowner, by its first excavator, Baron Arvid Kurck in 1875. Flattened oval in shape, the mound is located on a gentle slope surrounded by farmland. The earth is banked as high as the top of the entrance capstones; within it the burial chamber and its entrance are set slightly and strangely off-centre to the south-east.

The entrance is on the east side of the internal chamber and and its passage, which is 21ft (6.4m) long and up to 3ft (0.9m) wide, aligned east-north-east. The passage retains the only three capstones here, about 3ft 3in (1m) above the original floor. The one nearest the chamber measures 3ft 6in by 5ft 6in (1.1m by 1.7m), and its top surface is covered with 92

cup marks, 80 of which are round with diameters of up to 3½ins (9 cms). There are four pairs of portal stones, closed by a square boulder at the outer entrance.

The axis of the chamber is broadly north-west/south-east, and is a rectangular 17ft (5.2m) long and 7ft 6in (2.3m) wide, with rounded corners. There are ten uprights around the chamber, interfilled with drystone walling (with curious tall thin stones inside it).

Finds here include the remains of several skeletons, of which some may have been buried in a sitting position (concentrated at the southern end of the chamber), potsherds, flint heaps, flakes, and a knife. These were discovered at two different floor levels, demonstrating a long period of use.

RAMSHÖG

The absurdly large capstones are a famous feature of this site.

*Hagestad,
Löderup,
Skåne*

BURIAL CHAMBER AND
PASSAGE IN MOUND

D 1

Leave the south coastal town of Ystad travelling east. After 5 miles (8km), take the first right fork along the coast a few miles to Hagestad.

This marvellous site (the old name of which was Ramsbjer) was first excavated in 1875, and then more thoroughly, before restoration, in 1961–69. The earth tumulus is in the shape of a flattened circle, and contains a smallish chamber and, by comparison, a long passage. The entrance passage is orientated east-north-east; it is 21ft 6in (6.6m) long and up to 2ft 6in (0.8m) wide. It has five pairs of opposing boulders, dressed on their insides and packed with drystone walling and smaller stones. There are also 14 fine paving slabs, and two of the capstones nearest the chamber survive.

The oval chamber to the south-west is aligned north-west/south-east. It has nine uprights, dressed on the insides, and measures 17ft by 8ft 6in (5.2m by 2.6m), at the widest inner

points. Its three massive capstones seem to perch in dramatic profile on top of the earth mound.

Some interesting finds here, uncovered to the left of the chamber entrance and to the right and far right of it, were several potsherds, amber beads, flint tools and flakes, a knife blade, and, from a later period, cattle and horse bones. Around the entrance, there were 5214 ceramic pieces. The fascinating human remains in the burial chamber, in piles and very mixed up, consisted of seven to nine individuals, including one or two children, two or three young people, and four adults.

One adult bone at Ramshög has produced a radiocarbon corrected date of 2590 BC.

RÖSSBERGA

Valtorp,
Falköping,
Västergötland

PASSAGE-GRAVE

C 5

This grave was excavated by C. Cullberg in 1962. The chamber is 29ft 6in by 6ft 6in (9m by 2m), and it was found that the floor had two strata. The older one revealed a 1ft (0.3m) deep pile of disarticulated human bones from about 40–45 individuals. This confirms that skeletons in a burial were simply swept to one side if space was needed for further inhumations (the adult body has 206 separate bones in its body, so piles soon build up!). The discovery of a complete skeleton therefore usually indicates a last use of the site.

Here the secondary floor level was found to contain no less than 17 compartments, some as small as 3ft 6in by 1ft 6in (100cm by 50cm); this could imply that each was made to fit an individual, and for various positions. Their 33 dividing slabs were 12in–19¾in (30cm–50cm) in length, and averaged 1ft 6in (0.5m) high.

According to early reports of similar graves to Rössberga, skeletons were found in a sitting position. If this was true, it would establish the constructions as true Funnel Beaker Culture (TRB) graves, and not just simple ossuaries or depositories for bones. However, most likely the bones arrived here as already disarticulated skeletons.

Take the 184 south-east from the north coastal town of Lidkoping for 31 miles (50km), through Skara, to Falköping. There turn north-east on to the minor road through Torbjörntorp, just west of Valtorp. The signposted site is on the right.

TÅGARP 5

Tågarp Östra Tommarp,
Skåne

PASSAGE-GRAVE

E 1

Near the south-east coast in Skåne; Tågarp is 6¼ miles (10km) west of the port of Simrishamn after Östra Tommarp.

This passage-grave received considerable restoration, following its excavation in 1970.

This Middle and Late Neolithic site yielded much that was unusual and fascinating during its excavation in 1970. It was in bad condition, and the restoration thereafter was on a considerable scale.

The central grave alignment is north-south; its 12 uprights and the drystone walling between them, in a stretched ovular setting, surrounded an area of 18ft by 6ft 6in (5.5m by 2m) Outside this is a low, kerbed cairn. The insides of the uprights were dressed, and lined a floor holding 13 compartments (perhaps for specific ranks in the community), made with both small, thin slabs (as for individual cists) or lines of piled up stones.

A strange stone and the only one of its kind on the site was found here: it was of arrow-shaped quartzite, measuring 17in by 5in by 3in (42.5cm by 12cm by 6.5cm); an exactly similar one was found at another local grave, and also in drystone walling between two uprights here.

The short passage to the entrance faces east, is 16ft 6in (5m) long, and consists of three pairs of portal boulders, septal stones, and a single capstone. In front of the entrance and either side of it, soot-filled ditches were uncovered which contained Middle Neolithic potsherds and burnt human bones. There were also six hearths, all of different ages.

In the chamber, below the secondary level (the compartments), there was found, in the northern section, a heap of firestones, together with a single unburnt rib bone. At the secondary level, in only one of the compartments, there were small piles of tiny shreds of red cloth (which has also occurred at RAMSHÖG, Löderup). Unhappily, the oxide content in the material was so low that dating by radiocarbon methods was impossible. In this same compartment lay a Funnel Beaker pot lid.

There were two exciting conclusions here: it has been proved that flint was not used for cutting or dressing the stones at this site. And charcoal remains have indicated the intriguing possibility that the primary pebbled floor of the chamber could have been partially boarded over. This is another example of the use of wood within Neolithic tombs.

IV
Iberia and the Balearics

There is still no certainty about the origin of the first Neolithic settlers on the Iberian peninsula. Were they indigenous – spontaneously commencing agriculture about 7500 years ago? Or did the builders of, for example, ANTA DE POÇA DA GATEIRA in Portugal's Evora province in 4510 ± 360 bc, come from the eastern end of the Mediterranean Sea, and by way of the Balearics, or not? Both may be true. On the other hand, at the beginning of this century it was proposed that the early Iberian megalithic monuments were erected by Atlanteans from Libya inter-married with native Iberians!

Minorca (Menorca in Spanish) has, over its 271 square miles (702 sq km), an astonishingly diverse array of monuments to offer a megalith hunter – and all of them can be seen in a day or so. Yet similar monuments are not found in the countries nearest to the island, although the distances between them are not great: Majorca an intervisible 30 miles (48km), Spain 124 miles (200km), Algeria 199 miles (320km), Sardinia 211 miles (340km) and France 230 miles (370km). Majorca (Mallorca in Spanish), the largest of the Balearic Islands with 1405 square miles (3639 sq km) of land, is only 104 miles (167km) from the Spanish mainland, yet it did not export the *talayot*; nor did Minorca the *naveta* to Majorca.

It can be surprising to discover that the Iberian peninsula and Balearic Islands possess thousands of megalithic tombs, some of which are among the oldest in the world. The *antas* (dolmens) and *cuevas* (corbelled chambers) in Evora, for example, date back to about 5500 BC, and even then succeeded a tradition of megalithic single cist building.

Iberian passage-graves

In spite of the scarcity of radiocarbon dates for Iberian megalithic sites, it now seems clear that passage-graves with single chambers were evolving around that time (*c*.4500–4000 BC) in both the north-west and south-west with no discernible direct cultural influences from northern Europe. They are detached from the passage-grave's traditional forms in western France, because no covering mound in Portugal or southern Spain has ever been found to contain more than one primary (as opposed to a later second) passage-grave. *See*, for instance, BARNENEZ, France, and elsewhere.

In spite of this, the temptation to award contemporaneity to passage-grave construction in northern Europe and the Iberian peninsula can be resisted. The French corbelled roofing systems appeared in Brittany and many parts of Britain at the time of the earliest Evora *antas*, but not for several hundred more years in Portugal and southern Spain (to the north of Almeria). The absence of corbelled roofed chambers in northern Spain appears to rule out such a route south.

The most spectacular of the corbelled passage-graves which followed is CUEVA DEL ROMERAL, near a sugar refinery outside white-walled Antequera, north of the southern Spanish tourist centre of Malaga. It is dated at about 3500 BC, and its enclosing mound is about 285ft (87m) across. This is one of the three best known *cuevas* of a type that does not exist in northern Spain. The others are CUEVA DE MENGA (where one of the capstones weighs 180 tons) and CUEVA DE LA VIERA, which is a *tholos* type, over 100ft (30m) long, and containing three port-hole slabs.

Tholoi tombs arrived in southern Iberia later still, around 3000 BC: *see* LOS MILLARES, Spain, and REGUENGOS DE MONSAREZ, Portugal, for example. The Greek name invented by the famous archaeologist Louis Siret for these beehive-shaped tombs should not persuade one to look to the east of the Mediterranean Sea for their inspiration; most likely they were an indigenous variation by talented builders.

Los Millares

The most famous type-site in Iberia and the Balearics is LOS MILLARES, on its bleak and rocky prominence, some 14 miles (22km) north of the coastal resort of Almeria. Although sometimes marked as a necropolis, this huge site was also a fortified settlement, complete with an aqueduct and forts. Here was one of the first great copper mining centres in Europe. Between about 3100 and 2600 BC, before the Beaker culture succeeded it, the Millaran culture spread throughout southern Iberia. Unfortunately treasure hunters, with their metal detectors, and other human predators, have in recent years made a tragic nuisance of themselves. The consequence for such an important site came in 1990, with the erection of a 1¾ miles (3km) long wire fence all around it. Access is therefore now restricted to bona fide visitors.

Megalithic art

The most famous megalithic art in Iberia is in the 886ft (270m) long Altamira cave, which is 18½ miles (30km) west of Santander, and 1¼ miles (2km) south of Santillana-del-Mar, on the northern Spanish coast. The cave was discovered by accident in 1868; a local girl was the first to spot the artwork eleven years later. It was only accepted as genuine

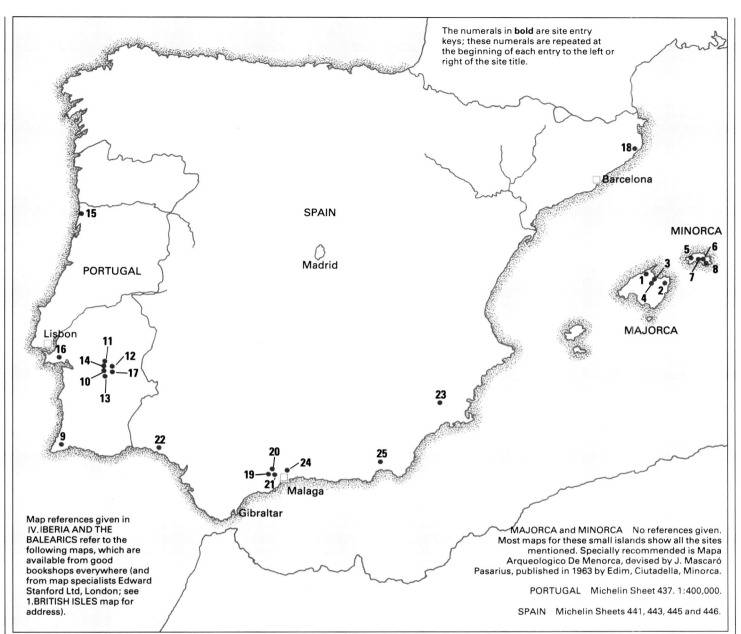

The numerals in **bold** are site entry keys; these numerals are repeated at the beginning of each entry to the left or right of the site title.

SPAIN

Madrid

PORTUGAL

Lisbon

MINORCA

MAJORCA

Barcelona

Malaga

Gibraltar

Map references given in IV. IBERIA AND THE BALEARICS refer to the following maps, which are available from good bookshops everywhere (and from map specialists Edward Stanford Ltd, London; see 1. BRITISH ISLES map for address).

MAJORCA and MINORCA   No references given. Most maps for these small islands show all the sites mentioned. Specially recommended is Mapa Arqueologico De Menorca, devised by J. Mascaró Pasarius, published in 1963 by Edim, Ciutadella, Minorca.

PORTUGAL   Michelin Sheet 437. 1:400,000.

SPAIN   Michelin Sheets 441, 443, 445 and 446.

Quaternary art (dating back to 30,000 bc) after discoveries of paintings and engravings at La Mouthe, and Font de Gaume and Combarelles, in the Dordogne area of southern France (in 1895 and 1901 respectively) and their subsequent verification by the abbé Henri Breuil. The cave at Altamira, which has 150 or so paintings, is now closed to the public most of the time because of the effects of its popularity (like France's Lascaux caves), but the nearby Cueva de la Estalactitas can be visited.

Majorca and Minorca in the Balearic Islands

On both Majorca and Minorca, the earliest third millennium burials were in settlement caves. At first they were in natural openings, such as Cueva de Muleta, Majorca, where a radiocarbon date of 3984 ± 109 bc has been obtained. Rock-cut tombs followed, such as CALA SANT VICENÇ, Majorca, with corridors, side chambers, and ledges inside. There are many more of these in Majorca than in Minorca.

The successive Talayotic cultures in both islands were broadly contemporary, stretching from about 1500 BC through to Roman times, though there were variations in them. A *talayot* (or watchtower) is a round cyclopean construction which was either solid or contained a single round chamber with a corbelled roof. Later versions were sometimes square, and with a second chamber above the first. The 72 well-excavated tombs in the cemetery of SON REAL, Majorca, have three different chamber shapes. At SES PAÏSSES, Majorca, a *talayot* can be seen within a walled settlement, and also at TALATI DE DALT, Minorca, though in some cases they occur just outside enclosing walls. At the latter site an indigenous megalithic Minorcan monument is also to be found. This is a *taula*, a T-shaped structure consisting of a dressed, almost rectangular upright supporting a cross beam, also dressed. The largest of these on Minorca is TREPUCÓ.

The first-ever study of prehistory to be published in Spanish, in 1818, took Minorca as its subject; this bestows a fitting pedigree on a small island crammed with megalithic riches. Its author, Juan Ramis y Ramis, gave the cleverly logical name *naveta* (boat) to its most famous single monument, ELS TUDONS. This extraordinary boat-shaped chamber tomb is claimed to be the oldest above-ground building in either the Balearics or Spain.

MAJORCA

CALA SANT VICENÇ

Pollença

ROCK-CUT TOMBS

Majorca is 62 miles (100km) east to west, and 46 miles (74km) north to south.

These tombs were the natural successors to caves as settings for burials, in the pre-Talayot period (*see* SES PAÏSSES). They were an obvious and common development throughout the Mediterranean, although the kinds of entrances varied widely in accordance with local geology, as did the layouts of the passages and chambers.

There are nine tombs in this group (as they generally occur), and quite the most interesting of them is Tomb 7. Its rectangular carved façade and forecourt face directly south. A short passage leads to a rectangular antechamber; another short passage leads on to a second chamber of the same shape but the other way about, and with one chamber at each side. Its principal gallery is 29ft 6in (9m) long, has a rounded roof, and has a rare but sensibly utilitarian ledge running along each wall. Even as far back as 2000 BC the islanders were showing signs of order.

2¹/₂ miles (4km) west of Port de Pollença on the 710, turn right, north-east, towards Cala de Sant Vicenç. The tombs are 1¹/₄ miles (2km) along on the right.

SES PAÏSSES

Artá

TALAYOT SETTLEMENT

Leave Artá south-west on the 715. The site is almost immediately on the left.

Part of the settlement's still complete oval wall, and the large south-east gateway.

The Talayotic culture in Majorca (*talaia* means watchtower) produced a form of housing within walled settlements, with *talayots* (round, tapering stone towers) either inside or adjacent to them. It possibly commenced around 1400 BC, lasted no more than 1500 years and was first identified by Emille Cartailhac, who held that the slightly different *talayots* in neighbouring Minorca were broadly contemporary.

This fascinating site on a hill by a spring was excavated not long ago by the Sardinian archaeologist Giovanni Lilliu. The settlement's containing wall, roughly ovular in shape, is complete; this is extremely rare for a Bronze Age site. The area within it, at its widest points, measures 348ft by 308ft (106m by 94m). It has four unevenly spaced gateways, of which the main one on the south-east is hugely impressive. There are very small housing 'units' in the centre, built over more than a millennium, a small passage and a solid *talayot*, which today is 14ft 9in (4.5m) high. It must once have had an external winding stairway to a platform area at the top.

SON REAL

*Can Picafort,
Santa Margarita*

CEMETERY

*Take the 712 coastal road
south-east from Alcudia; after
7 1/2 miles (12km) turn left
into the town of Can Picafort.
Park, and walk less than 1
mile (1 1/2km) south-east
along the beach. Wear rubber
boots.*

*The burial chambers in the cemetery
on the Bay of Alcudia have many
different shapes.*

Son Real is one of the few Majorcan examples of a substantial mass burial site. It dates back to about 8–6 BC, the end of the Talayotic period. It was built in three approximate stages at today's water's edge in the Bay of Alcudia; at that time the level of the sea was several metres lower (as more tombs on a nearby islet indicate).

Extensive excavations since 1957 have revealed that the earliest burial chambers were boat-shaped, somewhat in the manner of the Minorcan *navetas* in plan (*see* ELS TUDONS). These are distinctive for two unusual features. In some of them, two or three very small rectangular holes occur side by side. In others there are shallow trenches at each end, between

which crouched skeletons were laid, always with their heads facing to the east, and to the carefully dressed stone 'bows'. Collective burials have been found in the second oldest, circular, stone chambers.

The slightly more recent rectangular tombs vary in their methods of construction and form. More than 100 of all these types were built, and sometimes so close together that they share common stretches of wall. Disappointingly few grave goods have been uncovered at this remarkable cemetery, although many 'tools for the job', such as fragments of axes, blades, chisels, daggers, knives and swords, have been found. The tombs here are relatively young.

VERNISA

*Vernisa,
Santa Margarita*

CAVE BURIALS

Majorca has been inhabited for nearly 7000 years, as evidence of inhabitation and use in these caves has proved. Burials commenced here in the Late Neolithic period, being, as ever, one of ancient man's major preoccupations.

The cave culture was succeeded in about 1400 BC by the Talayotic way of life and, judging by pottery finds at this site, the caves were in almost continuous use for a further 1000 years. Flint flakes, buttons, a bronze dagger, and both plain and decorated pottery sherds have been found here.

Other natural caves in Majorca, similar in basic respects to the Vernisa cave are Cas Hereu, Cueva dels Bous, Sa Canova, Son Marroig, and Son Torrella.

*Leave Artá (on the east of the
island) on the C712 north-
west towards Puerto de
Alcudia. After 9 1/4 miles
(15km) turn left on to the
PM340. Take the first
turning on the right, then
right on to the PM341, then
left towards Muro. Vernisa is
now on the right.*

ELS TUDONS

Ciutadella

NAVETA

Minorca is 30 miles (48km) east to west, and 8½ miles (14km) north to south.

A *naveta* is a form of chamber tomb which is unique to Minorca. The name was invented by Spain's first serious prehistorian, Juan Ramis y Ramis, when he explored this tomb in 1818; at the time he concluded that it was a temple of Isis, the moon goddess of ancient Egypt. It was then the only known construction of its kind on the island, and it had the clear outline shape of an upturned boat. In Minorca today, *navetas* are sometimes confusingly called 'talayetas'. Els Tudons means the wood pigeons; perhaps they wisely used it, when all burial activity had ceased. It is held to be the oldest

Leave Ciutadella eastwards on the island's only major road, the C721. The naveta is signposted at the second track on the right.

Els Tudons is easily the finest of Minorca's 50 or so remaining navetas.

above ground 'building' in the whole of Spain and the Balearic Islands; it is also the Balearics' grandest monument.

From its exterior, the multicoursed stone mound tapers slightly inwards towards the entrance, as the chamber does within. The high and unique, inward curving façade contains a small, very low outer doorway; it faces almost south-west and has a great lintel stone above it, which projects slightly outwards. It leads into an antechamber or narrow corridor. From the outside, Els Tudons is 46ft (14m) long and 21ft 3in (6.5m) wide at the middle. Large, squarish semi-dressed stones form its foundation; eight layers of flatter stones lie above, tapering inwards as they rise. A big, flat, stone slab forms a platform at the back of the chamber and there is also a remarkable low, upper chamber, entered from the antechamber.

Navetas were constructed as tombs, and today some 50 are known to survive in Minorca. There is a fine group of these remarkable *navetas* around Alayor; they include Biniac 1 and 2, Cotaina, Llumena, Rafal Rubi 1 and 2, Torralbet, and Torre Llisa Vell. Els Tudons, in the area of the greatest concentration of them, has yielded the remains of more than 100 humans on pebble layers, as well as associated grave goods. Among the mysterious finds were discs bearing circular patterns.

The closed end of the monument, at the north-east, completes a spectacular piece of architectural design; its semi-dressed 'upturned prow' is most beautifully made. Els Tudons is roofless today, and exactly why is part of the monument's fascinating history. Some 30 years ago it was in terrible disrepair – mostly fallen, with many stones plundered for the ubiquitous Minorcan field walls, and with olive roots tearing at its great foundations. After much fund raising,

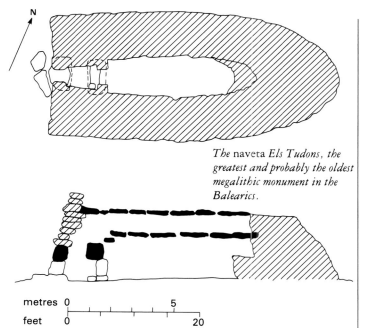

The naveta *Els Tudons, the greatest and probably the oldest megalithic monument in the Balearics.*

| metres | 0 | | | | 5 |
| feet | 0 | | | | 20 |

excavations took place in 1958. Then restoration commenced in 1959–60 under the direction of a remarkable servant of Minorcan archaeology, Maria Luisa Serra Belabre, who died before her time in 1967. She was never convinced by an original drawing of the site by Ramis, lodged in archives in Mahon, and therefore refused to accept unconfirmable conjecture about the roof's construction beyond the vestibule (it was probably corbelled). And so today Els Tudons is finely restored, after two years' work, but remains without a roof.

TALATI DE DALT

IV.6

*Algendar,
Mahon*

TAULA AND TALAYOT

The T-shaped taula *might represent a bovid (cattle-like) head.*

Leave Mahon westwards on the main C721; after 2½ miles (4km) turn left for Algendar. Take the first right fork, and then the site is on the left, about ½ mile (1km) from the main road. Not signposted.

This sloping, heavily-wooded and hard-to-find site disguises its megalithic excitements. Within a D-shaped enclosure there are remains of a stone circle around a fine *taula* (which has a tall stone leaning against it, cushioned by another). Its

rectangular, horizontal capstone has the same wonderfully dressed shape as the one at TREPUCÓ (see the reference to Stonehenge), and is the largest in Minorca; it measures 13ft by 5ft by 2ft (4m by 1.5m by 0.7m).

This site also contains buried chambers, standing stones (possibly supports for wooden roofs), and one distant, individual stone with a port-hole. Added to this, the remains of a substantial *talayot* dominate the prehistoric hamlet. Quite a building site over 3000 years ago!

Whatever the elegant and mysterious *taulas* were used for, it is generally accepted that they were neither roof supports nor sacrificial altars. One authority, J. Mascaro Pasarius (whose archaeological map of Minorca is recommended), has suggested that *taulas* were emblems of bull worship.

TORRE D'EN GAUMÉS

Alayor

PREHISTORIC VILLAGE

From the town of Alayor, 7½ miles (12km) west of Mahon on the main C721, take the road south-west to Son Bou. After the hamlet of San Isidro, take the turning south, as signposted.

A fine view of this prehistoric village in its rural setting.

This prehistoric settlement is sometimes referred to as 'Sa Comerma de Sa Garita', which is actually the name of the tomb at this site.

The village contains one of the four chamber tombs on Minorca, and, like the others, it is in a pitiful state with its capstone gone; its chamber measures 13ft 9in by 8ft 3in (4.2m by 2.5m). Also in the enclosure are standing stones, a stone pillared hall, three *talayots*, and a *taula* which has no capstone, but a candidate lies nearby – although the tomb may have had a wooden covering.

Dated between 2000 BC and 1000 BC, the site yielded, during excavations in 1974, an Egyptian bronze statue of Imhotep, the god of medicine, along with primitive surgical instruments, and also a bronze spearhead – a unique artefact in the Balearics.

This is a most tranquil place, and is watched over by a huge and brooding farmhouse, shutters ever closed against the elements.

TREPUCÓ

*Trepucó,
Villa Carlos*

TAULA

Take the main road PM702 south from Mahon to San Luis. After 1¼ miles (2km), turn left for Trepucó, and then left again; the round tower is now visible.

The most elegant of about 50 taulas on the island. Its top surface is 15ft (4.6m) above ground level.

This is the largest *taula* on Minorca with a pedestal 13ft (4m) above the ground and 9ft (2.7m) wide. Its rectangular, horizontal capstone measures 12ft by 6ft by 2ft (3.7m by 1.8m by 0.6m). The shape of the capstone is distinctly similar to the lintels of the Sarsen Trilithon Horseshoe (c.2000 BC) at STONEHENGE, Wiltshire, England.

Other impressive *taulas* on Minorca with the same capstone shape include Torralba d'en Salort (with a 'spine' running up its pedestal on one face – a familiar sight on standing stones around the world), Torre Trencada (with a separate stone 'spine' behind it), and Torre Llafuda.

There are some 50 *taulas* on the island; like many of the others Trepucó is enclosed by a stone wall, within which there are also tables stones and standing stones. A mostly ruined round tower stands nearby. Funerary practices have not been traced.

The site was excavated during 1928 and 1930 by the English archaeologist Margaret Murray.

IV.9

ALCALÁ GROUP

Monchique	*Monchique is 15 miles*
CHAMBER TOMBS	*(24km) north of the south-*
4 U	*western port of Portimao.*

BELOW: *Tomb 7 at Alcalá.*

This important group consists of 13 clusters of beehive-shaped chambers or *tholoi* (*see* LOS MILLARES, Almeria, for the origins of the term) which date back to about 3500 BC. Their first great excavator was Estacio da Veiga. In most of them the chambers average 8ft 3in by 9ft 9in (2.5m by 3.0m).

Tomb 1 at the site is unlike the others in the group, in that a double ring of stones forms the chamber. Tomb 3 has a handsome closed vestibule at its south-east facing entrance and two compartments within its passage, the last part of which has a septal slab before its chamber is reached. This has a niche to the east of it, which was found to contain seven long flint knives. Chisels, four daggers, awls, pieces of ivory and phallae made of clay were among other finds.

Two niches were found in Tomb 4, which contained two pieces of thin gold, probably finger rings. Tomb 7 is notable for the double rows of drystone walling all around it. Its entrance, as usual, faces the south-east, and the narrowing passage is punctuated, as in Tomb 3, with three pairs of opposite slabs. The chamber here is set lower than the entrance, as is the case in Tomb 9. It has a corbelled roof, the heavy top slab of which is broken. A 'cell' opens off either side of the chamber, at right angles to the axis of the passage. This grave also features the arrangement of double stones along its 14ft (4.3m) passageway.

ALMENDRAS

CROMLECH (STONE
CIRCLE)

5 Q

This is generally considered to be the largest and most complete cromlech in Portugal.

Take the N114 westwards out of Evora towards Montemor-o-Novo. After 6¼ miles (10km) turn left for Guadalupe 1¾ miles (3km) down the road. At the crossroads in the village, continue over on to the good dirt road, and follow the site signs thereafter. Turn right almost immediately, and then left just over ½ mile (0.8km), until it reaches Almendras Farm.

farm the road turns left and follows a winding route through woodland. After another ¾ mile (1km), the *cromlech* (as a stone circle is called in Portugal) can be seen to the left of the road.

Almendras is the largest and most impressive *cromlech* in Portugal, so it is claimed. It lies on an east facing slope with panoramic views, and is made up of about 95 stones, up to 8ft 3in (2.5m) high, with the enclosed area measuring about 197ft by 98ft 6in (60m by 30m). They are arranged in a main double oval setting, with a small 'lobe' at the western end and a larger one to the east.

Recent excavations and restoration (which caused the dirt road approach to be created) have cleared away vegetation, raised some of the fallen stones and revealed several more decorated stones, to add to those already known. The decoration ranges from simple cup marks on the flat top of one stone (near the road), to more elaborate compositions of circles, curves, zigzags, and wavy and straggly lines. Overall the designs fit into the general range of Portugese megalithic art, with the cup marks in particular providing a link both to standing stones and passage-tombs. This is a most rewarding site, and a visit should be completed with a picnic.

At the farm, in the directions above, a fine standing stone, 10ft 6in (3.2m) high, can be visited; it is in an olive grove near the grain silos to the south of the farm. This pleasurable megalithic quest now continues back on the road, which turns north through the farm. Along the way, a Roman altar and milestone can be seen. After another 220yds (200m) from the

ANTA DE PAVIA

PASSAGE-GRAVE
(REMAINS)

5 P

In the small square in the centre of the modest town of Pavia there is to be found one of the more startling sights as well as sites in this book! The massive chamber of a passage-tomb rears up some 13ft (4m), to the level of surrounding rooftops. Hidden from view on the far side, where the passage would have led off, a tiny chapel (dedicated to St Dennis) has been built up against the chamber – and indeed using its interior.

The chamber is characteristic of central Portugal, with its tall pillar-like stones abutting and curving in towards the top, kept in place by a massive capstone.

A true megalithic curiosity!

Take the N4 north-east from Montemor-o-Novo for 15½ miles (25km) to Arraiolos; then turn north on to the N370 to the town of Pavia.

ANTA DE POÇO DA GATEIRA

*Reguengos de Monsaraz,
Evora*

PASSAGE-GRAVE

7 Q

Leave Evora south-eastwards on the N256. The site is near Reguengos de Monsarez, about 23 miles (36km) along the road. Guide books and maps to the monuments in the area are on sale locally.

Anta is the Portuguese word for a burial chamber, and this is one of the most important of its type in the Iberian peninsula. It has an astounding thermoluminescence date of 4510±360 bc, which makes it one of the earliest monuments in this book (see DATES AND DATING pages 12–13). The first serious excavation of this grave was conducted in 1948–49 by archaeologists Georg and Vera Leisner.

The covering circular cairn, kerbed in places, was 39ft (12m) in diameter. The short, low passage was lined with just two upright slabs and leads to the central chamber, which measures 10ft by 6ft 6in (3m by 2m). The most unusual discovery in the chamber was a line of 11 plain pots and one other – corresponding possibly to 12 corpses destroyed by acid soil – which doubtless once contained human remains. Many other pottery sherds were uncovered, along with polished axes, flint cutting blades, and a beautiful plain hemispherical Neolithic bowl.

ANTA GRANDE DO ZAMBUJEIRO

*Valverde,
Evora*

PASSAGE-GRAVE

5 Q

Take the N114 westwards out of Evora towards Montemor-o-Novo. After 6¼ miles (10km) turn left for Guadalupe, 1¾ miles (3km) down the road. At the crossroads in the village turn left and proceed south continuing on a good dirt road. Valverde is reached in

2½ miles (4km). Now turn left down the hill through the village in the direction of Evora, cross the river, turn left past the agricultural station on the right. The site is signposted on the left, and a car park is soon reached to the north.

Part of the substantial chamber, with unusually tall uprights.

The huge mound, which lies across a stream (dry in the summer), is now protected by tin roofing. Much of the mound has been removed, leaving exposed an enormous chamber, constructed of typical in-curving pillar-like uprights reaching 19ft 9in (6m) in height – perhaps the tallest to be recorded in this book. The vast passage is well preserved, and contributes to the 'monumentality' of this extraordinary site.

About 65ft 6in (20m) to the south of the mound lies a long stone slab showing cup marks. There has been a recent excavation at this site, and two main periods were revealed. The earlier yielded a stone axe, a microlith and callis beads, and only the succeeding one produced the rich array of decorated schist plaques, flint and stone tools, and pots so often associated with central Portugese passage-tombs.

This site is not to be confused with the village of the same name, 21 miles (34km) east of Evora and south-west of Redondo.

CABEÇAS

*Arraiolos,
Evora*

PASSAGE-GRAVE

6 P

This 28ft (85m) long grave has some interesting characteristics. Its entrance vestibule is just south of east and the passage is lined with upright slabs, which increase in height towards the chamber at the north-west. This passage is 8ft (2.4m) long but its maximum height, before the antechamber, is only 2ft 3in (0.7m) high. What a gloomy crawl! There were probably seven capstones. The largest and domed slab covers the four-sided chamber, the uprights of which lean inwards; the chamber's entrance was through a narrow gap at the north-east. A large paving stone on the chamber floor reflects the 6ft (2m) high roof area.

Leave Evora north-westwards on the N114-4, and then turn north on to the N370. Arraiolos is about 13½ miles (22km) from Evora. Local guides and maps on sale.

CUNHA BAIXA

Espinho,
Oporto

PASSAGE-GRAVE

J4

This dolmen, with its chamber and corridor, is one of the largest and best preserved to be found in Portugal. The polygonal chamber, which is surrounded by nine orthostats carrying one capstone, is 10ft 6in (3.2m) high by 9ft 9in (3.0m) wide. There is evidence of ochre painting on the orthostats, and the chamber was once paved.

The passage, which is about 5ft (1.5m) lower than the chamber, is bounded by a double row of eight uprights carved with incised cup marks and other engravings. These uprights are still partly covered in the area next to the chamber by one of the large stone slabs which originally covered the whole corridor.

The majority of the artefacts found on the site are now in the National Museum of Archaeology in Lisbon; they consist mainly of polished stone axes, flint blades, microliths, pottery sherds, and a granite supporting stone. This stone, which is 4ft (1.2m) tall, has 15 parallel incisions carved on its sides.

Beside the bridge over the brook (castelo) on the road from Cunha Baixa to Espinho, a concrete footpath is on the left of the road; this leads directly to the dolmen, about 650ft (200m) from the road.

PALMELA

IV.16

Quinto do Anjo,
Palmela,
Setubal

ROCK-CUT TOMBS

3 Q

The entrance to one of the tombs, now badly desecrated. Finds have though been of importance.

This site is about 31 miles (50km) south-east of Lisbon, over the Tagus estuary, and some 5 miles (8km) north-west of the coastal town of Setubal. Leave this town north-west on the N252, then take the second turning on the left, on to the N379. The signposted site is about 3 miles (5km) along the road, off to the left.

This small group of tombs (sometimes spelt Palmella) has given its name to a type of fine developed Beaker pottery, dated about 2500–2000 BC. Four of them (two complete and two sliced in half) have been excavated. Three of their entrances face to the east, and one is aligned almost north/south, with its entrance just east of north. Their kidney-shaped chambers are reached through long, very low passages, which probably had one or more door slabs at their entrances, or through roof manholes, which are unique to the Iberian peninsula. They were used for successive multiple burials, then sealed; afterwards they were entered, almost emptied and, finally, it seems, deliberately and badly damaged.

Finds have happily been made, however. Notable among them is a unique arrowhead design; it has an almost circular blade and a long tang, and its type is known now as the Palmela point. The later Beaker burials brought copper daggers and flat axes. Remains have also been found of reddish and brownish decorated vases, sherds of low wide bowls, hanging vases with inturned rims, a small beautiful mixing bowl, a strange carved ball of limestone with a recessed waist around it, and beads for a necklace, perforated discs and other sundry amulets.

There was also a thin cylindrical idol-like figurine, which tapers towards its 'head'. It has four incised bands around the top, five more a third of the way down, then an inverted crescent less than the width of the object, followed by six bands all around, like the others and, finally, at the base but above a single band, what may be a representation of a human face. This may be artistic licence or mathematics expressed.

REGUENGOS DE MONSARAZ

*Reguengos de Monsaraz,
Evora*

PASSAGE-GRAVES

7 Q

*A tall menhir stands at the centre of
the large Xarez stone sanctuary.*

There are several important tombs here, set to the west of and among the tributaries of the Rio Guadiana. As a group they are well worth a visit (*see* also ANTA DE POÇO DA GATEIRA).

The *Antas* of Da Comenda Da Igreja, to the west of Evora, and away from this group, are fascinating. The circular cairn here, Anta Grande (which was excavated in the 1930s), contains a primary passage grave with very large upright slabs, and a secondary *tholos*, like POÇO DA GATEIRA near this site. The earlier grave is approached from the south-east by a low passage 34ft 6in (10.5m) long and at one point only 20ins (50.8cms) high. The once capstoned megalithic chamber is 8ft 3in (2.5m) high, with a maximum diameter of 11ft 6in (3.5m). This tomb has been tentatively dated back

*Leave Evora south-eastwards
on the N256. Reguengos de
Monsaraz is about 23 miles
(36km) away. Guide books
and maps to the monuments
are on sale locally.*

Anta 2 da Olival Da Pega, near this Evora group.

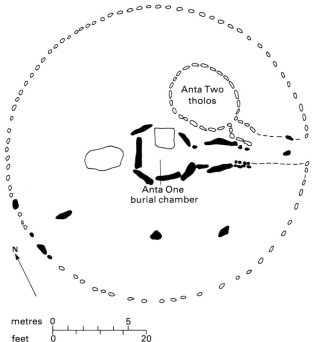

RIGHT: *Antas One and Two within the circular mound at Farisoa, one of a group at Reguengos de Monsaraz, Evora. (After G. and V. Leisner).*

The crook motif is thought by some to be a symbol of authority. It may also have been a horizon-measuring device and in this respect the apparent association with sun symbols is interesting. Crooks with zigzags were found at Anta Grande de Olival da Pega, close to this site.

to before 3500 BC.

Many centuries later a *tholos*, Anta 2, was built into the enclosure to the south of it but at a distinctly lower level. This chamber, which once had a corbelled roof, in accordance with its type, is 11ft 6in (3.5m) long and 9ft (2.7m) wide and is reached by a 6ft 6in (2m) long passage, which is actually parallel to the passage of Anta 1.

Nearby, there is a standing stone known as Abelhoa. Although the bottom part has been replaced, the top two-thirds of this typically-shaped menhir has some intriguing carvings on its surface. A crook is clearly discernible, with its handle to the right; this motif was often carved (*see* GAVR'INIS, Morbihan) and is a puzzle. More explicable is a representation of the sun shining above it, and there are also wavy lines, which possibly represent the ripple effect of water. The stone stands 8ft 9in (2.7m) above the ground. Other standing stones in the area include the 19ft 9in (6m) high Outeiro to the north, and Xarez, which stands at the centre of a huge stone sanctuary.

In plan, Antas 1 and 2 Da Farisoa (a few miles south-west of Da Comenda) are rather beautiful. The round mound which encloses both is perfectly circular and about 65ft 6in (20m)

across. At its centre, the passage and burial chamber was constructed first and, secondly, a *tholos* to its north. The oval chamber, Anta 1, is approximately 10ft (3m) in diameter, and seven uprights survive. Anta 2, with a diameter of 14ft 9in (4.5m), is the *tholos*, which shared an entrance at the south-east with the passage of the earlier grave; dated at about 2750 BC it is a neat oval, some 15ft (4.6m) at its widest, and is set, as customary, lower than the earlier grave. Its narrow orthostats are unusually thin and are shaped to fit their contiguous neighbours almost perfectly. They average 4ft (1.2m) in height, and would have been a fine sight beneath the corbelled roof of the *tholos*. Mysterious slate plaques have been found in both graves.

The earliest passage-grave in the Reguengos De Monsaraz Group is Anta 1 Dos Gorginos, which was excavated in 1949 by the Leisners. It has yielded a thermoluminescence date of 4440±360 bc. Its almost round, kerbed mound is some 40ft (12.2m) across. Other early graves in this remarkable area include the two Antas Da Pega, where more than 60 fragmented, engraved slate plaques were found; their patterns were mostly abstract, but some were anthropomorphic in design. These were probably prehistoric good-luck charms.

IV.18

COVA D'EN DAINA

Romañyá de la Selva,
Sant Feliu,
Gerona

GALLERY GRAVE

Sheet 443:38 G

Take the C250 from Sant
Feliu on the coast north-west
towards Llagostera and
Gerona. After about 3 miles
(5km) turn right along a
minor road to Romañyá de la
Selva. The site is to the north
of the village.

The interior of the gallery grave,
with its remarkable doorway.

This grave is set within a kerbed circular mound, which has a diameter of about 36ft (11m). The ring of stones, even if most are fallen, make an impressive sight. The parallel sets of orthostats inside are reminiscent of the French *allées-couvertes*. A single capstone, measuring 27ft (8.25m) in all, with a width of 5ft (1.5m), remains over the end of the gallery.

To the west, at the right of the entrance, stands the distinguishing feature of the site: a huge slab, second in size only to the endstone. The slab is the first of seven (one of which has fallen) around the quadrant. Finds here have included plaques – notably a bone plaque which is beautifully incised with abstract patterns and dated at 1500 BC, plain Almerian bowls, awls made of copper and Beaker sherds.

IV.19

CUEVA DE MENGA

Antequara,
Malaga

UNDIFFERENTIATED
PASSAGE-GRAVE

Sheet 446:16 U

Take the N351 northwards
from Malaga towards
Antequara. At the junction
with the C337, turn left
towards Antequara; the site is
signposted on the right.

One of the three monolithic supports.

This has long been one of the most famous chamber tombs in Spain; its main features are its huge length of over 82ft (25m), and the monoliths in its passage. Three large roughly square stones of slightly different dimensions stand in a row at approximately equal intervals down the centre of the passage, supporting capstones. There are five of these, and the end one over the chamber is estimated to weigh an incredible 180 tons.

The chamber's trilithon entrance faces north-east, with a vestibule; the passage is lined with twelve upright slabs on each side, averaging 9ft 3in (2.8m) in height. This great gallery is 20ft 3in (6.2m) at its widest, and the central pillars undoubtedly add to the grandeur of the interior. The tomb was once covered with a mound some 164ft (50m) across.

Being well-known over many centuries, it must have been thoroughly plundered, because no finds are recorded. But there are traces of carvings and paintings on the insides of the uprights; they include faintly human cross shapes, and one of them sports a kind of skirt.

Cueva del Romeral

*Antequara,
Malaga*

Passage-Grave

Sheet 443:16 U

*Take the N351 northwards
from Malaga towards
Antequara. At the junction
with the C337, cross over on
to the minor road, and the site
is signposted on the left.*

*A drystone passage leads to the
narrow trilithon doorway and on to
the round* tholoi *chamber.*

Here is perhaps the most impressive passage-grave in Spain, and it has been dated at about 3500 BC. For a start, the enclosing mound is some 285ft (87m) across, and reaches 30ft (9m) in height. There are only six upright megaliths here, plus three near the entrance.

Regular drystone walling lines the 5ft (1.5m) wide and 6ft 6in (2m) high pasage, this leads north-east towards a lower narrow trilithon doorway. This gives on to a drystone walled circular *tholoi* chamber, the first and larger of two here at 15ft (4.6m) in diameter. A capstone, 12ft 6in (3.8m) high above the ground tops the vaulted corbelled roof. A second, short, funnel-like passage, slightly west of the main passage axis, leads to the much smaller chamber between two uprights, beneath roofing capstones in the walling. Again, a capstone lies astride the corbelling. Del Romeral is a typical *cueva*, of a form that does not exist in northern Spain.

Cueva de la Viera

IV.21

*Antequara,
Malaga*

Passage-Grave

Sheet 446:16 U

*Take the N351 northwards
from Malaga towards
Antequara. At the junction
with the C337, turn left; the
site is signposted on the right.*

*The entrance down into this fine
passage-grave.*

This is another handsome tomb in the Antequara group which, archaeologically, is very important. Its mound is some 200ft (61m) across, and within it lies an 80ft (24.4m) long passage. This is lined with a parallel set of contiguous uprights, of which 22 survive. The entrance vestibule is at the south-east, and a port-hole transversal slab gives on to the passage.

A second, four-sided, port-hole stone slab gives access to the 2 sq yds (1.7 sq m) end chamber. This is covered by a massive 170-ton capstone which slightly overhangs an open area in the mound behind a huge capstone. This ambulatory space is reached by a third port-hole entrance in this endstone.

Port-holes are, incidentally, a particular feature of the Alcaide rock-cut tombs nearby; there are seven of them and each incorporates this almost square-shaped, carved access. The chamber here is most notable for its security, derived from some impressive vertical grooving on those port-hole stones – a Late Neolithic design triumph for a clearly important client.

DOLMEN DE SOTO

*Trigueros,
Huelva*

UNDIFFERENTIATED
PASSAGE-GRAVE
Sheet 446: 9 T

The so-called 'dolmen' is called Cueva del Zancarrón de Soto on some maps. This communal tomb with a stone rubble cairn is now partly depleted, but this does not detract from the majesty of the place. Indeed, light pouring down into the roofless end of the gallery adds to its drama.

There are about 32 pairs of contiguous uprights, (the final seven have lost their capstones) which gradually rise away from the entrance. The odd one is the twenty-second on the left; it is easily twice the width of the others except the endstone, which is about 9ft 9in (3m) in width.

The gallery is some 69ft (21m) long and is partially covered by a remarkable 19 capstones of which the penultimate one is by far the largest. Beneath the seventh capstone from the entrance, about a quarter of the way along the passage, two internal uprights act as portals, to produce a narrowing or neck; just ahead of them is another upright, just off-centre, and its purpose is difficult to guess at. Of the uprights, 21 bear carved decorations some of stylised human faces. In terms of tonnage, this is a mighty megalithic monument indeed.

Leave Huelva north-east on the N431. At San Juan del Puerto turn left north on to the N435 to Trigueros 3¾ miles (6km) away. A trackway leads south-east to the site. Take a torch.

LOMA DE LOS PEREGRINOS

*Alguazas,
Murcia*

ROCK-CUT TOMB
Sheet 445: 26 R

This name literally means 'pilgrims' mound', and about 20 skeletons of them have been found in articulated form inside this rock-cut tomb. The entrance is, typically, at the south-east. After a short passage, two lateral side cells occur before the main chamber opens out; this is oddly elongated to the south-west and measures 13ft by 10ft (4m by 3m). This arrangement is very similar to the rock-cut tomb Praia Das Maĉás (Estremadura, Spain) now mostly destroyed.

Finds have included rectangular Millaran copper awls, which are rare in tombs of this date (about 3400–3100 BC), plain Almerian pottery, and flint arrowheads.

Leave Murcia northwards on the N301. After 8¾ miles (14km) turn left over the River Segura, to Alguazas, where the site is signposted.

LOS CASTILLEJOS

*Montefrio,
Granada*

CHAMBER TOMBS AND
SETTLEMENT
Sheet 446:17 U

The directions here guide you into a beautiful limestone valley, with great cliffs rising along the right hand side of the road. Eventually a track is signposted on the right, and this leads to a parking place (and picnic area). From here begins a memorable archaeological ramble along the foot of the cliffs. Amidst a jumble of crags and meadows, with fine views across the valley, megalithic tombs are strewn over more than ½ mile (1km). At least 20 sites are known, not individually large or spectacular, but often with splendid 'dog kennel' and port-hole entrances. They are generally simple passage tombs, with short passages widening into small, low, wedge-shaped chambers. In their midst, on a defensible crag detached from the main scarp, is a deeply stratified settlement. Excavation, penetrating to a depth of 16ft 6in (5m), revealed a lengthy sequence of Neolithic and Copper Age layers, followed by long abandonment in the Bronze Age. During the final, Iron Age, phase the settlement was defended at one end with a fine bastioned, ashlar wall, probably of Greek inspiration.

Leave Granada westwards on the E902. After about 21 miles (34km), at Loreto, turn north on to the C335. Montefrio is then 15½ miles (25km) along the road. In the village take the road for Penas de Los Gitanos.

LOS MILLARES

Santa Fé de Mondújar, Almeria

CEMETERY AND
DEFENDED SETTLEMENT

Sheet 446: 22V

A partially restored area at this vast famous site.

This wild, desolate site certainly does not provide an easy-going day's outing. In the summer months it is very hot, the stream, Rambla de Huechar, is dried up, and a quick glance across the rocky spur might not reveal any man-made constructions. But they are there, and in great numbers.

The Los Millares site, which is 790ft (240m) above sea level, consists of a 12-acre (4.8 hectares) cemetery attached to three or more forts, which are to the west of an ancient partly-walled hut settlement. Los Millares was a seat of great power from about 3100 BC for some 500 years thereafter; the scale of the place and the fortifications make this clear. There was even a long aqueduct running east and then northwards to the village ramparts to meet the needs of the village inhabitants on the harsh spur overlooking the confluence of the Rio Andarax and the Rambla de Huechar.

There are up to 100 individual burials in passage and circular graves, spread about either side of the aqueduct, to the

Models and finds from this important site can be seen in the Archaeological Museum, Almeria. Take the N340 north from Almeria, on the coast. At Benahadux, turn left north-westwards on to the N324. The large mountainous site is over on the right on the spur between the river valleys of Andarax and Rambla de Huechar. This signposted site has been fenced in recently, but there is a manned entrance.

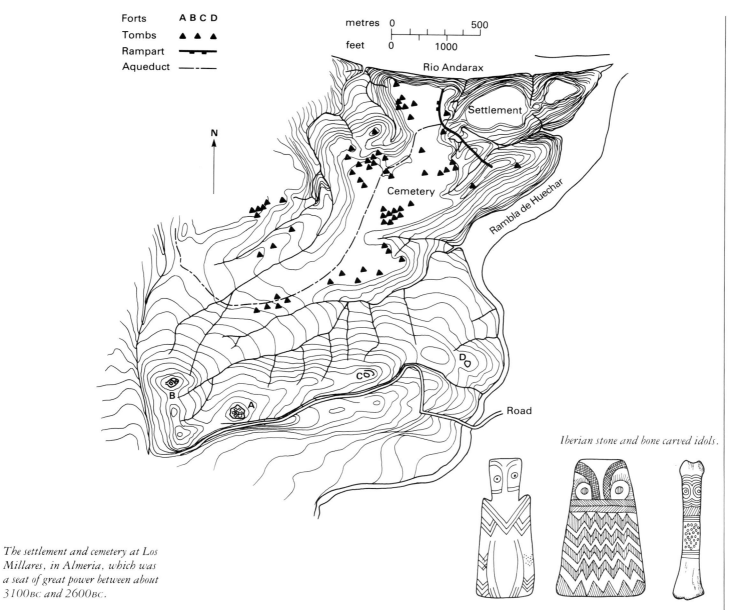

Forts   A B C D
Tombs   ▲ ▲ ▲
Rampart
Aqueduct

The settlement and cemetery at Los Millares, in Almeria, which was a seat of great power between about 3100 BC and 2600 BC.

Iberian stone and bone carved idols.

north of the forts and, naturally, outside the village ramparts. The site was first seriously excavated at the beginning of this century by Louis Siret who was able to demonstrate the copper mining industry at Los Millares, to the astonishment of archaeologists at that time.

Among the 80 or so circular chamber tombs here, there are distinctive, beehive-shaped, drystone walled, corbel-roofed chambers; to describe them in one word, Siret came up with the Greek word *tholos* (plural *tholoi*). He had related such tombs to Mycenaean equivalents, but, as radiocarbon dating has subsequently proved, Los Millares graves are far too old for such a design influence. However, the corbel-roofing can be related to architecture in the Mediterranean basin – to the Sardinian *nuraghi* (*see* LI-LOLGHI and SANT' ANTINE, Sardinia), the *sese* of Pantelleria (the often-ignored island lying between Sicily and Tunisia) and the *talayots* of Minorca (*see* TALATI DE DALT).

Los Millares was next excavated by M.J. Almagro Gorbea and Antonio Arribas, and also examined during 1953/55 by Georg and Vera Leisner who designated the tomb numbers used here. Many have notable features. Tomb 7, for example, yielded the usual copper artefacts but at the south side of the entrance ten small betyls (flat topped, cone-like stelae), about

1ft (0.3m) high, stood in a group – a mysterious minilithic huddle. These were often painted with a red substance, and elsewhere have measured up to 2ft (0.6m) high.

Tomb 17 is a well-known *tholos*. The flat-topped circular cairn was probably constructed in two stages and had four levels of kerbstones, with a semi-circular entrance forecourt at the east breaking into the first two levels. The passage was equally compartmented by septal port-hole slabs; most unusually two rectangular side chambers open out either side of the third western compartment. The circular chamber is 11ft (3.4m) in diameter, with contiguous uprights and a corbelled roof. A low monolith was set at the centre, and was perhaps once a platform for a wooden roof support.

Tomb 19 has provided the important date of 3100 BC. Tomb 40 was revealed to contain about 40 burials, and Tomb 63 was rich, not in bones, but in grave goods, behind its square port-hole slab at the chamber entrance. Los Millares has been well served over the last 100 years or so by both architects and publishers. Settlements and camps which are set on hill spurs at the confluence of rivers (*see* also VILLENEUVE-TOLOSANE, Haute-Garonne) have proved to be major contributors to an increased understanding of interactions between small local prehistoric communities and their ways of life.

V

Southern Europe

In cultural matters richness can lie in diversity. The basin of the Mediterranean Sea contains islands and mainlands which are strewn with megalithic remains of the greatest interest. Iberia and the Balearic Islands are dealt with separately in this book, as are France and the coastal African Maghreb countries of Morocco, Algeria and Tunisia.

Early burials and pottery

Rock-cut tombs present the earliest evidence of single and double burials only, perhaps as far back as late in the fifth millennium BC, throughout the central and western Mediterranean. It is an odd fact that no rock-cut tombs have been found in Corsica, although a few miles to the south lies the island of Sardinia, where well over 1000 such tombs have been recorded.

Equally strange is the fact that none occur north of Tuscany, 51 miles (82km) across the sea from Corsica. In Campania, south-west Italy, near the walled coastal town of Paestum (famed for its Greek temples), are three of the most sophisticated rock-cut chamber tombs (*hypogea*) in Italy. They have yielded corrected radiocarbon dates ranging from 3350 BC to 2500 BC. This type site of Gaudo was discovered in 1943, when United States military bulldozers were seeking rock for an airfield after the Salerno landings; it was quickly explored by the British Army's Mobile Archaeological Unit. There were 25 graves, clearly used in succession, as their earlier occupants were disarticulated and simply piled up in a corner. Around the walls of a kidney-shaped tomb, 25 complete skeletons were found (almost equally male and female). There were 33 pots and other vessels of great beauty. They included a double cup, made by fusing the handles together, and an *askos*, a vessel with a top opening off-centre and a carrying handle extended to the middle of the pot top. The same pottery, now known as Gaudo ware, was found in a tomb nearby, Mirabello Eclano, where a chieftain was buried with many primitive weapons at his side for the great journey, and a dog at his feet. Sadly, this site at Paestum cannot be visited today.

Also in Campania, but very much open to those hardy enough to explore it, is the site known as LA STARZA, or sometimes Ariano. It is outside the village of Ariano Irpino, but best reached from Benevento. This huge rocky gypsum hillock overlooking the Ariano Pass was excavated in 1957–61 by David Trump, a notable contributor to European archaeology. He established that the site was in human occupation from the Early Neolithic to the Early Iron Ages, and that trade in those far-off days was vigorous.

There are no megaliths and no mysteries here, but plenty of remarkable pottery finds to demonstrate such trading. They included Lagozza ware (from near Milan in the north, and dating back to 3800 BC), Piano Conte (from the island of Lipari, north-east of Sicily), Connelle (from the Marche, east-central Italy), Rinaldone (from a Copper Age site near Lake Bolsena, north of Rome), and Gaudo ware. There was also the site's own pottery; this has a distinctive white band around the waists of the pots – bands made of gypsum from the hill itself.

As usual, in southern Europe, natural and then artificial cave and rock-cut burials were succeeded by interments in single stone cists. At about 2500 BC the building of megalithic chamber tombs commenced.

Corsica

This rugged island of 3368 square miles (8722 sq km) lies only 7½ miles (12km) north of Sardinia, across the strait of Bonifacio, and yet their two cultures differed in many ways. Some remarkable megalithic monuments remain from the Chalcolithic Age (c.2800–1700 BC). Chief among them are the two rows (remains of seven) of some 90 statue-menhirs at PAGLIAIU (or Palaggiu). These are the survivors of 258, out of an island total of about 450 (and not one of them shows any part of the female body). The Middle Bronze Age statue-menhirs, unique to Corsica, reached their zenith at FILITOSA, south of Ajaccio. Although spoiled, this is one of the more instructive as well as beautiful archaeological sites in southern Europe. The statue carvers were succeeded here by the Torreans – builders of circular cyclopean towers (which are also unique to Corsica) of which there are 120 dotted around the island. Chamber tombs, known here as *dolmens* (as in France, of which the island is a *département*), include SETTIVA. It is unusual in having two stones standing outside its forecourt entrance.

Italy

Rock-cut tombs in mainland Italy have already been mentioned. Later came the builders of *specchie*, Italy's own form of burial chamber. One spectacular example, even if tragically harmed during its discovery, is GIOVINAZZO, near Bari. It is counted as one of the so-called Bari-Taranto group of tombs in the region of Apulia, on Italy's heel. Almost all of these collective grave sites mysteriously feature an associated standing stone (*pietrafitta*), though not at Giovinazzo. *Specchie* is also the name given to larger non-burial cairns.

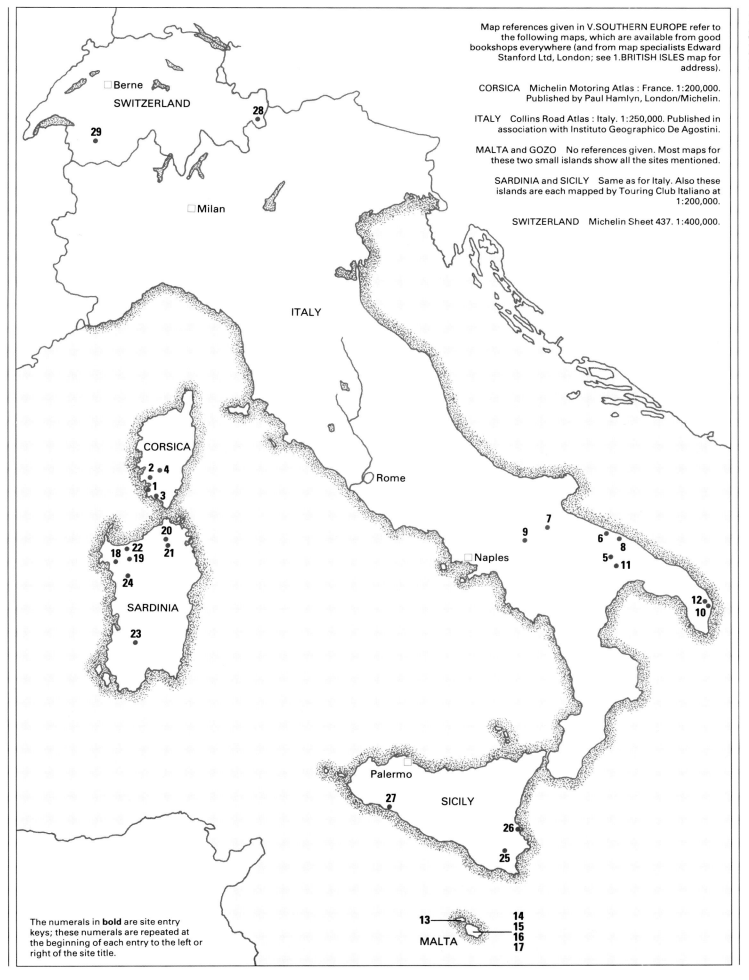

Map references given in V.SOUTHERN EUROPE refer to the following maps, which are available from good bookshops everywhere (and from map specialists Edward Stanford Ltd, London; see 1.BRITISH ISLES map for address).

CORSICA   Michelin Motoring Atlas : France. 1:200,000. Published by Paul Hamlyn, London/Michelin.

ITALY   Collins Road Atlas : Italy. 1:250,000. Published in association with Instituto Geographico De Agostini.

MALTA and GOZO   No references given. Most maps for these two small islands show all the sites mentioned.

SARDINIA and SICILY   Same as for Italy. Also these islands are each mapped by Touring Club Italiano at 1:200,000.

SWITZERLAND   Michelin Sheet 437. 1:400,000.

Berne
SWITZERLAND
28
29

Milan

ITALY

CORSICA
2 4
1
3

20
22
18   21
19
24

SARDINIA

23

Rome

7
9
6
5 8
11

12
10

Naples

Palermo
27
SICILY

26
25

13
14
15
16
17
MALTA

The numerals in **bold** are site entry keys; these numerals are repeated at the beginning of each entry to the left or right of the site title.

LEFT: *One of the 'holes' at*
MNAJDRA, Malta. The southern
temple at this site is the best preserved
on the island.

ABOVE: *One of the most interesting*
chamber tombs in Corsica is
Fontanaccia, south of Sartène in the
south-west of the island on the remote
Cauria plateau.

RIGHT: *The dramatic, well-*
preserved Nuraghe Su Nuraxi at
Barumini, south-east of Oristano,
in Sardinia.

Although there are no rock-cut tombs north of Tuscany (nor indeed in Corsica to the west), they occur in the south. In one at ALTAMURA, Bari, a strange bone plaque has been found, showing six bosses (possibly breasts). Similar plaques have been found elsewhere in southern Europe, at TARXIEN, Malta, for instance, and CASTELLUCCIO, Sicily.

Apulia has a concentration of tombs worth visiting. BISCEGLIE, Bari, is typical of the Bari-Taranto Group, and 12 in the different Otranto Group are located near Lecce. Of the latter, SCUSI was the first to be recorded in the whole region, in 1867, and it has been broadly dated between 2500–1800 BC.

Malta and Gozo
The islands of Malta and Gozo attract thousands of visitors each year to their 30 or so rock-cut and cyclopean temples. Their construction started in about 3500 BC and suddenly ceased for ever in about 2400 BC. Some are in pairs, such as HAGAR QIM and MNAJDRA. Perhaps the most extraordinary is HAL SAFLIENI (partner TARXIEN), south of Valletta. Twenty chambers were accidentally discovered in 1902, hewn out of solid rock; there were about 7000 disarticulated skeletons, red ochre paintings, and curious oracle holes (perhaps the world's earliest confessionals). There are also dolmens on the islands.

Sardinia
This is another island with unique megalithic monuments. The oldest site is LI-MURI, near Arzachena, in the north, which has five intersecting stone kerbed circular platforms. In the centre of each is a *coffre* (an open-ended high-sided rectangular stone slab cist). Near them are the remains of a Giant's Tomb – one of the many *tomba di giganti*, collective burial chambers, in Sardinia. They were constructed by the *nuraghi* builders for well over a millennium starting in about 1900 BC and perhaps as early as 2300 BC.

Nuraghi are Late Neolithic high round stone defensive towers, built from about 2500 BC; there are more than 6500 of

them spread over this 9,301 square miles (24,089 sq km) island (*see* SANT' ANTINE, near Thiesi). One of the most extraordinary and complex of them all is Nuraghe su Nuraxi, at Barumini in Cagliari, with its 13 towers, surrounding walls and a hut settlement; it is dated at about 1800 BC. Not to be missed in Sardinia are well temples, such as SANT' ANASTASIA, near Campidano, and the atmospheric so-called temple mound of MONTE D' ACCODDI, near Porto Torres, with its stone egg.

Sicily

This fascinating country, a fifth larger than Wales, is known for its rock-cut tombs, such as the coastal THAPSOS, near Siracusa, and the huge inland site of CASTELLUCCIO. The Castelluccian culture has been placed in the First Siculan period (about 2500–1700 BC), but may be earlier; it gives its name to the buff-coloured pottery with black linear patterns found there. More than 200 small, round oven-shaped (*a forno*) chambers were cut into the hillside for collective burials. Some

of the doorway slabs bear decorative motifs which are unique in Sicily. Seven bone plaques have been found here (with six bosses or breasts) out of the ten discovered so far on the island.

Switzerland

One of the most interesting Swiss megalithic sites is LE PETIT CHASSEUR, Sion, in the Valais; here there are chamber tombs, statue-menhirs and cists. A date of 4000 BC has been obtained from one of the two excavated stratified levels. There was a very early re-use of anthropomorphic statue-menhirs here which is unusual (but which also occurred at FILITOSA, Corsica).

Physically-fit megalith afficionados might enjoy trekking up to the rock carvings at CARSCHENNA in the canton of Graubünden. The ten carved surfaces are well worth reaching. The eventual pause for breath would be a good moment to reflect upon the fact that every single motif carved here is also found in every other country in this book.

CAPU-DI- LOGU

*Belvédère-Campomoro,
Propriano*

CHAMBER TOMB WITH
CARVINGS

180 C 3

This is one of about 100 chamber tombs in Corsica, where (as in France) they are called *dolmens*. They are mostly in the south of the island, where such building commenced in about 2900 BC.

Usually, dolmens were simple rectangles formed by stone slab uprights, but one or two have short passages facing east and some were covered by an earth mound. Most Corsican examples are in a ruined state, because of looting by treasure hunters through the ages.

This dolmen, with incised decoration, has a horned forecourt, which is similar in design to TINKINSWOOD, South Glamorgan, Wales, and, much nearer, to many Sardinian *tomba di giganti*, such as LI-LOLGHI, Arzachena.

Take the N196 south from Propriano. Turn right onto the D121 along the Golfe de Valinco. After 10 miles (16km) just beyond Belvédère-Campomoro, the site (also known as Capo di Luogo) is down a signposted track on the left.

FILITOSA

*Filitosa,
Sollacaro*

STATUE-MENHIRS AND
TORRI

180 C 2

Three of the many statue-menhirs at this site. None of them are 'female', and nor are there any in Corsica.

Take the N196 south from Ajaccio. 6¼ miles (10km) south of Petreto-Bicchisano, take the next turning right on to the D757 running south-west along the Taravo to Sollacaro, and on to the site of Filitosa, which is signposted. Car park and museum.

Though a much disturbed site, Filitosa is easily the best known in Corsica, and one of the most famous in the Mediterranean basin. In its beautiful setting above the Taravo river, it has a lasting 'presence' which perhaps recalls its original use as a sanctuary. (Prehistoric sites without question possess characters of their own; some are simply 'not nice': ST LYTHANS, South Glamorgan, Wales, is, the author feels, one example). Filitosa was discovered as recently as 1948, and led to a modest flurry of interest and activity in Corsica's prehistoric monuments under the direction of Roger Grosjean.

The sanctuary site was probably occupied in three different stages between about 4000 and 500 BC. For the first 2000 years, it was in the hands of Neolithic and then Early Bronze Age tribes, who were megalith builders. During the next 1200 years, from about 1800 BC to about 800 BC, it was the province of indigenous creators of Corsica's *torri*.

A *torre* is a circular tower constructed of cyclopean masonry, with a large entrance giving on to a short access passage which leads to a large single chamber, with a false-corbelled roof. Variations incorporated small niches within the chamber and additional passages, especially if they were built around natural rock formations (as one is at Filitosa). There are about 120 *torri* on the island, and tourist literature rightly displays them as Corsica's principal contribution to Mediterranean prehistory (just as Minorca has *navetas* and *talayots*, Sardinia *nuraghi*, Italy *specchie*, and so on). Here they date to the Middle and Late Bronze Ages.

The final period of Filitosa's active occupation saw the 'arming' of some of its many statue-menhirs, with daggers, swords, coats of chain mail with strange grooves, and depictions of helmets carried on the menhirs. These helmets have two holes which may have accommodated horns.

The site is approached along a path past the museum. The East Monument, the first *torre* of three, incorporates a narrow gateway in a wall of cyclopean blocks which encircles the site on its rocky spur. The Central Monument is reached through hut remains. This consists of a ruined *torre* (dated at about 1800 BC) resting on a larger low round cyclopean platform.

Today statue-menhirs almost surround it; they were excavated from the *torre*'s foundations and date from about 2000–1500 BC. Unlike France, Spain, and elsewhere, there are no 'female' statue-menhirs, showing breasts, at Filitosa or anywhere in Corsica (among a total of about 450 carved and uncarved menhirs).

Further to the north-west on the spur lies the West Monument, a *torre* dated to between 1400–900 BC. This soft stone 20ft (6.1m) high outcrop with deep, rounded fissures driven into it by weathering, is surrounded by now ruined cyclopean walling. Below it and nearby are five intriguing statue-menhirs of great age. But their positions in the peaceful sylvan arena are modern, like statues in a public park — which is just what they are.

A vividly carved statue-menhir from the group opposite, with the familiar necklace. Below it are rare symbols of defence or attack, which were perhaps carved during the fifth of their six development stages.

RIGHT: *The sanctuary site at Filitosa, notable for its statue-menhirs (one shown) and its Torrean monuments.*

BELOW: *There are about 450 carved and uncarved statue-menhirs in Corsica. A carved dagger can be seen below the mysterious visage.*

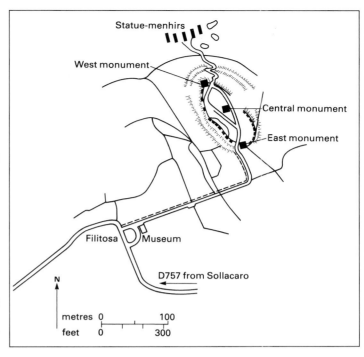

PAGLIAIU

Sartène

STONE ROWS
(ALIGNMENTS) OF
STATUE-MENHIRS

180 C 4 (marked as
Alignements de Palaggiu)

*Standing and fallen stones among
the rows. About 90 of them are
carved.*

These two stone rows, or *alignments*, are sometimes collectively referred to as 'Palaggiu'; there were originally 258 carved granite standing stones placed in seven groups, out of an island total of about 450. Unusually, not one depicts the female body, or any of its parts. They are dated around 2000 BC, and seem to have developed, according to R. Grosjean, in six broad stages; only in the fifth stage were weapons depicted.

Recalling the stone rows of Brittany (*see* KERMARIO and MÉNEC, Morbihan, France), many of the 90 or so statue-menhirs here are placed in alignments oriented north-south, with the carved surfaces facing east. The Carnac rows are uncarved, and are set east to west. It has been proposed that the Carnac rows formed an astronomical instrument; perhaps these Corsican menhirs are simply memorial stones.

At Pagliaiu there is also a cup-marked cist (known here as a *coffre*), with a small stone circle around it, which probably acted as a revetment around a covering earth mound; it could date back to 2500 BC. Rare for Corsican sites, this cist yielded artefacts in the form of Beaker-type fragments. Carved dolmens are also to be found here.

Leave Propriano in the Golfe De Valinco southwards on the N196. Sartène is 8 miles (13km) south. South-west of the town, turn right on to the D48; after 5½ miles (9km), take the right fork on the D48. The rows are signposted on the right.

SETTIVA

Petreto-Bicchisano

CHAMBER TOMB
(DOLMEN)

180 C 2

This is one of three Corsican dolmens which have port-holes in their entrance slabs. Its wide outward curving forecourt faces south-east, and unusually two stones, rather than one, stand a few feet in front of the entrance.

A tiny antechamber leads into a square chamber, which has an extra rectangular upright slab in its north-west corner. The original cist (dated at about 2250 BC), from which the tomb evolved, was in this chamber.

Remains of five individuals were found here, as well as beads, pottery sherds, obsidian and flint blades, axes, and also 20 cups from the earliest layer of deposits. They are of a type which indicates 3250–2750 BC as the probable date for the first use of Settiva.

Petreto-Bicchisano is 14 miles (22km) up a winding mountain road, the N196 north of Propriano on the road to Ajaccio. Ask in the town for local directions.

ITALY

ALTAMURA

Altamura,
Bari,
Apulia

ROCK-CUT TOMBS

62 B 4

These tombs are set in to the side of a hill. Neolithic sherds of pottery have been found, coming from the Diana-Bellavista period, (4th millennium BC), and from the Bronze and Iron ages, in the higher tombs. Lower down, disturbed deposits have occurred from the Late Paleolithic period; there were also stones carved with distinct geometric patterns, and both impressed and painted pottery.

In the vicinity of the tombs, a bone plaque with some intriguing characteristics has been discovered. It is 3½ins (8.9cm) long and has six protuberances, bosses or breasts. Exactly similar plaques have been found at Troy, TARXIEN, Malta, and CASTELLUCCIO, Sicily.

Leave Altamura south-
eastwards on the S171
towards Santéramo in Colle.
The tombs are 5½ miles
(9km) along the road on the
left before the station at Casal
Sabini.

BISCEGLIE

Corato,
Bisceglie,
Bari,
Apulia

GALLERY GRAVES

61 J 1 (Chianca); 63 G 4
(Tavole dei Paladini)

Near the seaside town of Bisceglie, just to the west of the ferry port and city of Bari (capital of Apulia; its archaeological museum is in the Piazza Umberto), are a dozen burial chambers, which are sometimes (thanks to John D. Evans) called the Bari-Taranto group. They are all collective grave sites, housed in parallel-sided, narrow, galleried structures, with endchambers of the same width. In this respect they are like the French *allées-couvertes*, and similar Neolithic tombs are found all over Europe, including the Mediterranean basin. In this group, rather mysteriously, almost all of them have an associated standing stone or menhir, some of which are statue-menhirs.

Chianca was discovered in 1909. It
lies on an exact east/west axis in a
shallow trench.

V.5

V.6

Take the straight road south from the coastal town of Bisceglie, beneath the regional road, towards the E55 autostrada. Turn left before it, and Dolmen Di Chianca (as marked on the map) is on the right. Albarosa is just over ½ mile (1km) away. Tavole dei Paladini (as marked on the map), is south-east of Bari, just north of the S16, between the towns of Fasano and Ostuni.

The chamber of Chianca at the western end is unusually tall at 6ft (1.8m).

The finest grave in this group is Chianca (not to be confused with another Chianca, at Maglie, south-east of Lecce). It was discovered in 1909, excavated by M. Gervasio and A. Mosso and dated at 2300–1750 BC. The whole tomb is 24ft 6in (7.5m) long, set exactly on an east/west axis, with its entrance at the east. The western chamber is particularly tall at 6ft (1.8m), and measures 12ft 6in by 8ft (3.8m by 2.4m) beneath a thin capstone. The chamber and passage are set in a shallow trench, and were most likely once covered by a stone cairn. Such cairns, and other stone towers (often with exterior spiral stairways) which were never tombs, are known as *specchie* and are characteristic of southern Italy. *Specchie* apparently never had compartments; here, handsome pairs of uprights line a passage now open to the sky.

There have been many finds in and around Chianca, including the usual broken votive pottery, a strange bronze disc and amber beads. There were also 13 skeletons, one of them complete and in a flexed position. This individual was no doubt the last to arrive. Chianca is set in a delightful olive grove, but is now bounded by unattractive stone walls.

Tavole dei Paladini, though not in the immediate vicinity of Chianca, is counted as one of the Bari-Taranto group. This gallery grave has a very short passage, with a vestibule facing east; a septal slab gives on to the antechamber. The sloping capstone survives, as do the huge side slabs.

Albarosa, another notable gallery grave about ½m (1km) away was also enclosed by a huge *specchia*. Curiously, its height in the chamber, at 6ft (1.8m), is the same as at Chianca; the length of the whole is only slighter shorter, at 23ft (7m), and its entrance also faces east (though this is very common).

Frisari, nearby, is a good example of a simple burial chamber, with just four uprights; the widest of them is 11ft 6in (3.5m), and one of the others has fallen. Dolmen di Giano was once in this loose group, but it has now vanished without trace, due to the economic demands of agriculture and therefore for big flat fields for farmers.

Man has been in the area of Bisceglie for a long time. Neanderthal human remains have been found in the nearby Grotta S. Croce, which is somewhat similar to caves in the Cheddar Gorge, Somerset, England; bones of rhinoceros and hyena were found there by L. Cardini during excavations in 1939, and again in 1954–56. During the following six years he explored a similar inhabitation, Cave di Mastro Donato. Its quaint name seems to be unconnected with the astonishingly long period of its use – its excavator uncovered both Neanderthal remains and SERRO D'ALTO pottery.

CASTELLUCCIO DE' SAURI GROUP

Castelluccio De' Sauri,
Foggia,
Apulia

PREHISTORIC
SETTLEMENTS AND
STATUE-MENHIRS

56 D 6

RIGHT: *A statue-menhir from the*
prehistoric settlement at
Castelluccio De' Sauri. (After
Philip Howard)

This site, on the huge plain of Tavoliere (which means 'chessboard' and is a reference to its Roman field system) is one of a number of prehistoric settlements in the area for those with sharp eyes. Others include La Quércia (to the north-east), which is ringed by no less than eight ditches, and Passo di Corvo, which is a veritable township of 100 dwelling places. Another important prehistoric settlement is on the Adriatic coast, north-west of Foggia, outside the village of Manfredonia.

There are three statue-menhirs from the Copper Age from this site in the Archaeological Museum in Foggia. The early ones are primitive and mostly faceless, as in Sardinia (*see* FILITOSA). They become more elaborate and detailed as the centuries pass, very often featuring necklaces – or are they token belts, displays of wealth and status (see CRECH-QUILLÉ, Côtes-d'Armor, France, and LE CÂTEL, Channel Islands).

Other recurring decorations, both incised and in low relief, are weapons such as daggers and axes and anatomical features such as breasts, arms, heads and eyes, and also navels. Grave goods or local finds are very rarely found with statue-menhirs, and yet they must have been megalithic memorials.

Leave Foggia southwards on
the S655. After about 12½
miles (20km), turn right on to
the S161 for the village of
Castelluccio De' Sauri, 3¾
miles (6km) away. Then ask
for local directions.

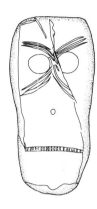

V.8

Giovinazzo,
Molfetta, Bari,
Apulia

GALLERY CAIRN
(SPECCHIA)

62 B 2 (marked *dolmen*)

Leave the coastal town of
Giovinazzo south-westwards
on the largest road towards
Terlizzi. Cross over the S16,
and then over the E55
autostrada and the site is
visible on the right. It is 11
miles (18km) from Bari, and
not signposted.

GIOVINAZZO

One of the most impressive specchie in Italy.
It was inadvertently discovered by a farmer.

This splendid *specchia*, sometimes called San Silvestro, was only discovered in 1961, when a farmer attempted to flatten what he thought was simply a long high mound of earth. Smashed in two though it is, it is still regarded as one of the grandest *specchie* in their native southern Italy and forms one of the Bari-Taranto group (*see* BISCEGLIE, Bari).

It has been dated at about 1750 BC, but is probably earlier. Most likely it was constructed for a tribal or family group, and was in use for some 1500 years. It boasts a substantial semi-circular forecourt, the walling of which is so thick that it is difficult to believe that its top surfaces were not used, in conjunction with the courtyard below, for some ceremony or ritual, perhaps involving votive offerings.

The original covering cairn of dressed drystone was 90ft (27.4m) long and set on a north/south axis, with the grave entrance at the south – which is extremely rare. The round antechamber consists of inward leaning square stone blocks. Beyond this lies the 53ft (16.1m) long gallery passage, topped by six surviving capstones and lined with substantial leaning flat slabs; it measures only 3ft (0.9m) at its widest, and is divided into compartments by septal slabs. In one, human bones of nine adults, two adolescents and at least two children were found. The roof of the chamber, now destroyed, was probably of the *tholos* type.

Many skeletons have been identified at this *specchia*, and also pottery from the Mycenaean I and II periods. This is an archetypal southern Italian megalithic site, although it has no associated standing stone (*pietrafitta*). Many of these are to be seen around the nearby village of Terlizzi. Apulia offers an excellent 14 day megalith hunting holiday.

LA STARZA

Ariano Irpino,
Benevento,
Avellino,
Campania

PREHISTORIC CAVES

59 I 2

Sometimes called Ariano, this huge and dramatically situated site is a rocky gypsum hillock overlooking and commanding the Ariano Pass. It was excavated in 1957–61 by David Trump, a notable contributor to European archaeology. He established that the site was in human occupation from the Early Neolithic to the Early Iron Ages, and that trade in those far-off days was vigorous.

There are no megaliths and no mysteries here, but plenty of remarkable pottery finds. They included final Lagozza ware (from near Milan in the north, and dating back to 2850 BC), Piano Conte (from the island of Lipari, north-east of Sicily), Connelle (from the Marche, east-central Italy), Rinaldone (from a Copper Age site near Lake Bolsena 50 miles (80km) north of Rome), and Gaudo — all implying considerable movement.

On one terrace there was a large rubbish heap, giving 16ft (4.9m) deep of stratified finds, including the site's own Ariano pottery; this has a distinctive white band pressed around the waists of the pots — bands made of the gypsum of the very hill.

Leave Benevento eastwards on the E842 autostrada; turn off northwards at the Grottaminarda exit on to the S90 going northwards to Ariano Irpino. Then ask for local directions.

SCUSI

V.10

Minervino di Lecce,
Otranto,
Lecce,
Apulia

CHAMBER TOMB

69 I 4 (marked *Dolmen di Scusi*)

This charmingly situated dolmen is one of 16 in the Otranto area (*see* also TERRA D'OTRANTO). It was, in fact, the first such tomb to be recorded in Apulia, in 1867, and has been dated between 2500–1800 BC. It was thought by its excavator, M.A. Micalella, that its name might have been derived from a local dialect word *scundere*, measuring 'hiding place'. It is very similar to other Otranto group sites, which have clear affinities with Maltese and Sardinian tombs.

Its thick flat, perforated capstone, which is 12ft 6in (3.8m) across, rests on one upright slab and eight piles of up to four courses of large stones, all of which stand on a platform of natural limestone. In this platform, near the tomb, there is a small rectangular hole, which once almost definitely held a menhir; this would have been consistent with the tomb's type.

Leave Otranto south-westwards for 3¾ miles (6km). At Uggiano la Chiesa turn right towards Minervino di Lecce. The signposted site is 1¼ miles (2km) beyond the village on the left.

This charmingly situated chamber tomb was the first Apulian megalithic site to be recorded. The capstone pillar supports are unusual.

SERRA D'ALTO

*Serra d'Alto,
Matera,
Basilicata*

CAVES, ROCK-CUT
TOMBS AND OPEN
VILLAGE SETTLEMENTS

62 B 4 (marked
Villaggio Neolitico)

Caves hewn out of rock faces in valley ravines are known as *sassi* in this region which forms the arch in the foot of Italy. The *sassi* La Murgecchia and Tirlecchia to the north and east of Matera, below the 13th-century cathedral, number more than 3000 and, incredibly, more than 17,000 people occupied this honeycomb until the beginning of this century, when American funds sponsored their removal. Some were excavated by D. Ridola in 1900–10 and by U. Rellini in 1919.

High on a limestone escarpment a hut settlement, dated at about 3750 BC, was found. Pottery, now known as Serra d'Alto, was made here. In design terms it was amazingly advanced for the Neolithic period; its painted detail varied but often featured meanders and spirals, while always conforming to a simple yet distinctive general style. The museum at 24 Via Ridola in Matera displays fine examples of this classic prehistoric ware.

Leave Matera north-eastwards on the S271. The site is signposted about 1¾ miles (3km) on the left.

TERRA D'OTRANTO GROUP

*Otranto,
Lecce,
Apulia*

BURIAL CHAMBERS
(DOLMENS) AND
STANDING STONES
(PIETREFITTE)

69 I 4 Giurdignano;
69 H 3 Gurgulante and
Placa (all as marked)

The coastal town is the most easterly in Italy. It is reached by the autostrada running south-east from Brindisi to Lecce, and then on the S16 to the town.

The Gurgulante dolmen, one of the smallest in this book.

There are 12 tombs (out of 16 recorded) in the so-called Otranto Group, and they are markedly different from the Bari-Taranto tombs (*see* BISCEGLIE, Bari). Here there are menhirs (called *pietrefitte* in south-east Italy) which are almost always associated with *dolmens*. They are generally about 10ft (3m) tall, slender and finely dressed rectangles, with their longer faces to the east and west.

The chambers much resemble French dolmens in construction. They consist simply of a sub-rectangular capstone (sometimes with a port-hole), about 6ft (1.8m) across, supported by uprights and pillars of stones, with no passage. They were probably covered with earth. There are few carvings, and, oddly, no finds have been recorded. This is

disappointing, because associated radiocarbon dates might have provided links with similar French Atlantic-seaboard megalithic tombs.

Prominent among the Otranto tombs is a group of seven, with standing stones, outside the village of Giurdignano near a farm called Masseria Quattro Macini. On one of the *pietrefitte*, about 4ft 6in (1.4m) from the ground, there are carvings of two differently shaped crosses, one above the other, indicating modest attempts at Christianization.

Other tombs in this coastal area include Gurgulante, next to a wall in an olive grove, and Placa, with a tree growing against it, just west of the village of Melendugno (between Otranto and Lecce, via the coastal road). SCUSI is also in this group.

GGANTIJA

Xaghra,
Gozo

TEMPLE

Malta and Gozo are only 121sq m (313sq km) in total land area.

Cyclopean walling looms over small trilithons in the temple.

Malta is justly world famous for its unique temples, of which there are about 30 on Malta and its smaller neighbour Gozo. They were all built between 3500 BC and about 2400 BC, when all work abruptly ceased: just why is one of the great megalithic mysteries yet to be solved.

The temples were generally built in pairs. The two here are side by side in a great cairn 50yds (46m) long. The southernmost is the earlier, and has five apses. Like its partner, it has a fine curved forecourt at its entrance with enormous stones around the bases and cyclopean drystone walling above. The length of the southern temple is 86ft 3in (26.3m) and its width is 77ft 9in (23.7m).

The temple tomb to the north has only four apses and is altogether smaller, being 61ft (18.7m) long and 57ft 6in (17.5m) wide. The apses are rounded, have virtually no entrances and in plan are rather beautiful, spreading like the petals of a flower.

Take the road (no numbers used) directly east from Victoria; take the first left for the village of Xaghra. The temple is signposted on the right. A hypogeum was discovered opposite this site in 1991.

Many authorities now accept that the temple ground plans depict the Great Goddess in outline. The Earth Mother is, of course, a key motif in Maltese archaeology.

HAGAR QIM

Zurrieq,
Malta

TEMPLE

This superb temple's pair is the neighbouring MNAJDRA. Hagar Qim was constructed in two stages between 3500 BC and 3300 BC. Four giant stones, irregular and much gnarled by the Mediterranean elements, form the curved frontage together with some lintels. The great trilithon entrance survives, together with the base course of huge dressed stones; the other courses and roofing are long gone. There is a stone kerb all around the temple.

The two lobed chambers inside are of different periods and contain altars, a slab with a port-hole, a betyl, and a huge central passage lined with dressed uprights and a few lintels, but no roofing. The central four apse chamber is 56ft 3in (17.1m) long and 65ft 6in (20.0m) wide. The northern chamber is much narrower, but has five apses; it measures 52ft 6in (16.0m) in length and 24ft (7.3m) wide.

Seated female figures, carved in local limestone, have been found here; their greatly exaggerated proportions suggest a Mother Goddess depiction of about 3000 BC. They manifest a mystery: why are they virtually always headless? Perhaps their neck holes were for receiving the latest Goddess's head?

Take the road south from Zurrieq, near the south coast; turn right, north-east, before the Blue Grotto. The signposted temple is down the next track on the left.

A seated figurine from Hagar Qim (now in the National Museum of Malta, in Valletta).

Hal Saflieni

Tarxien,
Valletta,
Malta

Rock-cut Temple
(hypogeum)

Go south from Valletta,
through Marsa to Paolo.
Continue straight on; the
temple is signposted a few
streets along on the left in
Burials Street.

The dramatically lit interior of the
underground temple.

The *hypogeum* at this site is one of the most remarkable prehistoric monuments in the whole of Europe — and yet surprisingly little is known about what went on inside it. The three-level site was discovered accidentally by workmen in 1902 while they were working on a drainage system for this suburb of Valletta. Its nearby partner, TARXIEN, was not discovered until 1914. The excavations of 1905–09 produced a date of between 3500 BC and about 2400 BC, the now accepted period for all Maltese temple building.

In the 20 chambers cut out of the rock, reached by one entrance shaft, remains of some 7000 disarticulated human skeletons were found. The *hypogeum*, at the lowest level and reached through a carved 3ft 3in (1m) high doorway, reflected many of the characteristics of the buildings above it.

It contains shallow port-hole niches surrounded by trilithon entrances, amazing paintings of cattle in red ochre, local pottery, personal ornaments, animal bones, carvings in relief, and strange so-called 'oracle holes' connected to hidden chambers like confessionals. One of the most spectacular finds here was of two terracotta 'sleeping women' statuettes.

Although its specific uses may still be a mystery, this temple was being carved out of solid rock to a pre-planned design of great sophistication probably before the beginning of STONEHENGE or the Great Pyramid at Giza.

Mnajdra

Zurrieq,
Malta

Temple

Take the road south from
Zurrieq, near the south coast;
turn right, north-west, before
the Blue Grotto. The temple is
down the next track on the
left, past Hagar Qim by the
coast.

The north temple.

These three temples are set in a hollow, just below their 'pair', HAGAR QIM. The southern and central temples are faced with the familiar and substantial dressed base-stone courses, with courses of cylopean drystone walling above; they share a common wall between them.

The southern one is 49ft 9in (15.2m) in length, and 45ft (18.7m) in width; it has a substantial 'reception area', with four apsidal chambers leading of it. One of them containing two betyls (pillar altars), and another two port-hole slabs.

Its central partner to the north is the largest here, with a length of 59ft (18.0m) and a width of 54ft 6in (16.6m), and also four apses. The third, north-eastern temple has three apses, and is the oldest, at about 3400 BC, and the smallest, at 27ft 3in (8.3m) long and 38ft 6in (11.7m) wide.

As the best preserved temple complex in Malta, the one to visit here is the southern one; it bears witness to an astonishing period in megalithic history, which was most likely a completely indigenous occurence.

TARXIEN

*Tarxien,
Valletta,
Malta*

MEGALITHIC TEMPLES

*The four temples at Tarxien were
built in succession, and became the
best decorated temples in Malta and
Gozo. The 30 or so were all built
between 3600BC and 2400BC.*

This famous group of temples has HAL SAFIIENI as its pair, a few hundred yards away in this built-up suburb of the island's capital. Dating from about 3300 BC, this is the only Maltese site of the time of the temple builders (3600–2400 BC) which was subsequently used after they were gone, in the Bronze Age. The site was discovered in 1914 and excavated by Sir Themistocles Zammit in 1915–17; it covers about 59,200 sq ft (5500sq m). The four temples, which adjoin each other, were built from the island's fairly soft limestone — and not all at once, but in succession. They were once all roofed.

The southernmost, at the west and called Tarxien South, (also Tarxien West!), is 74ft (22.8m) long and 60ft (18.3m) wide. It has two pairs of opposing chambers (known here as

*Go south from Valletta,
through its suburbs to Marsa
and Paola. Continue straight
on to Tarxien, turn left, and
then left again at the signpost
into Old Temple Street.*

As so frequently at prehistoric sites, the enigmatic spiral motif appears in this temple, and was the work of a master carver.

Part of an altar carving at the temple of Tarxien South.

apses), many abstract and literal carvings, a font and a most unusual altar. This is robustly carved in sunken relief with an interleaving swirling pattern of great beauty; it is 4ft (1.2m) high, and has a mysterious recess in the front in which a flint sacrificial knife was found. Another surprise in this astonishing temple, is a massive and rather unattractive Goddess (of fertility?) statue (today in replica: the original is in the National Museum of Malta in Valletta). It is broken off horizontally across the waist (the top part has never been found); two grotesquely swollen legs descend from a voluminous pleated skirt and seem to rest upon tiny feet that one expects to be cloven.

In the same period the four-apse East temple was constructed, containing the finest decorated stones in Malta, often with the enigmatic spiral motif prominent. It is 51ft (15.6m) long, and 41ft (12.6m) wide. The adjoining Far East temple here is smaller at 39ft (12.0m) long, and was probably once 19ft (6.0m) at its widest. In about 3200 BC, the largest temple, Tarxien Central, was inserted between the South and East ones. Its entrance led from the southern end, and it features six apses within a total length of 75ft (23m) and a width of 61ft (18.6m).

Megalithic temple architecture on Malta and Gozo is unique to the islands and justly famous. Although Sicily is only some 62 miles (100km) away, there is nothing of it to be found there. The Maltese builders used their stone in an amazingly sophisticated manner from about 3600 BC, some 1400 years after the first Neolithic farmers settled on the island. No more than 20 foreign pottery sherds (of Sicilian origin) have ever been found, compared with thousands of fragments of indigenous ware.

Skorba, another Maltese site, has produced an early date of about 4000 BC. Rock-cut tombs were probably being used for collective burials at much the same time as at TRANCHINA, Sciacca, Sicily, and were probably inspired by Sicilian immigrants. By this time large-scale temple building was commencing, with the subterranean trefoil plans made of massive cyclopean masonry going up above ground. Skorba West is a trefoil temple where the end apse later acquired an internal open doorway. Five-apsed temples followed (*see* GGANTIJA, Gozo).

In later temples, the end apse shrank in size, so that, by the time of the unique six-apsed Tarxien Central, it had become a cupboard-like extension only, perhaps a sanctuary, the innermost sacred shrine. There seems little doubt that the Tarxien constructions, like most of the 30 or so on the island, were never used for funerary purposes. They incorporated, from the beginning, altars, statues, 'oracle holes', and shrine areas. The earliest are believed to be among the oldest above-ground, roofed buildings in the world.

Although constructed soon after the very earliest megalithic tombs in north-west Europe, these temples were immensely more sophisticated in their design and layout. It seems that there really were architects and master carvers at work, at least at Tarxien, which is the best decorated temple group on Malta or Gozo. Interestingly, a fragment of a clay model for a building (now in Valletta Museum), showing rectangular rooms and doorways, has been discovered at Tarxien. Perhaps it was too advanced for its time, because no such building has ever been found. Nevertheless, the main façade at Tarxien, with its raised trilithon doorway and courses of immaculate cyclopean masonry, was once a mighty and beautiful thing.

V.18

ANGHELU RUJU

This cemetery is one of the best-known in Sardinia. On this site, which was formerly a quarry, more than 35 tombs have been found, made from sandstone extracted from the fields around. They share some common design features – such as steps down from the entrance, and then a descending passage to a large burial chamber, with small chambers leading off it. The main chamber's closing slabs were often decorated and were surrounded by a sort of trilithon carved in relief.

A particular feature of the carvings are long-horned bulls' heads in low relief, and they were sometimes painted in red ochre. These cult symbols, which occur in Tombs 19, 20 and 30, for example, have been interpreted in different ways. Mycenaean influence is naturally detected, but the finds here date at around 2900 BC, which is too early for that theory.

The exotic array of artefacts include obsidian, barbed and tanged flint arrowheads, an axe and awl from Ireland, maceheads and a ring from East Europe, copper-tanged daggers from Spain (*see* LOS MILLARES, Spain), spiral wire beads, buttons, small marble statuettes, and stone bracers.

Pottery finds included Beaker ware, Chassey ware (Neolithic pottery found all over France; the type site, Chassey-le-Camp, is west of Dijon in central France and the ware reached Sardinia during the Ozieri culture), and Ozieri (or San Michele) ware (Copper Age Sardinian pottery showing links with the Maltese Tarxien Cemetery phase [about 2500–1500 BC]). Some of these finds can now be seen in the Museo Nazionale, Sassari.

Marked on the map 'Necrop Anghelu Ruiu'. Leave the coastal north-west town of Alghero northwards towards Porto Torres. The cemetery is on the left after about 5¹⁄₂ miles (9km).

The antechambers and oval main chambers were originally roofed in this cemetery of more than 35 tombs. Most had steps leading down to their entrances.

ENA'E MUROS

*Ossi,
Sassari*

LONG CIST (TOMBA A
POLIANDRA)

86 D 5

This is one of over 200 such cists in Sardinia, dating from the early nuragic period. In Sardinian this site's name implies a large number of bodies, and, indeed, more than 30 skeletons were found at this site. A most unusual feature here is the fine collection of pottery found with the burials. It was Bonnanaro ware, dated to about 1750 BC, and named after the rock-cut tomb in which it was first discovered.

What today would be regarded as a full set of kitchenware was evidently carefully designed, manufactured, sold or exchanged, and also exported to Italy. It has been found in giants' tombs on this island (*see* LI-LOLGHI, Arzachena). Although the surfaces are undecorated, there is a definite style in the basic shapes of upturned handles, drinking cups, cooking and serving pots; one notable example is a fine, handled serving bowl supported on three square legs. The pottery's brown finish has a 20th-century look, and is in striking contrast to the much more decorative and colourful Monte Claro ware (local Sardinian pottery dated to about 1850 BC but perhaps earlier), of which sherds have also occurred at Ena'E Muros.

Take the minor twisting road southwards out of Sassari, under the 131 main road, to Ossi. In the village turn left for Muros, just down the road.

LI-LOLGHI

Arzachena

GIANT'S TOMB

87 I 3

*Signposted, and near
Li-muri — see below.*

Giants' tombs (*tomba di giganti*) were constructed all over Sardinia by the *nuraghi* builders for some 1000 years from about 1900 BC until the destructive invasion by Carthage. Their collective burial chambers were long, with upright slabs, and covered with stone or earth, and robustly kerbed.

The tombs generally featured a horned semi-circular forecourt, which, as elsewhere in both the Mediterranean and

north-west Europe, was doubtless used as an open arena or meeting place for ritual, forms of worship and/or celebration.

The boat shapes of the wedge ends of the tombs are reminiscent of the Minorcan *navetas* (*see* ELS TUDONS, Ciutadela), which some think might have inspired them; others believe that giants' tombs are indigenous developments of the earlier dolmens.

Construction probably began at Li-lolghi in about 1500 BC; the passage-grave is about 88ft 6in (27m) long in total. Its gallery is 49ft (15m) long, and some 5ft (1.5m) in width. The paved, raised chamber at the end of it is a further 13ft (4.0m) long, and, most interestingly, cathedral-style, has an ambulatory around it.

LI-MURI

*St Oddastru,
Arzachena*

STONE PLATFORMS
WITH CISTS AND
GIANT'S TOMB

87 I 3

In the far north-east of the island, a third of the way along the road from Arzachena leading to Luogosanto, and signposted to the right; far up a trackway, through farmland, over a wall to the right. 20 mintues from the car park.

This is a high, remote and dramatic site. Though tentatively dated at 2500 BC, work probably began here some 1000 years earlier, making it the oldest megalithic site in Sardinia.

There are four distinct but intersecting circular stone platforms here (and remains of at least one more), which recall common walls elsewhere, notably at the large cemetery at SON

REAL, Majorca. Each of them has a *coffre* (an open-ended high-sided rectangular stone slab cist) at its centre, the open ends of which, in three, lie in the northerly direction. There are another eight or so around the circles.

The largest circle is the western one at about 25ft (7.6m) across. Finds here include human bones in one *coffre*, and the usual motley hoard of pottery sherds, beads, polished axes, perforated maceheads, flint knives, obsidian flakes, and a steatite cup. It is impossible to say whether or not collective burials took place here.

Near the Li-muri circles is a Giant's Tomb which is worth viewing. It must have been a massive structure when its original earth mound covered it. However, all the stone constructions in this area are now in poor condition, partly due to the simple passage of time in the harsh, baking Mediterranean climate, and also because of the islanders' ancient belief that treasures still lie hidden in these resting places.

MONTE D'ACCODDI

*Porto Torres,
Sassari*

TEMPLE MOUND

86 C 5

The temple mound area is also host to a mysterious stone.

This is a puzzling place. The high, broad and most peaceful setting is host to an earth mound with nothing inside it. It is just possible that there may be a concealed entrance, but it remains to be discovered. It is two-tiered, square, 29ft 6in (9m) high, and its very substantial cyclopean drystone walling is 121ft (37m) along a side. A similarly kerbed broad earth ramp leads to the top of the mound from the south. Perhaps it was a sighting platform, or a place for initiation or fertility rituals (with spectators standing on the surrounding tier ledge).

A number of standing stones are to be found in the area around the mound, but their association, if any, is unclear. Just to the east of the ramp lies a beautiful dome-shaped stone, like a flattened planet.

Take the 131 south-east from Porto Torres (on the north-west coast) towards Sassari. After about 3¾ miles (6km), take the signposted track on the right to the site.

SANT' ANASTASIA

Sárdara,
Campidano

WELL TEMPLE

90 D 2

Not marked on the map. Take the 131 north from Cagliari for 33 miles (53km), and then turn off for the village of Sádara where the church is.

Campidano is the undulating farmland which stretches from the River Tirso in the north to Cagliari in the south. This is a prehistoric spa, and the earliest of many in Sardinia. It takes its name from the nearby church, which is dedicated to a saint now rarely commemorated except in Byzantine churches. The

church dates back to about 7th–8th century AD, but the tradition of healing at the waters goes back at least a thousand years before them.

Steps beneath ground level descend to the well, which was once covered by a stone roof in the form of a cupola. A stone building stood at ground level. The area around the well was quite large and paved – implying the 'use' of the waters by many people at the same time.

Finds have been made in a pit in front of the well; they include nuragic pottery sherds, animal bones and much decorated pottery, which confirm its long use. Also, excavated was the rough outline of a stone bull's head, which perhaps clarifies the dedication of that church. Other fine sacred wells in Sardinia (among 30 or so) include Santa Vittoria, Serri, and Su Tempiesu, Orune.

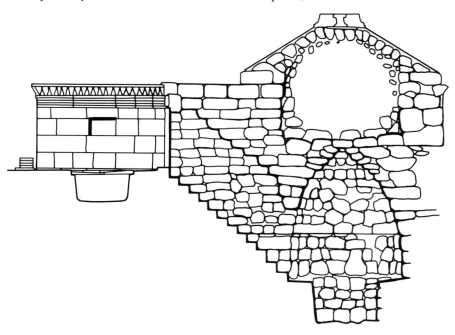

SANT' ANTINE

Torralba,
Thiesi

NURAGHE

88 D 2

Nuraghi are Late Neolithic high, round, stone defensive towers, peculiar to Sardinia; this is one of about 6500 on the island, and in better repair than most. They are somewhat similar to, but more elaborate than the *talayots* of the Balearic Islands and the *torri* of Corsica. (The medieval peel towers on the borders of England and Scotland served similar purposes.) This one is set on a larger, triangular tower, and, like most, it is built of cyclopean drystone.

Some *nuraghi* were quite complex, such as Palmavera, Alghero. The formidable stonework gave adequate defence for the chambered living quarters in these towers. The cyclopean walls surrounding their settlements complete a profile of a warring people, intent on preserving territorial gains.

The *nuraghi* culture on Sardinia reached its height during 1100–600 BC. Other *nuraghi* near Sant' Antine are Ránas, Monte Longo, two separate Tres Nuraghes, Póltolu, S'Ena, Sant' Sisto, and Oes (very near this one). The Italian Touring Club 1:200,000 map is recommended to *nuraghi* hunters.

Take the 131 road south-east from Sassari. Nuraghi are visible either side of the road. Turn off the road at Mores, and take the minor road west and south. Go through Torralba village, and take the third turning left, under the 131. The nuraghe is now on the right, before the railway station.

SICILY

CASTELLUCCIO

V.25

Castelluccio,
Noto,
Siracusa

ROCK-CUT CHAMBER
TOMBS

85 G 5

The useful Italian Touring Club 1:200,000 map labels this site a prehistoric village which it never was. The present village occupies the top of a rocky spur. According to Professor Bernabo Brea the Castelluccian culture flourished broadly between pre-2000–1400 BC, but it may well have started earlier. This site gives its name to a buff-coloured pottery, bearing simple linear patterns painted in black, which perhaps betrays Greek inspiration. It is physically related, not to the present village at all, but to the cemetery cut into the limestone walls of the nearby Cava della Signora valley.

The first excavations here were conducted by Professor Paolo Orsi in 1891–92. More than 200 small round oven-shaped (*a forno*) chambers (called *Cava della Signora*), which average 4ft 6in (1.4m) in diameter, were cut into the hillside, often with vestibules beneath galleries 'hanging' over them. One such gallery is supported by four portal stones with carved double spiral motifs. They were collective burial tombs and, after use, were sealed with either drystone walling or blocking slabs.

Some of these have finely carved decorations on them, and they are the only examples of prehistoric carving to be found

Leave Noto (near Avola on the south-east coast of the island) on the 115 main road south-west towards Ragusa. After 4¼ miles (7km) turn right, north-west, for 8 miles (13km). Then turn right to the signposted village of Castelluccio.

LEFT: *A carved stone slab from Castelluccio; now in the Museo Nazionale Archeologico in Siracusa, where many examples are held. This 3ft (0.9m) high stone may have blocked a chamber.*

One of more than 200 a forno *tombs cut into the limestone in the Cava della Signora valley.*

Some tombs had less elaborate entrances in the valley cemetery.

anywhere in Sicily. Why this should be is a mystery, unless one allows for a 'closed' community, entirely self-sufficient. These doorway slabs feature a fascinating variety of motifs, but their creators must have travelled, or else been employed outside any such community or tribe, because similar incised and relief designs such as spirals and lozenges are found throughout Europe (*see* GAVR'INIS, Morbihan, France).

Some of the stone slabs here display heads, breasts, and arms uplifted; such captured poses, in an apparent worshipping position, have been found in the Near East, Crete, Malta, Spain, Brittany and Guernsey. The Museo Nazionale Archeologico in Siracusa holds examples. One slab in particular, some 3ft (0.9m) tall, can be closely compared with one at TARXIEN, Malta, and another at ALTAMURA, Italy. Finds, apart from human remains, have included pottery sherds with clear Aegean connections. There were also seven (out of ten found so far in Sicily) of the mysterious, carved bone plaques, found at FILITOSA, Corsica, and elsewhere. Like others, they are 3½ins (8.9cm) long, but showing six, not seven, oval breast-like protuberances, surrounded by finely incised line decorations. Such amulets were burial objects and no sign of human inhabitation has been found here.

THAPSOS

V.26

Thapsos,
Penisola Magnisi,
Siracusa

ROCK-CUT TOMBS

85 I 4

Leave Siracusa (Syracuse) north-west on the coastal road. After about 9m (14km), at Priolo Gargallo, turn east for Thapsos which is 2¾m (4½km) away. The site is signposted.

Sicily is the largest of all the Mediterranean islands, with almost exactly 10,000 sq miles (25,900 sq km) , which is 20% larger than the land area of Wales. Several millennia ago this promontory site was an island in the Golfo di Augusta. Professor Paoloa Orsi, the first great Sicilian archaeologist (who devised the Siculan periods) excavated this perhistoric trading post in 1894; it evidently flourished around 1800–1300 BC. Below the old village, he found hundreds of rock-cut tombs, for which Sicily is famed. There were two types. Those away from the shoreline had vertical entrance shafts, with a convenient carved step. The typical tomb let into the cliffs facing the sea mostly had grooves to accomodate a sealing stone, and then a short passage (*dromos*) giving on to a recessed door case. Beyond was the cool, dark tomb, where pottery was found among the detritus of centuries.

Thapsos is the type site for a local incised grey pottery; it is highly distinctive – delicate bowls set on tall thick cylindrical pedestals, with handles placed high up beneath the rims (excellent examples can be seen in the Museo Nazionale Archeologica, Siracusa). Also occuring in the tombs at Thapsos were Borg in-Nadur pottery from Malta and Mycenaean pottery (dated at 1400–1200 BC).

At Pantalica, north-west of Siracusa (between the villages of Sortina and Ferla), there is a cemetery of some 500 rock-cut tombs on a plateau site overlooking the River Anapo.

TRANCHINA

V.27

Tranchina,
Sciacca,
Agrigento

ROCK-CUT CEMETERY

79 F 5

Tranchina is 7 miles (11km) from Sciacca, on the south-west coast.

years from about 3300 BC.

Of the total number of tombs, 33 had mostly single and some double burials in carved-out holes in their floors. The other three, of a later date, were used for collective burials. The usual range of grave goods was found, and they included broken Bell beakers, flint flakes and metal weapons of war.

Rock-cut chamber tombs, out of all classes of burial place, are the earliest in the central Mediterranean area, and moreover they were used for the longest period of time. Inexplicably, none occur in Corsica. In Sicily, the most common type to be carved out of rock was oven-shaped, *a forno*, which was entered either through the rock face, or through a roof shaft.

There are 36 tombs at this hillside cemetery (sometimes called Sciacca), which was excavated by S. Tinè in 1959. It has subsequently been calculated that it was in use for some 1000

V.28

Carschenna

Sils,
Thusis,
Graubünden

Rock Carvings

Michelin sheet 427:
M 5

There are no less than ten separate rock surfaces at this hard-to-find site, and they are well worth discovering (which, naturally, can only be achieved in the summer months). They are located on the northern side of a mountain overlooking Carschenna and the farmland around. This is no doubt a most difficult megalithic site to locate, but a most attractive one for keep-fit enthusiasts!

The rock surfaces were accidentally uncovered in 1965 by a forest surveyor. Here there are horsemen, cup marks, cup-and-ring marks, concentric circles (plain and divided into quadrants), bulls' eye marks, semi-circles, sun-wheels, both straight and wavy lines – and, of course, spirals, the most ubiquitous and mysterious motif of all.

That these sets of carvings may be maps of sacred places, such as springs, or local spots where lines of an earth energy may intercross, have to remain pure speculation. But the simple fact persists that every one of these strange patterns occurs in prehistoric sites all over the world (see ROUGHTING LINN, England).

Leave Chur (west across the mountains from Davos) on the motorway, going south-westwards, and then south beside the Hinterrheim for about 14 miles (23km). Leave it at the Thusis exit for the short distance east to Sils. Ask for walking directions in the town.

Many authorities think that spiral motifs are related to celestial, especially solar, motions.

LEFT AND BELOW: *Rock surface carvings.*

LE PETIT CHASSEUR

Michelin sheet 427:
G 7

*Sion,
Valais*

CHAMBER TOMBS,
STATUE-MENHIRS AND
CISTS

*One of the many simple four-sided
cists at the second level.*

This important site, by the Rhône, in the Valais, was thoroughly excavated by Olivier Bocksberger, and then by Alain Gallay (with Geneva University). At this oddly-named site ('the little hunter'), there are two stratified levels. The lower has been dated at about 4000 BC, one of the earlier dates in this book; it consisted of a hut settlement, a cemetery of cists, and an alignment of standing stones. The later, higher level has over ten, perhaps 12 cists and megalithic tombs.

The earliest and most impressive is Tomb 6, dated Late Neolithic. It is an extended triangular horned grave, 52ft (15.8m) long, built along a north-south axis, with an antechamber and single capstoned chamber. The entrance, however, is through a holed stone in its eastern flank, and the

The N9 autoroute south from Lausanne, through Montreux and Martigny, ends at Sion. Enter the town on Avenue de France, turn left along Avenue de Petit Chasseur. The restored site is in the courtyard of St. Guérin School, past church. Finds are in the Musée d'Arhéologie, 12 Rue des Chateaux.

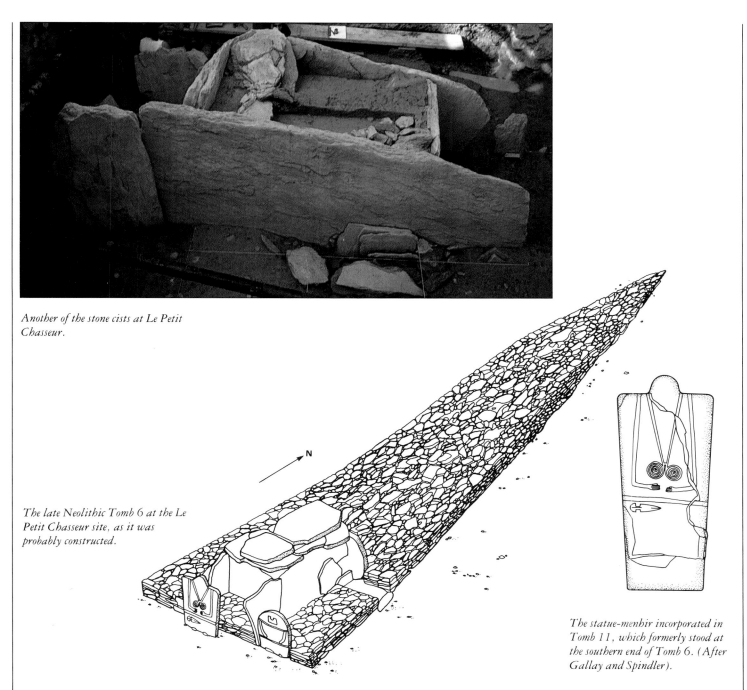

Another of the stone cists at Le Petit Chasseur.

The late Neolithic Tomb 6 at the Le Petit Chasseur site, as it was probably constructed.

The statue-menhir incorporated in Tomb 11, which formerly stood at the southern end of Tomb 6. (After Gallay and Spindler).

general plan shows great affinities with Scandinavian long dolmens. The tomb was later abandoned, and then re-used by the Beaker people in about 2500 BC. Flint daggers have been found here from the great mine and factory of blank and finished pinkish flints at Le Grand Pressigny, Indre-et-Loire, France, which exported flint for megalithic builders' yards all over Europe.

The stone-covered cairn over Tomb 11, on the same site, incorporates decorated statue-menhirs, taken from Tomb 6 and re-used in Tomb 11's construction. Tomb 11 is particularly known for them, and they probably originally stood at the southern end of Tomb 6. They date back to about 3200 BC, and perhaps further. The more elaborate of them (which stands apart from the revetment) features a lower neck, at the top of the stone, and carvings of two arms and hands, a necklace with two ornaments with spiral shapes hanging from it, and finally a dagger.

This secondary placing of anthropomorphic statue-menhirs occurs elsewhere (*see*, for example FILITOSA, Corsica), but this

is one of the earliest dated re-uses.

Stone cists were later dug in against the south-west and south-east sides, and Early Bronze Age pottery vessels were found in the traditional votive position. The capstone has a hole in it, the damage of tomb robbers no doubt, after it was, like Tomb 6, re-used by the Beaker people.

Finds from their burials, apart from human bones, included carvings on boars' tusks and silver earrings; these demonstrate the more elaborate nature of Early Bronze Age burial customs.

There is also evidence, from revealed post-holes, that the tomb site was probably once covered with a wooden roof, and almost certainly ringed with wooden posts.

It is only when such roofing timbers are burnt, and the charcoal remains subsequently preserved in the right soil conditions, that radiocarbon calibrated dating techniques can be applied (*see* DATES AND DATING, pages 12–13). This was possible at a site in Denmark (*see* TUSTRUP GROUP), where the 'temple' was burnt down after, it is thought, a single funerary ceremony.

VI
North Africa

The root of the word Maghreb, which comprises Morocco, Algeria and Tunisia, is the spoken Berber word *gharib*, meaning to travel to the unknown. Tourists are, in ever-increasing numbers, attracted by the harsh and ancient ways. Nomadic life continues away from the great cities, kasbahs and ksour (fortified Berber villages) in accordance with the seasons and market days. Pottery for sale at roadsides is likely to be decorated in styles which are literally thousands of years old. It is a different world on a different continent – and yet the ferry boat takes only 75 minutes to cross from Gibraltar to Tangier. This is the passage where the Mediterranean Sea becomes the Atlantic Ocean, between the two Pillars of Hercules. One of them is the Rock itself; the other is Mount Acho (Abyla), the highest of the seven hills at Ceuta, a visible 14 miles (22.5km) away. Over this short distance many cultural influences and practices have passed.

In comparatively recent times, the contribution of the French Army to the archaeology of its North African colonies has been notable. French tomb builders, some thousand years ago, had brought their funerary habits to the whole of the old Maghreb, and so there still survive local versions of *allées-couvertes*, such as Aït Garet on the Algerian coast, for example, which has a 41ft (12.5m) long, narrow, paved chamber. Egyptology is widely published, but less is known about Libyan megalithic tombs and cemeteries. There are of course riches in stone throughout the African continent; Ethiopia is a scholar's lifetime; the name Zimbabwe means chief's graves and comes from the Shona for stone houses.

Second millennium BC chamber tombs in Morocco, Algeria and Tunisia are concentrated in two broad areas. Those in two coastal districts in northern Morocco are very early in that millennium and unsurprisingly derive from the Iberian peninsula. Then there are the Algerian cemeteries on the central coastal area, and the Tunisian groups to the north. Compared with the coverage of European sites, little has been published in English about them. Even popular accounts of a well-known tourist attraction such as, for instance, DOUGGA (THUGGA) in Tunisia, virtually ignore the 13 Neolithic graves just outside its massive walls.

Berber *djoulas* are fairly simple above-ground dolmenic burial chambers, consisting of uprights and drystone walling, or only the walling, which support capstones (as found throughout Europe); they were not covered by mounds. They are, however, often set on stepped revetted plinths (up to four

in number); this makes them reminiscent of Mediterranean island tomb structures, such as the Sardinian *nuraghi*. Berber tradition has them built by giants, manifesting a common worldwide belief about megalithic monuments which is often reflected in their names.

Berber *redjem* are present in their thousands all over North Africa in raised places. These are simple stone cairns, sometimes shapeless, sometimes made in distinct cones, covering burials, which may be within cists. On precarious sites, such as steep slopes, these may have a revetment of bigger boulders, always undressed. The burials were single or multiple, and with or without poor grave goods. In summary, they varied in both structure and purpose; indeed the more recent Moslem *marabouts* were even placed to mark tribal territorial bounds.

Most countries have indigenous kinds of megalithic burial chambers and other forms of monument. Cyclopean constructions, using very large, precisely fitted, mortar-free blocks of dressed masonry are common throughout the Mediterranean basin and yet, strangely, are almost unknown for funerary purposes in North Africa. There is though a fascinating cyclopean burial chamber at DJEBEL MAZELA, Algeria. *Bazinas* occur at the same site, and Bazina XXII is a beautiful example. Its concentric stepped circles of stone retaining walls, on its sloping position, show great similarities to cairns as far away as the Orkney Islands (Wideford Hill, for example, though this has an entrance passage).

The Algerian *chouchet* (singular *choucha*) are unique to the north-east and Kabylia regions of Algeria and northern Tunisia. These are stone-walled cylinders, rising to about 10ft (3m), capped by one slab, and containing a four-sided chamber just large enough to accommodate a single contracted burial (unlike *bazinas*). The other north African burial tomb is the *hypogeum* (sometimes charmingly called *haouanet*, Arabic for small shops). These Late Bronze Age cliffside tombs greatly resemble Sardinian and Sicilian sites; the oldest African ones have a short passage in front, with a shaped ceiling above it. They are common in northern Tunisia, and on Cap Bon, which faces Pantelleria and Sicily.

Most North African guide books cater for the needs of young travellers. They form much the same market that crowds the Wessex complex of megalithic monuments in England and the hundreds around Carnac, in Brittany, but rarely do guides mention these fascinating sites, lying unregarded a few miles from Europe.

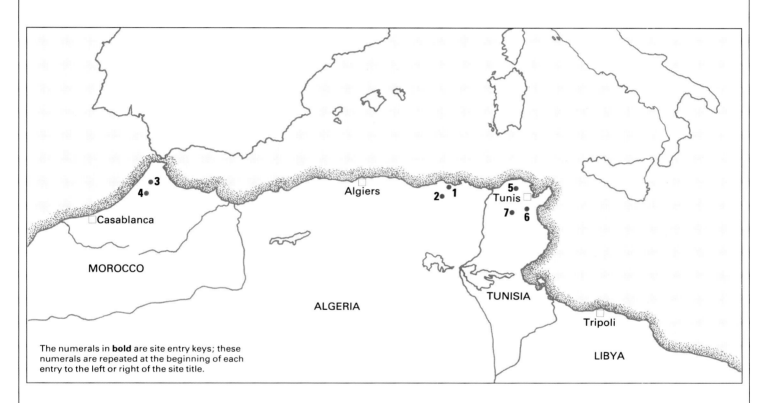

The numerals in **bold** are site entry keys; these
numerals are repeated at the beginning of each
entry to the left or right of the site title.

Map references given in VI.NORTH AFRICA refer to the following maps, which
are available from good bookshops everywhere (and from map specialists
Edward Stanford Ltd, London; see I.BRITISH ISLES map for address).

ALGERIA   Michelin Sheet 972. 1:1,000,000.

MOROCCO   Michelin Sheet 969. 1:1,000,000.

TUNISIA   Michelin Sheet 972. 1:1,000,000.

DJEBEL MAZELA

Bou Nouara,
Oued Berda,
Constantine

MEGALITHIC CEMETERY
(BAZINAS, DJOUALA
AND THE CYCLOPEAN
MONUMENT)

Michelin Sheet 972

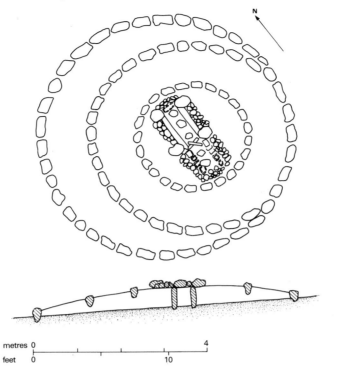

Leave Constantine south-east
on the N3. After 9¼ miles
(15km) turn left on to the
N20. Bou Nouara is about
26¾ miles (43km) away
from Constantine. Ask for
local directions.

Bazina **XXII** *at the megalithic*
cemetery at Djebel Mazela. Its
sloping site is 220yds (200m)
north-east of the Cyclopean
Monument. There were many finds
in the chamber and antechamber,
including (not noted anywhere else
in this book), bird bones. (After G.
Camps).

metres 0   4
feet 0   10

The Djebel (mountain range) Mazela stretches from west to east and south-east, north of the lowland village of Bou Nouara. Lying along it, and a little to the north, east and south of the ridge, is a cemetery which is not only the largest in Algeria but also contains a greater number of tombs than almost anywhere in the world. It is perhaps more important than ROKNIA, located not far away, and is much larger than the other Algerian cemeteries of Beni Messous and Gastel.

Bou Nouara was so-named by Général Faidherbe in his 1868 account of the site, but he was actually referring to a small area on the southern slope near the present village. He could not have known then that the cemetery extends over more than 1000 acres (400 hectares). What is known today about the area is derived from the definitive account by Gabriel and Henriette Camps, following their exhaustive surveys and restoration work in 1954 and 1963. They estimated that there are between 3000 and 4000 tombs, but point out that it is difficult to spot sites from aerial photographs, when they are only 9ft 9in (3m) or so in diameter. Many sites have also been completely destroyed on the lower levels of Djebel Mazela.

The greatest concentration of tombs is in the centre of the range, along the ridge called Chabet-El-Ameur (sometimes Kef-El-Ameur on maps). The Camps actually located a rather grand megalithic entrance to this huge area — and so, again, one is faced with the incontrovertible facts of a high degree of design, order and discipline of Neolithic times. These thousands of tombs would appear to be randomly distributed; often they are only a few feet from each other. Material was easily managed, because the plateau consists of stratified limestone. Finds have been few; through the centuries Berbers have taken all they could find, and even today one is offered potsherds from the tombs.

In their survey the Camps gave an account of only a small number of tombs, the sophistication of which is most impressive. Their Dolmen VIII, for example, is set on a fairly steep slope on a circular platform 13ft (4m) in diameter and has two surrounding stone boulder walls. The exterior one has two courses: apparently the builders put one huge upright wall stone in place and decided not to trim it down to the size of its neighbours, so up went another course of stones to match the height of its top surface! The exterior western faces were neatly dressed, and the whole provided for a horizontal surface into which a dolmenic chamber was placed, so that the capstone alone showed. It measured 7ft 6in (2.3m) in length, and 3ft 3in (1m) in width.

The chamber is rectangular, measures 4ft by 1ft 6in (1.2m by 0.5m), and is orientated exactly north/south (which is *not* dictated by the topography). The rectangular shape is standard here — at ROKNIA, not far away, polygonal chambers are seen. Finds in Dolmen VIII included snail shells, a bowl, potsherds, and, beneath them, human bones (but in poor condition, as always here), and skull fragments. One body had been placed on its side, with its face to the east.

Algeria's chamber tombs are called *bazinas*. They are basically similar to the *djouala* of the Maghreb (that is, a revetted mound, with one or two stepped platforms as it rises, and containing a dolmenic chamber). The *bazina* has a high retaining exterior wall, its shape in plan may be circular or four-sided, and it most often has multiple burials. The Algerian *chouchet*, on the other hand, contain single burials in their 10ft (3m) high cylindrical stone towers.

Bazina XXII on Djebel Mazela overlooks the railway (the construction of which led to the ruin of so many of the tombs on the lower slopes). It is very beautiful in design, taking

perfect account of its location on a slope. The lower platform is 19ft 9in (6m) in diameter. Inside this walled exterior are two concentric stone revetments all to provide rising flat surfaces. The rectangular north/south, chamber measures 4ft 3in by 1ft 3in (1.3m by 0.4m). Its uprights are all surrounded by drystone walling, and there is a small antechamber as well. Finds included disarticulated human bones and teeth, bird bones (an unusual find), and, lower down, a heaped up skeleton. Pottery was found at the south entrance.

The unique Cyclopean Monument lies 220yds (200m)

south-west of this *bazina*; it is a most striking construction, half way down the southern slope on the edge of the ravine. It is rectangular, with walls 6ft 6in (2m) high, 26ft 3in (8m) long and 6ft 6in (2m) wide and its southern wall has three huge courses of boulders, each measuring about 6ft by 3ft 3in by 1ft 9in (1.8m by 1m by 0.5m). It is bordered at the east by large stone blocks 13ft (4m) long, and at the west by blocks 26ft 3in (8m) long: cyclopean indeed!

Djebel Mazela is an ideal candidate for the world's first megalithic park.

ROKNIA

Hammam Chellala (formerly Meskoutine), Constantine

MEGALITHIC CEMETERY (BAZINAS, CHOUCHET AND DJOUALA)

Michelin Sheet 972

Take the N3 south-east out of Constantine near the coast. After 9¼ miles (15km), turn left on to the N20. After another 45 miles (73km), turn off northwards before Guelma on to the W122 to Hammam Chellala (until recently Meskoutine). The signposted site is about 6¾ miles (11km) of twisting road further on.

This remarkable megalithic cemetery lies on the western edge of a plateau, near a precipice overlooking the Oued Roknia. The 'oued' (river bed) runs between Djebel (mountain range) El Grar and Djebel Debar.

This 500ft (153m) high cliff is made of tufa, and is the same dimension in horizontal thickness. This unique stone has been curiously shaped into cones and cliffs, over many millennia by the action of the famous hot springs in the valley below the cemetery. The sulphurous water bubbles up from great fissures in the ground at about 97° Celsius, making it the hottest spring water in the world outside Iceland. Its most famous source is at nearby Hammam Chellala. Until recently this village was called Hammam Meskoutine, meaning 'the

accursed baths'. Hammam is a bathing place and a natural site for settlements. The Romans called the hot spring baths there Aquae Tibilitinae, and they gloried in the great falls of the waters (which are still to be seen today) down the cliff below the Roknia cemetery.

At this site (which was excavated in 1875), it has been estimated that some 3000 burial chambers are made of tufa. This extraordinary estimate dates from the very birth of Algerian archaeology. Before 1859 no dolmens were thought to exist in North Africa (the Maghreb), but in that year a paper was given to The Society of Antiquities, London, entitled 'Ortholithic Remains in North Africa'. Four years later an intrigued archaeologist, Henry Christy, travelled to Algeria, where an Algerian army interpreter led him to Roknia and a personal count of over 1000 dolmens in three days. A report of the expedition by M Féraud was subsequently published which awakened the interest of the academic world.

The cemetery at Roknia mostly comprises simple *djouala*; these chambers consist of a large capstone supported by two or three upright megaliths or drystone walling and are typical of the Maghreb, but reminiscent of the French dolmen or the Welsh cromlech. Burial chambers may also be resting on a one- or two-stepped platform (the Berbers' *choucha*, pl. *chouchet*), or within a close variant (*bazina*). They are not covered by earth mounds or stone cairns. Dated at about 2600 BC, their discernible design influences are from southern Italy, through Malta, and from Sardinia, home of the *nuraghi*. The early estimate of 3000 tombs is probably too high, but as Roknia is littered with megalithic wreckage, the original number will never be known.

MOROCCO

M'ZORA

VI.3

Chouahed,
Asilah,
Larache

STONE CIRCLE [WITH
TWO STANDING STONES]
Michelin Sheet 969

Leave Larache (El Araïche)
on the west coast, and take the
coast road northwards towards
Asilah (Africa's first fully
pedestrianised town). After
15½ miles (25km), take the
turning east towards Tétouan.
Cross the railway line, take

Here is a megalithic surprise! The so-called circle of stones is in fact a perfect ellipse, and is claimed to be the only one in the world outside the British Isles and Brittany, where there are many hundreds. Its dimensions of 177ft (54m), north to south, and 190ft (58m), east to west, indicate the use in the design of Alexander Thom's megalithic yard and the Pythagorean right-angle (long before his time!). There are three or more groups of stones outside the 'circle' as well as a curious earth platform, all of which makes it practically certain that M'zora was a prehistoric lunar or solar observatory, perhaps in use about 4000 years ago. The major axis of the ellipse is directly aligned to the summit of Djebel Si Habib, the highest mountain on that horizon. It is no wonder that M'zora in Arabic means holy place.

This site is also variously spelt M'Sora, M'Zorah, Mçora, Mezora, and Mzoura. It was excavated in 1935–36 by Cesar Luis de Montalban. Strangely, he left no account of his findings; worse, his trenches were not filled in, bequeathing a

the first left, and travel 2½
miles (4km) to a village called
Souk Tnine de Sidi el Yemeni.
With the aid of either a very
detailed map (obtainable in
Rabat or Tangier), or a guide
hired here, make your way 3
miles (5km) north-east over a
maze of rough tracks to the
very small village of
Chouahed and the site.

Part of the ellipse of 167 dressed
stones.

certain disarray inside the circle. There were rumours at the time of a possible sepulchral structure at its centre, but there is no trace of one today.

The elliptical setting consists of no less than 167 dressed monoliths, of varying shapes, mostly circular, ovular and rectangular, with domed tops; their average height is 5ft (1.5m). One of them is heavily cup-marked. On the north side of the 'circle', there is an extraordinary feature; in place of a standard monolith stands El Outed, narrow and 16ft 6in (5m) tall. Its name, which means stake or post (according to local tradition, for a god-king's horse) is sometimes given to the whole site. Beside it is a similar stone, 13ft 9in (4.2m) high. This setting of monoliths is surrounded by a huge wall, made of several courses of precisely shaped rectangular stone blocks. There is a model of this marvellous site in the museum at Tétouan in case you don't feel like reaching it.

VI.4

SIDI SLIMANE

Sidi Slimane,
Meknès

MORTUARY HOUSE

Michelin Sheet 969

The market in Sidi Slimane had to be enlarged in 1939 and, soon after work commenced, workmen revealed a strange rectangular structure to the south of what had appeared to be an earthen mound. It turned out not to be made of stone, but was very similar to the Cyclopean Monument at DJEBEL MAZELA, Algeria. Excavations soon started, led by A. Ruhlmann.

The exterior dimensions are 43ft (13m) long, nearly 28ft (8.5m) wide, and nearly 7ft (2.1m) high. The circular mound in which it was enclosed was made of clayey mud, and was 154ft (47m) in diameter and 19ft 6in (6m) high. It is made of mud bricks in precise courses, with earth as mortar between them, and is in three parts. The antechamber is 17ft (5.2m) long, 4ft (1.2m) wide at the entrance, tapering to 3ft 3in (1m) at the other end. Inside there are vertical grooves which held wooden posts, and an extended skeleton, lying on its left side was found. Was it perhaps a sleeping guard?

Next came the sepulchral chamber; on the wooden threshold to this lay another extended skeleton, without weapons. The chamber is 9ft (2.8m) long, 4ft (1.2m) wide, and 6ft 6in (2.0m) high. At the end was the funerary chamber, 10ft (3m) long and 9ft 9in (3m) wide. At the far end of this almost square chamber there was a shelf, similar to an altar and the floor was paved. The ceiling was formed by six tree trunks, covered in beaten earth. Two skeletons were found here, under the paving.

The distance from Tangier to Meknès, via Ksar-el-Kebir and Sidi Kacem, is 165 miles (265km). Sidi Slimane is north of Sidi Kacem; ask for local directions there.

Skeletons have been found in this mortuary house.

184
NORTH
AFRICA
Tunisia

TUNISIA

VI.5

Äin el Hadjar

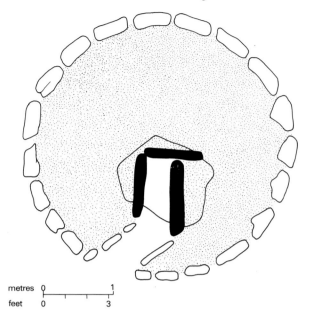

metres 0   1
feet   0   3

*Mateur is on the GP11 which
leads south-westwards from
the northern coastal town of
Bizerte.*

These two *djouala* are the most westerly to be found in Tunisia, and they probably represent the earliest form of North African burial chamber. This type (the simplest dolmen form) has a circular mound with a roofless passage leading to a central chamber, and *djouala* like this are also found in the cemetery of Tayadirt, Moyen Atlas, Morocco.

One at this site has 20 boulders in a circle enclosing the mound. Unlike its companion, the very short entrance passage (three stones on the left and just one large one on the right) is angled south-west to the rectangular chamber.

The other *djouala* is also circular, with a neat revetment of 56 small boulders and a straight, longer passage to the rectangular chamber. The unroofed passage is partly paved and has eight pairs of opposing small uprights. The tomb is sealed at the chamber entrance with drystone walling. Four slabs, which include a particularly large one directly opposite the entrance, form this late Neolithic capstoned chamber.

Berbers believe *djouala* were constructed by giants.

Dougga (thugga)

Dougga (its Latin name *Thugga* is still often used) is justly famed for some of the finest and most extensive Roman ruins in all North Africa. They are set on a plateau and steep hillside overlooking the Oued Khaled valley to the west of the old road from Carthage to Theveste. The site goes back to Neolithic times, but eventually became a Numidian settlement, under Carthaginian influence, until the third century AD. Roman colonists came, and Septimus Severus united the populations, and created a beautiful city. Visitors passing through it to the megalithic cemetery can see many of the splendid remains.

The only surviving wall section of the earlier Numidian settlement is at the northern and highest part of the plateau. Its 426ft (130m) length overlooks a cemetery of 13 dolmens, located north-east of the Temple of Minerva. They naturally predate the classical ruins all around, probably at about 1500–1000 BC. Among the finds in the cemetery have been human bones, funerary urns, Italian potsherds, unguent bottles and Punic coins and are in the Bardo Museum, Tunis.

Among the grave sites, there is one with two chambers inside a ring of 17 stone boulders; one of the chambers is directly north of the other. Both consist simply of three upright slabs forming three sides of a square, with the fourth sides open precisely to the east.

*Take the GP5 south-west out
of Tunis. After about 37
miles (60km) follow the same
road off to the south at
Medjez-El-Bab. About 22
miles (35km) later, turn right
on to the MC75 to Téboursouk
4½ miles (7km) away.
Dougga (Thugga) is clearly
signposted there just to the
south of the town.*

VI.7

ELLÈS

185
NORTH
AFRICA
Tunisia

*Ksour Toual,
Maktar*

DJOUALA (DOLMENS)
Michelin Sheet 972

This is the most important group of *djouala* in Tunisia, and perhaps in North Africa. An 1882 report by the archaeologist Professor J. Poinssot mentions 15 of them; today, just three, may be four, survive. They were first discovered by an American explorer, Frederick Catherwood, in 1839; his published plan of the best preserved of them was not very accurate, but a single accompanying comment rings true: 'I found this edifice inhabited by two Arab families, and the tradition is that it was always thus'.

This 'edifice' apart, the *djouala* are very similar in design and construction to the French *allées-couvertes*. They are up to 13ft (4m) in length and incorporate broad slabs and porticos.

The incomplete tomb mentioned by Catherwood is set on a slope, with compensating foundations. Either side of a narrow passage there are side chambers; five to the right and three to the left. At the passage end is a closing stone; there was also a now-vanished perambulatory apse beyond the stone, and possibly also an altar stone.

The exterior uprights supporting the roofing slabs in the style of trilithons, are huge dressed rectangular stones, with their broader faces inwards/outwards. The present structure measures 57ft 6in by 41ft (17.5m by 12.5m). This really is a unique megalithic structure, a second millennium BC achievement that is truly monumental in its formality.

The most monumental of the Tunisian djouala, *discovered by the American Frederick Catherwood in 1839.*

Leave Tunis on GP3, via the very beginning of the motorway (which runs south-east to Hammamet). After 33 miles (53km), at El Fahs, turn south-west on to the GP4. After 62 miles (110km), before reaching Maktar, turn north-west on to the GP12 towards Le Kef. After 17 miles (27km), at Ksour Toual, turn directly south to Ellès as signposted.

A Glossary of Terms

POULNABRONE, a fine restored portal-tomb on The Burren, a famous limestone pavement south of Ballyvaughan in County Clare, Ireland. It has been dated at about 2500 BC.

Alignment More or less straight row of standing stones.

Allée-coudée Allée-couverte with passage leading off at right angles before one end.

Allée-couverte French for stretched rectangular Late Neolithic megalithic burial chamber, beneath long mound.

Anta Portuguese for burial chamber.

Antechamber First section of tomb, with same width and height as chamber.

Anthropomorphic With human attributes.

Archaeo-astronomy Science of prehistoric astronomy, using megalithic sites. (Preferred to Astro-archaeology).

Arrowhead Made of bone, metal or stone (flint); occurs in many shapes, such as barbed-and-tanged, hollow-based, and tranchet.

Artefact Man-made object.

Assemblage Group of different but associated objects.

Avenue Two parallel rows of standing stones.

Awl Sharp point of bone, flint or metal, for making holes.

Barrow Round or long mound of earth over burial chamber or deposit. Many different shapes and often surrounded by a ditch.

Bazina North African concentric stepped circle of well-built stone walls over burial.

Beaker folk Prehistoric makers and distributors of distinctive pottery and copper artefacts all over Europe. Origins still uncertain and controversial.

Beaker Ware Generally handless deep pottery drinking vessels, or beakers, with many designs.

Betyl Small stone pillar, probably sacred, and often conical.

Bossed bone plaque Long animal bone with row of carved round or oval bosses, or 'breasts', in varying small numbers. Often finely decorated; function unknown.

Broch Scottish circular drystone fortified homestead.

Bronze Alloy of copper (dominant) and tin or lead.

Cairn Round or long mound of stones, often covering chamber or burial (sometimes used for earth mound).

Calibration Mathematical calculation in radiocarbon dating (see 'Dates and Dating').

Callais Western European greenish stone bead.

Capstone Horizontal stone on top of chamber or passage; dressed or otherwise.

Cardium Latin for cockle; shell edge used for decorating Impressed Ware.

Carination Distinct beaked profile of vessel and spout.

Chalcolithic Age between Neolithic and Bronze (sometimes Copper); used outside Britain.

Chambered cairn Chamber tomb covered with stones.

Chamber tomb Common form of tomb, comprising orthostats, sometimes with interstices filled with drystone walling, and megalithic capstone over burial chamber approached by passage.

Chassey French Middle Neolithic culture with several phases and pottery decoration designs.

Chevron V-shaped carving motif.

Chouche North African stone-walled cylinder containing four-sided burial chamber.

Cist Small box-like square or rectangular burial place.

Coffre Open-ended cist (Sardinian).

Collective tomb Contains more than one burial.

Compartment Internal sub-division of burial place.

Contiguous Adjoining, touching.

Corbelled Beehive-shaped style of roofing; each rising stone course projects inwards over one below, until one or two stones close it.

Court cairn Kind of long chamber tomb occurring in northern Ireland and south-west Scotland. Generally more elaborate than horned cairns.

Cremation Burning of the dead, before burial or disposal. Ashes often placed in urns.

Cromlech Dolmen in Wales; stone circle in France.

Crook Megalithic art motif, like walking stick handle.

Cueva Spanish for chambered mound.

Cup mark Cup shaped depression carved out from stone.

Cup-and-ring mark One or more concentric rings around a cup mark; sometimes with groove slashed out from cup centre.

Cursus Generally very long Middle Neolithic rectangular enclosure formed by parallel earthen banks with external ditches. Function unknown.

Cyclopean Substantial stone walling of large blocks fitted together, in courses, without mortar.

Danubian culture One name for first farming culture of eastern and central Europe.

Diffusion Spread of cultural influences

from places of origin. Subject of continual debate among archaeologists.

Discarnation Divestiture of flesh, by natural or manual means.

Djoula North African above ground burial chamber, without mound, often set on revetted plinth.

Dolmen Simple megalithic burial chamber with three or more uprights and one or more capstones.

Dressed stone Manually shaped and smoothed.

Dromos Entrance passage to tholos burial chamber.

Drystone walling Without any form of mortar.

Dun Small Scottish and Irish fortified structure with internal galleries and rooms.

Dyss Danish burial chamber.

Eclipse Partial, total or annular interception of light of sun by moon to earth, or of light of moon by earth's shadow before sun. Very important event in prehistory, and probably much feared.

Enclosure Area bounded by stones or earth banks.

Entrance grave Sometimes called Undifferentiated Passage Grave; no distinction between passage and chamber, within round mound.

Faience Baked clay and sand, becoming glass-like, in blues and greens.

False entrance Dummy entrance opposite real one in chambered long barrow.

Fogou Cornish name for souterrain.

Forecourt External concave entrance area of tomb.

Funnel beaker Vessel with expanded neck. In German Trichterbecher (TRB), which gave its name to early Neolithic culture in north Europe.

Gallery grave Stretched rectangular megalithic burial chamber, beneath long mound.

Ganggrab German passage grave.

Ganggrift Swedish passage grave.

Grave goods Artefacts buried with dead.

Grooved Ware Type of Late Neolithic pottery pre-dating Beaker Ware.

Hallstatt Austrian salt mines and cemetery which gave name to European Late Bronze Age periods (A and B).

Head stone Faces tomb entrance.

Henge Almost unique Late Neolithic British earth enclosure of bank and ditch (usually internal). Class I has single entrance; Class II has two or more entrances.

Horned cairn Partly enclosed façade of cairn; can be at front and back.

Hügel German tumulus or mound.

Hunebed Burial chamber type most often found in The Netherlands; long narrow chamber of trilithons, within kerbed mound, with entrance on one long side.

Hünengrab German equivalent of hunebed.

Hougue French dialect word for tumulus or mound, from Old Norse haugre (eminence); howe in Scotland.

Hypogeum Large underground

chamber, often carved out of rock; generally for burials.

Incised pottery Decorated by deep cuts in soft clay before baking.

Inhumation Burial of dead body (as opposed to exposure or cremation). Position may be extended, flexed, or crouched, and prone, supine, or on side.

Impressed Ware First Neolithic farmers' pottery.

Interstice Intervening space.

Jaettestue Danish passage grave.

Jet Black soft stone.

Kerb Ring of retaining stones against mound or cairn base.

Lagozza Italian Neolithic culture type site.

La Tène Swiss type site providing name of post-Hallstatt European Iron Age.

Lateral chamber Chamber set in side of tomb.

Le Grand Pressigny Unique French source of fine, honey-coloured flint.

Lintel Horizontal stone across tops of two orthostats (forming trilithon).

Lozenge Diamond-shaped carving motif.

Lug Handle on pottery.

Megalith Great stone; sometimes wrongly used to describe megalithic monument.

Megalithic yard Alexander Thom's proposed prehistoric unit of measurement, equivalent to 2.72ft (0.829m).

Mesolithic Middle Stone Age, between Palaeolithic and Neolithic.

Menhir French word for single standing stone, but sometimes used loosely for other megalithic monuments.

Michelsberg Low Countries' Neolithic culture.

Microlith Very small stone implement.

Midden Domestic or food refuse heap.

Monolith Single stone block, monument or pillar.

Mortuary house Sepulchre in shape of building made of stone or wood; for temporary body storage.

Mound Of either earth or stone pebbles or rubble, generally covering burial chamber or deposit.

Naveta Minorcan cyclopean upturned-boat-shaped chamber.

Neolithic Period when settled farming superseded nomadic life.

Nuraghe Sardinian round cyclopean tower.

Obsidian Very hard volcanic glass used for tools. It can be dated by measurement of thickness of its hydration layer on surface.

Ochre Natural red or yellow oxides of iron, used for art, and most probably body painting.

Oculus Common eye-like carved motif of paired spirals and circles.

Ogham (ogam) Ancient alphabet, in which letters are formed of parallel lines which meet or cross a base-line. Possibly of Irish origin.

Orientation Positioned to face a certain direction, not only the east.

Ossuary Place for human bones.

Outlier Single stone away from main setting (generally a circle).

Passage grave Passage (sometimes with lateral chambers) leading to broader burial chamber, often roofed, within round mound (which may be kerbed). Façaded forecourt entrance common.

Paving Stone slabs on passage and chamber floors.

Pecking Hammered shapes or decorations on stone.

Peristalith Retaining kerbstones around barrow or cairn.

Pietrafitta Italian standing stone (plural pietrefitte; sometimes two words).

Plaque — see Bossed bone plaque.

Portal dolmen Rectangular burial chamber which is narrower and lower towards back, with two portal stones at entrance. Mainly Irish and Welsh.

Port-hole Circular hole, often in entrance stone to chamber tomb, or made by semi-circular holes in facing contiguous stones. Also in orthostats and capstones.

Portico Entrance porch.

Post hole Socket for wooden post.

Potsherd Fragment of pottery.

Primary burial (or interment) Burial for which surrounding structure was initially created.

Quoit Cornish name for burial chamber.

Radiocarbon date Derived from techniques for measuring Carbon 14 remaining in organic matter. See 'Dates and Dating' at the beginning of this book.

Recumbent stone circle Unique Scottish and Irish circles with one large stone lying horizontally between two uprights.

Redjem Simple North African stone cairn covering burial (sometimes within cist), often on raised site.

Revetment Retaining wall of stones around base of mound.

Rock-cut tomb Chamber tomb cut out of solid rock.

Roofing slab Another name for capstone.

Sarsen Sandstone lying on Wiltshire Downs; used for Stonehenge and Avebury, though not exclusively.

Schist Fine-grained rock, altered after formation by heat or pressure or both, so that mineral content is in roughly parallel layers. Can therefore be split into thin plates.

Secondary burial Follows primary or first use of grave site.

Segmented cist With internal compartments.

Seine-Oise-Marne (SOM) culture Latest Neolithic culture phase in Paris Basin; gallery graves with port-hole slabs, which occur elsewhere.

Septal slab Slab set in ground dividing internal chamber compartment.

Serra d'Alto Southern Italian type site for pottery with geometrical patterns.

Sese Bronze Age tomb on island of Pantelleria.

Severn-Cotswold tomb Early Neolithic gallery-type grave, located east and west of Bristol Channel, England.

Shaft-and-chamber tomb Burial

chamber opening to side of pit bottom.

Sherd Sometimes shard. Broken piece of pottery.

Shield/idol Carved abstract version of anthropomorphic figure, as idol.

Slab Flat thinnish dressed stone.

Socket hole For holding orthostat.

Souterrain Underground megalithic storage room in prehistoric settlements.

Specchia Southern Italian stone cairn monument, sometimes with burial.

Spiral Common decoration motif carved on stone; sometimes interconnected. Meaning unknown.

Standing stone Lone vertical stone; see Menhir.

Statue-menhir Stone slab or pillar with anthropomorphic carving.

Stazzone Sardinian dolmen.

Stele Small stone slab or pillar, sometimes carved with abstract or literal decoration.

Stone circle Ring, which may not be circular, of spaced or contiguous standing stones; sometimes roughly (and very rarely completely) dressed.

Stone row Sometimes alignment. Line of regularly spaced standing stones.

Stratigraphy Interpretation of layered deposits.

Talayot Balearic circular cyclopean tower, sometimes with internal chamber, and corbelled roofing.

Taula Catalan for table. Minorcan vertical dressed pillar supporting dressed horizontal block.

Temple General term for megalithic buildings; used especially in Malta.

Thermoluminescence (TL) — see 'Dates and Dating' at the beginning of this book.

Tholos Greek for corbelled roof. Now name of bee-hive shaped burial chamber so roofed.

Three Age System Division by Thomsen in 1816–19 of prehistory into Stone, Bronze and Iron Ages.

Timber lacing Wooden framework strengthening earth or stone structure.

Tomba di giganti Sardinian chamber tomb.

Torre Corsican round cyclopean tower with single room.

TRB Commonly used initials for Trichterbecher (German for funnel beaker), the first northern European Neolithic culture, which developed in several phases and directions.

Transept Side chamber.

Trilithon Two orthostats with lintel across them.

Tumulus Latin for mound or barrow; generally covers a burial, in a chamber (as in French use of word) or not.

Upright Colloquial term for orthostat.

Vitrification Fusing together of stones by heat.

Wedge tomb Irish type of chamber tomb which tapers slightly from entrance inwards beneath mound; sometimes with parallel outer walls either side.

Wheelhouse Scottish Iron Age circular stone house with internal walls radiating from the centre.

Further Reading

Alimen, H., *The Prehistory of Africa*, Hutchinson, London 1957

Atkinson, R.J.C., *Stonehenge*, Pelican, London (2nd Ed.) 1979

Baillie, M.G.L., *Tree-ring Dating and Archaeology*, Croom Helm, London 1982

Balfour, Michael, *Stonehenge and its Mysteries*, Hutchinson, London (2nd Ed.) 1983

Barber, Chris, *Mysterious Wales*, David & Charles, Newton Abbot 1982

– , and Williams, John Godfrey, *The Ancient Stones of Wales*, Blorenge Books, Abergavenny, Wales 1989

Bender, Barbara (with Cailland, Robert), *The Archaeology of Brittany, Normandy, and the Channel Islands*, Faber and Faber, London 1986

Bord, Janet and Colin, *Ancient Mysteries of Britain*, Grafton, London 1986

– , *A Guide to Ancient Sites in Britain*, Paladin, London 1979

Bray, W. & Trump, D., *A Dictionary of Archaeology*, Allen Lane, London 1970

Brea, L. Bernabo, *Sicily Before the Greeks*, Thames and Hudson, London, Rev. Ed., 1966

Brennan, Martin, *The Boyne Valley Vision*, The Dolmen Press, Portlaoise, Ireland 1980

– , *The Stars and the Stones*, Thames and Hudson, London 1983

Burgess, Colin, *The Age of Stonehenge*, J.M. Dent, London 1980

Burl, Aubrey, *The Stone Circles of the British Isles*, Yale University Press, London 1976

– , *Prehistoric Avebury*, Yale University Press, London 1979

– , *Rings of Stone*, Frances Lincoln/ Weidenfeld & Nicholson, London 1979

– , *Megalithic Brittany*, Thames and Hudson, London 1985

– , *The Stonehenge People*, J. M. Dent, London 1987

Camps, Gabriel, and others, *Atlas Préhistorique de la Tunisie*, Vol.8, Maktar, Rome 1985

– , and Camps- Fabrer, Henriette, *La Nécropole Mégalithique du Djebel Mazela à Bou Nouara*, Arts Et Métiers Graphiques, Paris 1964

Cartailhac, M. Émile, *Les Ages Préhistoriques de l'Espagne et du Portugal*, Ch. Reinwald, Paris 1886

Champion, T., Gamble, C., Shennan, S., and Whittle, Alasdair, *Prehistoric Europe*, Academic Press, London 1984

Chippindale, Chris, *Stonehenge Complete*, Thames and Hudson, London 1983

Collum, V.C.C., *The Tressé Iron-Age Megalithic Monument*, Oxford University Press 1935

Crawford, O.G.S., *The Eye Goddess*, Phoenix House, London 1957

Daniel, Glyn, *The Prehistoric Chamber Tombs of France*, Thames and Hudson, London 1960

– , *The Megalithic Builders of Western Europe*, Hutchinson, London (2nd

Ed.) 1962

Darvill, Timothy, *Prehistoric Britain*, B.T. Batsford, London 1987

De Laet, S.J., *The Low Countries*, Thames and Hudson, London 1958

Dyer, James, *Discovering Archaeology in Denmark*, Shire Publications, Princes Risborough 1972

– , *The Penguin Guide to Prehistoric England and Wales*, Allen Lane, London 1981

Ellis Davidson, H.R., *Pagan Scandinavia*, Thames and Hudson, London 1967

Evans, J.D., *Malta*, Thames and Hudson, London 1959

Farinha dos Santos, M., *Pre-Historia de Portugal*, Editorial Verbo, Lisbon (2nd Rev. Ed.) 1974

Feacham, Richard, *Guide to Prehistoric Scotland*, B.T. Batsford, London (2nd Rev. Ed.) 1977

Fergusson, James, *Rude Stone Monuments in all Countries*, Murray, London 1872

Gibson, Alex, and Woods, Ann, *Prehistoric Pottery for the Archaeologist*, Leicester University Press 1990

Glob, P.V., *Danish Prehistoric Monuments*, Faber, London 1971

Guido, Margaret, *Sardinia*, Thames and Hudson, London 1963

– , *Sicily : An Archaeological Guide*, Faber and Faber, London 1967

– , *Southern Italy : An Archaeological Guide*, Faber and Faber 1972

Hadingham, Evan, *Ancient Carvings in Britain : A Mystery*, Garnstone Press, London 1974

Harbison, Peter, *Guide to the National Monuments in the Republic of Ireland*, Gill & Macmillan, Dublin 1970

– , *Pre-Christian Ireland*, Thames and Hudson, London 1988

Hawkins, Gerald, *Stonehenge Decoded*, Souvenir Press, London 1966

Henshall, Audrey, *The Chambered Tombs of Scotland*, 2 Vols, Edinburgh University Press 1963 and 1972

Johnson, Walter, *Byways in British Archaeology*, Cambridge University Press 1912

Johnston, David E., *The Channel Islands : An Archaeological Guide*, Phillimore, Chichester 1981

Joussaume, Roger, *Dolmens for the Dead*, B.T. Batsford, London 1988

Klok, R.H.J., *Hunebedden in Nederland : Zorgen voor Morgen*, Fibula-Van Dishoeck, Haarlem, 1979

Leisner, Georg and Vera, *Die Megalithgräber der Iberischen Halbinsel*, Berlin 1943 and 1946

Lockyer, Sir J. Norman, *Stonehenge and other British Monuments Astronomically Considered*, Macmillan, London (2nd Ed.) 1909

MacKie, Euan, *The Megalith Builders*,

Phaidon, Oxford 1977

MacSween, Ann, and Sharp, Mick, *Prehistoric Scotland*, B.T. Batsford, London 1989

Malagrino, Paolo, *Dolmen E Menhir di Puglia*, Schena Editore, Fasano 1978

Mallory, J.P., *In Search of the Indo-Europeans*, Thames and Hudson, London 1989

Marshack, Alexander, *The Roots of Civilization*, Weidenfeld and Nicholson, London 1972

Michell, John, *City of Revelation*, Garnstone Press, London 1972

– , *The View Over Atlantis*, Garnstone Press, London (Rev. Ed.) 1972

– , *The Old Stones of Land's End*, Garnstone Press, London 1974

– , *Megalithomania*, Thames and Hudson, London 1982

– , *A Little History of Astro-Archaeology*, Thames and Hudson, London (Rev. Ed.) 1989

Milisauskas, Sarunas, *European Prehistory*, Academic Press, London 1978

Mithen, Steven, *Thoughtful Foragers : A Study of Pre-historic Decision-making*, Cambridge University Press 1990

Mohen, Jean-Pierre, *The World of Megaliths*, Cassell, London 1989

Morris, Ronald W.B., *The Prehistoric Rock Art of Argyll*, Dolphin Press, Poole, Dorset 1977

Munksgaard, Elisabeth, *Denmark : An Archaeological Guide*, Faber and Faber, London 1970

Over, Luke, *Visitor's Guide to Archaeology in Scilly*, St. Mary's, Scilly 1974

Paget, R.F., *Central Italy : An Archaeological Guide*, Faber and Faber, London 1973

Paturi, Felix R., *Prehistoric Heritage*, Macdonald & Jane's, London 1979

Pearce, Susan M., *The Archaeology of South West Britain*, Collins, London 1981

Peet, T. Eric, *Rough Stone Monuments and their Builders*, Harper & Brothers, London 1912

Pericot, Garcia L., *The Balearic Islands*, London 1972

Phillips, Patricia, *The Prehistory of Europe*, Allen Lane, London 1980

Piggott, Stuart, *The Neolithic Cultures of the British Isles*, Cambridge University Press, 1954

– , *Scotland Before History*, Edinburgh University Press 1982

Poinssot, Claude, *Les Ruines de Dougga*, L'Institut National D'Archéologie et Arts, Tunis 1958

Ponsich, Michel, *Nécropoles Phéniciennes de la Region de Tanger*, (Études et Travaux D'Archéologie Marocaine : Vol.111), Éditions Marocaines et Internationales, Tanger 1967

Radmilli, Antonia Mario (Ed.), *Guida Della Preistoria Italiana*, Sansoni Editore, Florence 1975

Renfrew, Colin, *Before Civilisation*, Jonathan Cape, London 1973

– , (Ed.), *The Megalithic Monuments of

Western Europe*, Thames and Hudson, London, Paperback Edition 1983

– , *Archaeology and Language*, Jonathan Cape, London 1987

Roche, Denis, *Carnac*, Tchou, Paris 1973

Savory, H.N., *Spain and Portugal : The Prehistory of the Iberian Peninsula*, Thames and Hudson, London 1968

Scarre, Christopher (Ed.), *Ancient France: Neolithic Societies and their Landscapes : 6000–2000 BC*, Edinburgh University Press 1984

Schirnig, Heinz (Ed.), *Grossteingräber in Niedersachsen*, August Lax, Hildersheim 1979

Schuldt, Ewald, *Die Mecklenburgischen Megalithgräber*, VEB Deutscher Verlag der Wissenschaften, Berlin 1972

Service, Alastair, and Bradbery, Jean, *A Guide to the Megaliths of Europe*, Weidenfeld and Nicolson, London 1979

Souville, Georges, *Atlas Préhistorique du Maroc*, Vol.1, 'Le Maroc Atlantique', Éditions Du Centre National De La Recherche Scientifique, Paris 1973

Sprockhoff, Ernst, *Atlas der Megalithgräber Deutschlands*, 4 vols., Rudolf Habelt, Bonn 1966, 1967, 1975

Stenberger, Mårten, *Sweden*, Thames and Hudson, London 1962

Strömberg, Märta, *Die Megalithgräber von Hagestad*, CWK Gleerups Forlag, Lund, Sweden 1971

Thom, A., *Megalithic Sites in Britain*, Clarendon Press, Oxford 1967

–, *Megalithic Lunar Observatories*, Clarendon Press, Oxford 1971

– , and Thom, A.S., *Megalithic Remains in Britain and Brittany*, Clarendon Press, Oxford 1978

Thomas, Nicholas, *Guide to Prehistoric England*, B.T. Batsford, London 1976

Trump, David, *Central and Southern Italy Before Rome*, Thames and Hudson, London 1966

– , *Malta : An Archaeological Guide*, Faber and Faber, London 1972

– , *The Prehistory of the Mediterranean*, Allen Lane, London 1980

Twohig, Elizabeth Shee, *The Megalithic Art of Western Europe*, Clarendon Press, Oxford 1981

Waterhouse, John, *The Stone Circles of Cumbria*, Phillimore, Chichester 1985

Watkins, Alfred, *The Old Straight Track*, Methuen, London 1925

Weatherhill, Craig, *Cornovia : Ancient Sites of Cornwall and Scilly*, Alison Hodge, Penzance, Cornwall (Rev. Ed.) 1989

Weir, Anthony, *Early Ireland : A Field Guide*, Blackstaff Press, Belfast 1980

Whitehouse, David & Ruth, *Archaeological Atlas of the World*, Thames and Hudson, London 1975

Whittle, Alasdair, *Problems in Neolithic Archaeology*, Cambridge University Press 1988

Wood, John Edwin, *Sun. Moon and Standing Stones*, O.U.P., Oxford, 1978

Picture credits

The publisher thanks photographers and organizations for their kind permission to reproduce the following photographs in this book.

A: *Above* B: *Below* L: *Left* R: *Right* C: *Centre*
18(L) Michael Balfour; 18(R) Janet & Colin Bord; 19 Michael Balfour; 20(A) A. Weir/Janet & Colin Bord; 20(B) Bob Burns; 21(A) The Jersey Museums Service; 21(B) Bob Burns; 22 Robin Briault; 23 Bob Burns; 24–27 Bernd Siering; 28(A) Robert Estall; 28(B) Bernd Siering; 29(A) English Heritage; 29(B) Bernd Siering; 30(A) Robert Estall; 30(B) Janet & Colin Bord; 31 Bernd Siering; 32(A) Bernd Siering; 32(B) M. Jenner/Robert Harding; 33(A) Bernd Siering; 33(B) Robert Estall; 34(A) Bernd Siering; 34(B) Janet & Colin Bord; 35 Kevin Redpath; 36–42 Bernd Siering; 43(A) A. Kennedy/Janet & Colin Bord; 43(B) David Lyons; 44 David Lyons; 45(A) Bernd Siering; 45(C) H.M. Brown/Janet & Colin Bord; 45(B) A. Weir/Janet & Colin Bord; 46(A) Michael Balfour; 46(B) A. Kennedy/Janet & Colin Bord; 47(A) A. Weir/Janet & Colin Bord; 47(B) Office of Public Works, Ireland; 48–51 Bernd Siering; 52(A) Michael Balfour; 52(B) Bernd Siering; 53 Bernd Siering; 54 Michael Balfour; 55(A) Werner Forman Archive; 55(L) Patricia Macdonald; 55 (R) C. Tait/Ancient Art & Architecture Collection; 56–59 Bernd Siering; 60 Frank Gibson; 61(A) Frank Gibson; 61(B) Cornwall Archaeological unit; 62(A) David Lyons; 62(B) Bernd Siering; 63(A) David Lyons; 63(B) Mick Sharp; 64–65 Bernd Siering; 66 David Lyons; 67(A) David Lyons; 67(B) Bernd Siering; 68(A) Bernd Siering; 68(B) David Lyons; 69 David Lyons; 70(A) Janet & Colin Bord; 70(B) David Lyons; 71 David Lyons; 72(A) Chris Barber 72(B) Michael Balfour; 73(A) Bernd Siering; 73(B) Aubrey Burl; 74(A) Janet & Colin Bord; 74(B) Michael Balfour; 75(A) Michael Balfour; 75(B) Bernd Siering; 76 Bernd Siering; 77(A) Michael Balfour; 77(B) RCAHM, Wales; 80–81 Michael Balfour; 82 Colin Burgess; 83 Michael Balfour; 84 Robert Estall; 85 Michael Balfour; 86–88 Jos Le Doaré; 89–90 Chris Scarre; 91(A) Aubrey Burl; 91(B) Michael Balfour; 92(A) Colin Burgess; 92(B) Chris Scarre; 93–94 Bernd Siering; 95(A) Ronald Sheridan/Ancient Art & Architecture Collection; 95(B) Colin Burgess; 96 Bernd Siering; 97–98 Jos Le Doaré; 99 Bernd Siering; 100(A) Michael Balfour; 100(B) Aubrey Burl; 101(A) Colin Burgess; 101(B) Michael Balfour; 102 Michael Balfour; 103 Mick Sharp; 104(A) Michael Balfour; 104(B) Robert Estall; 105 Michael Balfour; 106(A) Jos Le Doaré; 106(B) Colin Burgess; 110–114 Bernd Siering; 115–116 Ministry of the Environment, Denmark; 117(A) Ministry of the Environment, Denmark; 117(B) T. Spiegel/Rapho; 118(A) James Dyer; 118(B) Ministry of the Environment, Denmark; 119–120 Ministry of the Environment, Denmark; 121(A) Forhistorisk Museum, Denmark; 121(B) Minsitry of the Environment, Denmark; 122 Landesmuseum, Schwerin; 123 Pfaltzer/Roger Viollet; 124–129 Bernd Siering; 131 S. Andersson/Scandibild Bildbyra; 132(A) Märta Strömberg; 132(B) ATA/Märta Strömberg; 133 Märta Strömberg; 136 Oronoz/Artephot; 137 David Trump; 138 Nimatallah/Artephot; 139 Robert Estall; 140(A) N. Saunders/Barbara Heller; 140(B) X. Miserachs/Firo-Foto; 141 Chris Scarre; 142–143 Colin Burgess; 144 R.J. Harrison; 145–146 Colin Burgess; 147(A) Firo-Foto; 147(B) Oronoz/Artephot; 148(A) Oronoz/Artephot; 148(B) Ministry of Culture, Spain; 150 Oronoz/Artephot; 154(L) Bernd Siering; 154(R) Percheron/Artephot; 155 Ziolo/Artephot; 156–157 Bernd Siering; 158 Percheron/Artephot; 159–162 Ruth Whitehouse; 163 Caroline Malone; 164–165 Bernd Siering; 166(A) Percheron/Artephot; 166(B) Bernd Siering; 167 Robert Estall; 168 Bernd Siering; 169 David Trump; 171 Fabbri Editori; 173–174 Caroline Malone; 175 Archaeological Photo Service, Canton of Graubuenden; 176–177 Alain Gallay; 180 G. Camps; 182 Bernd Siering; 183 A. Ruhlmann; 185 G. Camps; 186 Bernd Siering.

Every effort has been made to trace photographers. In the event of any unintentional omissions the publishers invite copyright holders to contact them direct.